DATE			
AUG 22 1994			

SAMUEL BECKETT:
the comic gamut

SAMUEL BECKETT:

the comic gamut

by RUBY COHN

RUTGERS UNIVERSITY PRESS,
NEW BRUNSWICK, NEW JERSEY

Library of Congress Catalogue Number: 62–13761
SBN: 8135–0402–3

This book has been published with the assistance of a grant from the Ford Foundation.

Manufactured in the United States of America
by H. Wolff, New York

Second Printing

To my parents and Jarvis,
who taught me to read

contents

1 *portrait of the artist as an old bum* 3

2 *early elegance* 10

3 *Murphy the morph* 45

4 *Watt Knott* 65

5 *the first burst into French* 95

6 *a trilogy of novels* 114

7 *brief fiction* 169

8 *Comment c'est par le bout* 182

9 *the dramatic shift to waiting* 208

10 *Endgame* 226

11 *dramatic contractions* 243

12 *Samuel Beckett, self-translator* 260

13 *a comic complex and a complex comic* 283

appendix 301

notes 311

bibliography 328

SAMUEL BECKETT:
the comic gamut

JAQUES. but it is a melancholy of mine own, compounded of many simples, extracted from many objects, and indeed the sundry contemplation of my travels, which, by often rumination, wraps me in a most humorous sadness.

As You Like It

Je n'ai pas entrepris à dire tout. . . . Mon dessein n'est pas de faire un gros livre, et je tâche plutôt de comprendre beaucoup en peu de mots–j'espère que nos neveux me sauront gré non seulement des choses que j'ai ici expliquées, mais aussi de celles que j'ai remises volontairement afin de leur laisser le plaisir de les inventer.

Descartes, *Géometrie*

1

portrait of the artist as an old bum

L'auteur, ça n'est jamais intéressant.
Quoted by Madeleine Chapsal

On Samuel Beckett's planet, matter is minimal, physiography and physiology barely support life. The air is exceedingly thin, and the light exceedingly dim. But all the cluttered complexity of our own planet is required to educate the taste that can savor the unique comic flavor of Beckett's creation. Our world, "so various, so beautiful, so new," so stingily admitted to Beckett's work, is nevertheless the essential background for appreciation of that work.

Beckett's stagnating heroes reflect comically upon our radio beams and rockets, hurtling through interstellar space. The solitary confinement of Beckett's heroes in chamber, bed, or container is ludicrous in a universe whose particles whirl, explode, and make cataclysmic contact. Automation and cybernetics provide hilarious contrast to the futile exertions, the violent incomprehension, of Beckett's characters. In Beckett's works his fictions eat out of, excrete into, and inhabit various pots, and within these circumscribed islands they are as absorbed as Robinson Crusoe in their possessions, as absorbed as we are in the properties with which we furnish our rooms, from gourmet pantry to palatial toilet, from delivery room to funeral parlor. Our new omnipotence, the power to destroy our planet with a cobalt bomb, is a grotesque outgrowth of the blows on the head that recur in Beckett's fiction. It is, finally, to blows on the head, trunk, and buttocks that Beckett reduces the vast areas of learning of the European university tradition—philosophy and philology, natural and unnatural science, reading, writing, and rhetoric. Language, too, seems ridiculously rudimentary in Beckett's later work, whereas our own neologisms proliferate; his simplified syntax mocks the simple-minded syntax of advertisements and abridgments in our contemporary Tower of Babel.

A postwar Frenchman in his artistic concern with man's metaphysical situation, an irrepressible Irishman in his comic astringency, a disillusioned student of the intellectual disciplines of the classico-Christian legacy, Beckett conveys alienation as the human heritage. His imaginative shrinking of the human horizon is a sardonic comment upon both the literal and metaphoric concepts of our expanding universe, but his humor beats against that expansion to obtain its raucous resonance.

By the middle of the twentieth century we have become skeptical about expansion, and Beckett writes from the cultural context of the mid-twentieth century. All faiths are tottering—religion and science, personality and ideology, family and nation, freedom and imperatives, subject and object—and Beckett's prose totters with them; he even plays up the slapstick comedy, like any competent clown. His plosives echo the puncturing of surface reality by atomic physics and psychoanalysis. Logical Positivists and Existentialists alike insist upon the failure of metaphysics, highlighting Beckett's comic and poignant portrayal of man as *animalis metaphysicum.*

Moreover, Beckett's metaphysics, like that of Aristotle,

comes "after the physics." Archimedes, Hippasus, Heraclitus, Democritus, St. Thomas Aquinas, St. Augustine, Galileo, Newton, Geulincx, Leibniz, all receive passing mention in Beckett's fiction, for his heroes have earned their *je m'en foutiste* ignorance in some dim classroom past, which would seem to resemble our present; they have been the victims of a considerable education, and now they victimize *it,* with savage if uncoordinated attacks. Although Beckett insists upon the negative know-nothingness of his heroes, their ignorance is assumed (in all senses of the word), and they cannot completely strip away Samuel Beckett's extraordinary erudition, upon which his comedy rests.

Waiting for Godot has attracted audiences all over our shrunken globe because it contains slapstick and theology, vaudeville and philosophy; it hits below the belt of logic and literature. Evocative of both compassion and derision, Beckett's bums present us with an image of ourselves. Shivering in the rags of our classico-Christian heritage, they sing frantically for an uncertain supper. Like Yeats's Byzantine soul, they sing louder for every tatter in their mortal dress; with Beckett as with Mallarmé, "le chant jaillit de source innée, antérieure à un concept"; to Beckett as to Rilke, "Gesang ist Dasein." Beckett's bums may sing off-key, in snatches, but Beckett himself pays strict attention to the individual notes and the total structure. Compared to music by his admirers, to gibberish by his detractors, Beckett's prose is a skillfully composed verbal texture, gravid with suggestion beneath a comically threadbare surface. A rich poverty.

Like other impressive composers, Beckett limits himself to a very few, almost obsessive themes, and central among them is his art. From his critical writings, one can cull explicit expressions of his commitment to art:

Here form *is* content, content *is* form. . . . He is not writing about something; he is writing something.[1]

the work of art [is] neither created nor chosen, but discovered, uncovered, excavated, pre-existing within the artist, a law of his nature. . . . Indeed he makes no attempt to dissociate form from content. The one is a concretion of the other, the revelation of a world.[2]

Art is the sun, moon, and stars of the mind, the whole mind.[3]

to be an artist is to fail, as no other dare fail.[4]

L'artiste qui joue son être est de nulle part. Et il n'a pas de frères.[5] (The artist who stakes his being comes from no particular place. And he has no brothers.)

Although written about other artists during three decades, all these phrases boomerang at Beckett. They link him to an old tradition of the Artist as Maker, in the image of God, or, in an areligious age, the Artist as Rimbaldian *voyant.*[6] But far from the Artist as God or *voyant,* Beckett's artists are clumsy, disgusting, grotesque. Their lives are cluttered with an incongruous collection of débris, to which even art gives no noticeable coherence. With increasing insistence through the years, Beckett's ideal of commitment to art is undercut by his awareness of the absurdity of that ideal (as of others, earlier abandoned) and of the inevitability of its failure.[7] Not only does he mock his artist-heroes but he turns his incisive wit against his own art:

There are many ways in which the thing I am trying in vain to say may be tried in vain to be said. I have experimented . . . both in public and in private, under duress, through faintness of heart, through weakness of mind, with two or three hundred.[8]

By means of his comic thrust, Beckett shoves the artist off a pedestal, down into our lowly human midst. "L'art pour l'art" becomes "L'art pour rien; c'est à rire."

This tension between the ridiculous and sublime, between the sacred task and the profane, filthy hands, is the source of

Beckett's most immediate, as well as enduring, impression upon the reader, and is therefore a suitable starting point for the critic. However, "literary criticism," as Beckett saw, "is not bookkeeping,"[9] and the literary critic can scarcely expect to discover in Beckett's work a neat mathematical equilibrium between an artistic mission and its comic concretion. In his early writings Beckett flounders around in each area, and it is only after many years that artistic commitment and an ironic deprecation of that commitment melt into each other, paradoxically, comically. Commitment is comic, but it is also compulsive for the Beckett hero.

As the quotations suggest, devotion to art constitutes a stable groundwork in Beckett's writing. Upon it he sets his awkward, comic artist-heroes, who move from virtuosity to profundity through a series of subtractions—subtractions from fictional formulae in the fiction, and from dramatic conventions in the drama. In examining Beckett's work, we find his development to be a relentless and ridiculous retrenchment. *Comment c'est* (1961) presents a comic hero who might have crawled out of Genesis—an Adam who is kin to dust, but who gives to all things their names. *Happy Days* (1961) presents a primordial, comic couple in a scorched Eden.

The remainder, after Beckett's successive subtractions from the conventions of fiction and drama, is remarkable both for its linguistic control and its comic tone. A uniquely bilingual creator, Beckett already has followers in both tongues; contemporary French fiction and contemporary English drama both contain works in the spirit of his subtraction, but none of the pupils has mastered Beckett's comic compression. As he moves from a baroque to a colloquial style, Beckett retains his comic vision. An analysis of his humor therefore traces an attitude that is pervasive in his work, at its complex core, and an understanding of that humor may elucidate the core.

Arbitrarily, for the sake of clarity, a distinction will be drawn between the *comic* or laughable, which has been a subject for both psychological and literary analysis through the ages, and *comedy,* which has called forth a more esthetic commentary.[10] In early criticism of the comic, the Greeks already distinguished between the liberal jest that gives pleasure to all, and the illiberal jest that inflicts pain upon a victim.[11] The liberal jest evokes laughter *with,* the illiberal jest laughter *at.* As a comic writer, Beckett employs both jests, but the illiberal dominates from the start.

The illiberal jest lies at the root of the corrective theory of comedy—the leading theory of comedy of the Western cultural tradition. By laughing at the comic defect in the victim, the laugher exorcizes that defect from his own make-up.[12] More recently, comedy has been interpreted as social consolidation, to which laughter is irrelevant. In the latter view, the comic hero is integrated (or reintegrated) into his society, whereas the tragic hero remains isolated from his.[13]

Since this study will be concerned with Beckett's treatment of the comic, it must be stressed that neither of the two major theories of comedy is applicable to his work. So ambiguous are Beckett's comic heroes that we scarcely know why we laugh, and whether we laugh *at* or *with.* So asocial are Beckett's heroes that they appear to exist in tragic isolation rather than comic consolidation. But can a work be labeled tragic when the isolation of the hero from his society is conveyed by recourse to various comic tricks of a literary or theatrical heritage? If tragicomedy be defined as "a play mainly of tragic character, but with a happy ending," perhaps Beckett's works should be called comitragedy.

At the end of Plato's *Symposium,* Socrates declares that the same author should write both comedy and tragedy, and many critics since Plato have recognized a mixing of the two modes.[14] Northrop Frye has recently suggested that there are four rather than two fictional modes: comedy, tragedy, romance, and irony.[15] Irony has been defined as the "painfully comic,"[16] and Professor Frye's own definitions of irony are applicable to Beckett's later work:

> The term irony, then, indicates a technique of appearing to be less than one is, which in literature becomes most commonly a technique of saying as little and meaning as much as possible, or, in a more general way, a pattern of words that turns away from direct statement or its own obvious meaning.[17]
>
> The literary structure is ironic because "what it says" is always different in kind or degree from "what it means."[18]

In our own age, often viewed as an age of irony, distinguished critics have illuminated ironic aspects of much of our literature, but often they have accomplished this by reference to techniques that used to be trademarks of the comic—twist of plot, exaggeration of character quirk, and such linguistic play as pun and paradox.[19] The formal study of irony is relatively recent, but that of comedy is at least as old as Aristotle. Since almost the entire comic range is present in Beckett's work, a catalogue of his comic techniques can be compiled empirically, but the convenient and widely known classification of Bergson is usable as a springboard.[20] This is not to imply that Beckett went to *Le Rire* for his comic devices, any more than he deliberately drew from the methods of Rabelais, Swift, Jarry, or Joyce, whose heir he is. Although he employs most of the devices analyzed by Bergson, and shares certain comic astigmatisms with the latter authors, the line of descent is subtle and irregular; he is, as well, a contemporary of the sick humorists of our cabarets. In this book, the focus is narrowed to the idiosyncratic structure that Beckett builds from often familiar materials.

2

early elegance

That's not moving, that's moving.
Whoroscope

Samuel Beckett was born in Dublin in 1906, into a middle-class Protestant family. He was educated at Wilde's school, Portora Royal, and Swift's university, Trinity College, from which he received his B.A. in 1927, an honor student in modern languages.[1] While still a student, he visited Paris and met James Joyce. In 1928 he returned to Paris as visiting lecturer in English at the Ecole Normale Supérieure, which had been or was to be ornamented also by Henri Bergson, Jean Giraudoux, Maurice Merleau-Ponty, Romain Rolland, Jules Romains, Jean-Paul Sartre, Simone Weil. Beckett made friends with Alfred Péron, an *Agregé* in English, with whom he undertook to translate into French the "Anna Livia Plurabelle" section of Joycc's *Work in Progress*. In 1930 Beckett returned to Trinity to teach French but soon resigned in order to write, and to tour Europe. He received a Master's degree from Trinity in 1931, having done research on Descartes.

From 1929 on, Beckett began to publish poems, criticism, and short fiction in Eugene Jolas's *transition* and other little magazines. In 1930 his poem *Whoroscope* won first prize for the best poem on Time, in a contest sponsored by Nancy Cunard's Hours Press in Paris, and it thus became Beckett's first separately published work.[2]

Even before one reads the poem, the punning title, *Whoroscope,* suggests a cheapened or lying prognostication of the future. Written in the Eliotic dramatic monologue, replete with learned footnotes, the poem is at once a tribute to and a mockery of its persona. René Descartes, Seigneur du Perron, is the speaker and protagonist of the monologue; the poem's tone is colloquial, its basis factual, and its erudition overwhelming. Whereas the obscurities of Eliot's *Waste Land* are elucidated by references to the whole Western literary tradition, the obscurities of *Whoroscope* are illuminated only by detailed examination of Descartes's career. But like Eliot's glossing, Beckett's is arbitrary. Thus, Galileo merits comment, but Gassendi does not, and no attempt is made to explain the relevance of Franz Hals and Francis Bacon. Such terms as "lead-swinging" for Galileo's Pisan experiment, "sun-red crystally cloud" for Gassendi's treatise on parhelions, "tolle et legge" from St. Augustine's *Confessions*—are explained neither by poem nor by notes.

Beckett does, however, supply three introductory notes that are crucial to an understanding of the poem:

René Descartes, Seigneur du Perron, liked his omelette made of eggs hatched from eight to ten days; shorter or longer under the hen and the result, he says, is disgusting.

He kept his birthday to himself so that no astrologer could cast his nativity.

The shuttle of a ripening egg combs the warp of his days.

The first two notes are accurate, but if the shuttle-egg combs the warp of Descartes's days, it may be with a yarn spun by Beckett, who uses the egg to give form to the free verse monologue. The form is also bolstered by the recurrent image of blood,[3] and by the repetition of short abrupt questions. Thus, in this poem ostensibly about Time, the titular horoscope is missing, and in its stead are egg, blood, and questions.

The poem opens suddenly: "What's that?" Another "What's that?" a "Who's that?" a third "What's that?" and a "How long?" each introduces a short stanza, and the series of questions leads to the opening of the final longer stanza: "Are you ripe at last?" It is suggested that the poem deals with a special kind of Time, *ab ovo* to death—a lifetime.

Descartes's plea at the end of his life, for a "second/starless inscrutable hour" is doubly ironic in terms of persona and title of the poem—that the father of modern philosophy should desire inscrutability, and that he should wish for starlessness when a horoscope depends upon the position of the stars.

For a writer whose commitment is to art rather than to philosophy, Descartes seems a strange protagonist. Not only is the name almost synonymous with rationalism, that un- and anti-artistic method, but Descartes himself was uninterested in all fields of art except music. On the other hand, the great Cartesian recognition of a mathematical order in the universe came to him suddenly and intuitively, like an artistic inspiration, "discovered, uncovered, excavated, pre-existing within the artist, a law of his nature."[4] Indeed, Descartes himself considered intuition the highest human faculty, although he thought it "springs from the power of reason alone."

At the lower level of Descartes's personal predilections, several of the poem's phrases are expanded in later Beckett works. Descartes's taste for a "hot-cupboard" will be shared by Murphy; his love for a "squinty doaty" by the hero of "Premier amour." Beckett and his French heroes are as "unmatinal" as Descartes himself. Other Cartesian interests are wheelchairs (*Endgame*), spectacles ("La Fin," *Waiting for*

Godot, and *Endgame*), and slaughterhouses (almost all Beckett's French fiction). The early French heroes of Beckett imitate the Descartes of *Le Discours de la méthode:* "I did nothing but roam from one place to another, desirous of being a spectator rather than an actor in the plays exhibited on the theater of the world." And all Beckett's work is an extrapolation of the Cartesian definition of man as "a thing that thinks," so that knowledge begins with consciousness.

In *Whoroscope,* Beckett's attitude towards Descartes is ambivalent, ironic.[5] Other than the final "and grant me my second/starless inscrutable hour," virtually the only non-ironic line among the ninety-eight of the monologue is "the lonely petal of a great high bright rose." The reference is both to the Rosicrucians and to Dante's synthesizing vision, which is implicitly contrasted with the dichotomizing view of Descartes. In some obscure context occurs another reference to Dante (in a play upon his phrase in the *Convivio,* "the master of those who know"). Dante's emotional and intellectual responses were closely tied to his sensual experience—a tie celebrated by T. S. Eliot as the "unified sensibility." Although the Descartes of *Whoroscope* seems, in the Dantesque passages, to admire that unity, much of the poem dwells on the exclusively intellectual activities of his life. Beckett mocks those activities by employing many of the comic linguistic techniques that Bergson catalogued.

Since the over-all effect of these devices is to present an ironic portrait of the protagonist, we may first consider those techniques that contribute most directly to the irony. One of the oldest weapons of the ironist is the pun, and in *Whoroscope,* we find the same pun repeated in two key lines: "That's not moving, that's *moving,*" and "Then I will rise and move moving." Other puns are more labored, and might better be classified in Bergson's category of misplaced literalism, in which a figurative expression is literally interpreted, or the material aspect of a metaphor is emphasized. Thus, "that cracked beater" designates both the heart and an egg beater. From a literal reading of Descartes's title, Seigneur du *Perron,* Beckett obtains a wry poignancy:

Oh Weulles spare the blood of a Frank
who has climbed the bitter *steps,* (my italics)

Descartes's actual words to Dr. Weulles and his colleagues were, "Messieurs, épargnez le sang français." Beckett's use of "Frank" rather than "French" is probably an ironic comment on Descartes's character, which tended to be devious in self-protection. Twice, in the notes, Beckett charges him with "sophistry"—"expedient" and "Eucharistic." In the poem, the latter sophistry is expanded through pun and paradox:

So we drink Him and eat Him
and the watery Beaune and the stale cubes of Hovis
because He can jig
as near or as far from his jigging Self
and as sad or lively as the chalice or the tray asks.

It is initially possible to take the first line at face value. In the second line "Beaune" is a French red Burgundy and "Hovis" a whole meal bread, but they are pronounced, respectively, like the English word "bone" and the French words "eau vie." Thus the line contains a cross-irony on solid and liquid, Body and Blood, which renders both of them "stale" and "watery." "Jig" has sexual connotations, relating to the title. The entire sacrament, Beckett implies in the last three lines, can be pragmatically arranged to suit the occasion. In the light of the remainder of the stanza, the first line must be read ironically.

"Not a syllogism out of him" twists the colloquial "Not a peep out of him," and the hidden "peep" suggests the egg that unifies the poem. A variant of the twisted cliché occurs in the hidden cliché. Ham and eggs may suggest death and birth, or flesh and spirit, but the combination is never baldly stated. Rather it is hidden in such lines as "In the name of Bacon will you chicken me up that egg?" or "Two lashed ovaries with prostisciutto." The last mention of the egg is, "I will eat it with a fish fork." Since fish has long been the symbol of Christ, the line probably implies Descartes's careful Catholicism, and his fear of antagonizing the Church.

Learned jargon links Descartes to St. Augustine. "He tolle'd and legge'd" uses the "Tolle et legge" from the *Confessions,* twisting it. Even more striking is the wrenching of the celebrated "Cogito" to the Augustinian "Fallor, ergo sum." (St. Augustine's exact words are: "Si enim fallor, sum.")

A poem-long irony is obtained by the juxtaposition of colloquial jargon (stinks, lead-swinging, Kip, zig-zags, jig, ripper) against the erudite context (Copernican, syllogism, exfoliation, redemptorist). For those familiar with Descartes's Latin or his Latinate French, the colloquial tone is itself an irony. Incongruity, too, provides several jests; thus, the egg is variously described as "a little green fry," "my slim pale double-breasted turd," and "abortion of a fledgling."

This virtual roster of comic devices in a ninety-eight line poem might lead one to expect a patchwork effect. Actually, however, the several techniques contribute to the tonal unity of a poem that is too diffusely dependent upon the details of Descartes's life. In the *Whoroscope* that purports to be about Time, the *hours,* except for one of inspired intuition, are treated as taunting *whores.* Through the progress of the poem, Beckett has converted Descartes's uncast horoscope into an irrevocable whoroscope, but the function of the ubiquitous egg remains problematical.

The embryonic nature of the egg is its fundamental attribute, but what kind of fowl is in Beckett's mind? My guess, in the shadow of the title *Whoroscope,* the ostensible subject Time, and the hindsight of Beckett's subsequent works, is that the egg hatches into the fowl of *our* Time, post-Cartesian time. Descartes himself found it difficult to explain time or duration, and came close to calling it miraculous. Miracle, however, has no place in Beckett's poem, and the passing of time is conveyed by the events of Descartes's life, and especially by repeated reference to the age of the egg. For all his caution, Beckett implies, Descartes broke the egg, severing mind from body so effectively that all the king's horses and all the king's men couldn't put them back together again. The final irony, then, is that the egg hatches into modern times, for which only a *W* horoscope can be cast.

Techniques of the comic, as used in *Whoroscope,* appear also in the fiction and criticism that Beckett published at this time. In an article on Joyce published the year before *Whoroscope* and a monograph on Proust published the year after, several comic linguistic devices are embedded.

In the Joyce essay,[6] a sudden tonal clash introduces a comic note:

Philosophy and Philology as a pair of nigger minstrels out of the Teatro dei Piccoli (242)

The collective noodle of the monodialectical arcadians whose fury is precipitated by a failure to discover "innocefree" in the Concise Oxford Dictionary (251)

Vice and Virtue . . . simply a series of stimulants to enable the kitten to catch its tail (253)

The longer, less embattled, and more reflective Proust essay[7] is written in the same superior, sneering tone, with occasional guffaws provoked by a sudden incongruous trope:

Memory and Habit are attributes of the Time cancer (7)

Curiosity is the safeguard, not the death of the cat, whether in skirts or on all fours. (18)

An anti-Irish remark:

if Habit is the Goddess of Dullness, voluntary memory is Shadwell, and of Irish extraction. (20)

Or a mild obscenity:

We say farewell to M. de Charlus . . . scorned in the full strength of his terrible pride as the Duchesse de Caca or the Princesse de Pipi (58)

The anti-Irish remark and the mild obscenity, uncatalogued by Bergson, become standard Beckett comic devices. Primarily, however, Beckett's wit darts forth in parenthetical remarks addressed directly to the reader, in a manner recalling the parabasis of Aristophanic comedy.[8]

The reader is cordially invited to omit this summary analysis of what is perhaps the greatest passage Proust ever wrote. (25)

And if you don't understand it, Ladies and Gentlemen, it is because you are too decadent to receive it. You are not satisfied unless form is so strictly divorced from content that you can comprehend the one almost without bothering to read the other. This instinctive skimming and absorption of the scant cream of sense is made possible by what I may call a continuous process of copious intellectual salivation. The form that is an independent and arbitrary phenomenon can fulfill no higher function than that of a stimulus for a tertiary or quaternary conditioned reflex of dribbling comprehension. (248)

Evident too in the latter quotation is Beckett's early penchant for dwelling on the disgusting in order to evoke laughter. Even as a young man, Beckett saw the comically repulsive aspects of sex, and they appear in this light in his prose poem entitled "Text,"[9] which reflects the influence of the multipuns of Joyce's *Work in Progress.*

It is in his fiction that Beckett first sustains an elegant comic style. In *More Pricks Than Kicks,* the linguistic techniques of *Whoroscope* are highly polished to be set in carefully wrought paragraphs. The ten stories collected under that title were written between 1932 and 1934, and it is not certain at what point Beckett envisaged the possibility of publishing them as a group. The opening story, "Dante and the Lobster," first appeared in *This Quarter* in 1932. "Sedendo et Quiescendo," which also features Belacqua Shuah, the picaresque hero of the series, was published in *transition* in 1932, but that story was not included in *More Pricks Than Kicks.*[10] Since the volume is extremely difficult to obtain, some introduction is necessary.

The hero, Belacqua Shuah, is a native Dubliner of Huguenot descent. Both his first name and his sloth come from Canto IV of Dante's *Purgatorio,* where, seated with his face between his knees—almost in the fetal position—and resting in the shade of a rock, he comments upon Dante's strenuous climb. Unlike Dante's friend, Beckett's Belacqua is a learned poet who has traveled widely, and his initials are the inversion of Samuel Beckett's own. His field of operations is Ireland, not Italy, but Beckett's mockery of Ireland and things Irish may derive indirectly from Dante's condemnation of Italy in Canto VI of the *Purgatorio.*

In the main, Belacqua is involved in adventures with various ladies. Although we follow him from his student days through his burial, there is a chronological vagueness that recalls early picaresque novels. The comic is no stranger to the picaresque, but rarely has a hero been more scurvily treated, less sympathetically approached, than Belacqua. Nor is Beckett more gallant to the ladies: Winifred Coates, Alba Perdue, Ruby Tough, Lucy, Thelma bboggs, the Smeraldina.

The incidents of the first story, "Dante and the Lobster," as Belacqua himself enumerates them, are lunch, lobster, and lesson, in that order. Each of these items is described in such meticulous and sardonic detail that the underlying theme, the difficulty of reconciling divine mercy with divine justice, frequently fades away. Dante's rare moments of compassion in Hell are both exemplified and mocked in Belacqua's feelings about McCabe (son of Cain and Abel?) the murderer, and then about the cruciform lobster that is boiled alive. Technically, the story is of special interest; for comparison of the versions in *This Quarter* and in *More Pricks* reveals that the main purpose of revision was to sharpen the comic.

In "Fingal," Belacqua's first lady friend appears. She is described in the opening sentence: "The last girl he went with, before a memorable fit of laughing incapacitated him from gallantry for some time, was pretty, hot and witty, in that order" (23). Although Winifred Coates enters on the comic note, she is not subjected to as merciless a mockery as Belacqua's later loves; she is merely abandoned by our pale shadow of a mythical hero (Fingal), who, having fled on a stolen bicycle to a pub, is there overcome by the mammoth laughter of the opening sentence.

"Ding-Dong" is purportedly narrated by a friend of Belacqua during the "last phase of his solipsism, before he toed the line and began to relish the world, with the belief that the best thing he had to do was to move constantly from place to place." During compulsive wandering, Belacqua sees a blind paralytic beggar, "a power in the Coombe," who might faintly foreshadow the French heroes. But Belacqua passes him by, arriving at a pub where he buys from a woman peddler four "seats in heaven," for "yer friend, yer da, yer ma an' yer motte." Significantly, there is no mention of a seat for himself, but after the woman's departure for her room in Townsend Street, he leaves for Railway Street "beyond the river."

"A Wet Night," some fifty pages long, exhibits Beckett's gift for social satire. The scene centers on a party, and sparkling dialogue enlivens many pages, with Beckett's wit flowing both in and beyond his speakers' lines. In this story, Alba

Perdue, the most dazzling of Belacqua's ladies, makes her first appearance, uttering a refrain, "See me home."

Ruby Tough merits a sentence in "A Wet Night," but she becomes the heroine of "Love and Lethe." She is to serve as Belacqua's partner in *felo de se,* since she feels she has nothing to live for, and the doctors have informed her that in any case, she is not long for this world. However, in spite of Belacqua's careful preparations, the act they consummate is that other death, which, as Beckett makes clear by quotation, "n'est qu'une mesme chose."

"Walking Out" reveals our hero engaged to be married to Lucy. Having presumably renounced both the white (Alba) and the red (Ruby) ladies, he is committed to marry the luminous Lucy, in spite of her reluctance to take a *cicisbeo.* So devoted is Lucy to Belacqua that, on her jennet, she follows him and his bitch to the woods, where he secretly exercises his hobby as *voyeur.* There Lucy is run down by a superb limousine, "a Daimler no doubt." In their marriage there can no longer be any question of *cicisbei.*

After Lucy's demise, Belacqua offers hand and heart to Miss Thelma bboggs, and, aided and abetted by his friend Hairy Quin, endures through the fifty odd pages of the wedding, ironically entitled "What a Misfortune." Like "A Wet Night," this story is primarily social satire, but the milieu has been moved from the intellectual-arty set to the Irish Protestant bourgeoisie, whose money originates in toilet requisites.

After Thelma's abrupt disappearance, comes "The Smeraldina's Billet Doux," which purports to be a love letter from Belacqua's German girl friend. Her sentimentality, lust, and misspelling are exploited by Beckett for comic effect. "Sedendo et Quiescendo," published in *transition* in 1932, but not included in the collected *More Pricks,* recounts Belacqua's trip to Germany to woo the Smeraldina.

"Yellow" takes place in the hospital where Belacqua is to undergo simultaneous operations on neck and toe. In spite of this grotesque combination (prefiguring a characteristic Beckett concern with ailing heads and feet), flaws of real fear mar the elegant surface of the hero's thoughts. Although yellow is an Americanism for frightened, it may well be a fear of death that lends color and name to the penultimate story. But absurd beyond fear and trembling is Belacqua's death under the anesthetic; his doctor, having hurriedly departed from a wedding where he served as best man, forgets to auscultate our hero, and allows his heart to stop.

"Draff" opens with Mrs. Shuah reading Belacqua's death notice in the newspaper, this Mrs. Shuah being no other than the Smeraldina, for "Thelma née bboggs perished of sunset and honeymoon that time in Connemara. Then shortly after that they suddenly seemed to be all dead, Lucy of course long since, Ruby duly, Winnie to decency, Alba Perdue in the natural course of being seen home" (255). Thus, of all the lively ladies and less lively lads of *More Pricks Than Kicks,* only draff remains, namely the Smeraldina and faithful Hairy. After dutifully burying Belacqua, they turn to each other for solace, and survey with equanimity the conflagration that destroys the house to which Belacqua brought three brides. At Belacqua's grave, only the groundsman remains: "The words of the rose to the rose floated up to his mind: 'No gardener has died, comma, within rosaceous memory.' He sang a little song, he drank his bottle of stout, he dashed away a tear, he made himself comfortable. So it goes in the world" (278).

The volume that opened in Dante's *Paradiso,* where the man in the moon was Cain with a crown of thorns, ends in the world, with the prick of the rose and the kick of the stout. The commentary on Belacqua post mortem precludes any tinge of sympathy that may have been aroused in "Yellow." The comic tone is maintained at the last.

More Pricks Than Kicks mocks everyone and everything; even on his bier the hero has a "timeless mock" on his face.

The comedy is mainly one of manners, and the two long pieces especially, "A Wet Night" and "What a Misfortune," are in the tradition of social satire. But unlike most comedies of manners, these imply no acceptable social norm, either bourgeois or Bohemian. Nor, by laughing at the hero, do we correct any specific comic defect of our own. Only two tales, "Dante and the Lobster" and "Yellow," faintly foreshadow Beckett's later, more serious concerns with suffering. Other stories appear to be stylistic exercises, and no opportunity is lost to arouse gratuitous laughter, having little or no function in context.

Since Bergson in *Le Rire* bases his analysis of the comic largely on the comedy of manners, it is not surprising that his framework best fits this Beckett book. Of the three domains, situation, character, and language, it is mainly upon the last that Beckett's comic effects depend. Nevertheless, a few laughs are elicited by inversion of "normal" plots. In "Fingal" the hero abandons his damsel more or less in distress; in "Love and Lethe" there is a turning from suicide to sex; in "Walking Out" the hero urges his fiancée to take a lover, only to have her incapacitated for all sexual love; the lady is lustful in "The Smeraldina's Billet-Doux"; in "Draff" the dead husband's best friend replaces him in the arms of his wife.

The comic of character is almost nonexistent in *More Pricks,* or, indeed, in any Beckett work. Neither moral norm nor moral deviation is suggested. The hero is not integrated into society, but we rarely penetrate deeply enough inside him to care about his isolation. Other characters are candid caricatures.

Of Belacqua, the hero, we learn that he is fat and pasty-faced; he has a spavined gait and a heart in the Portrane Lunatic Asylum. These few sentences from "Love and Lethe" are as close as Beckett comes to characterizing his hero: "For we assume the irresponsibility of Belacqua, his faculty for acting with insufficient motivation, to have been so far

tion of the same Smeraldina from "Sedendo et Quiescendo," published in *transition.*

Well really you know and in spite of the haricot skull and a tendency to use up any odds and ends of pigment that might possibly be left over she was the living spit he thought of Madonna Lucrezia del Fede. Ne suis-je point pâle? Suis-je belle? Certainly pale and belle my pale belle Braut with a winter skin like an old sail in the wind. The roof and the source between and behind the little athletic or esthetic bit of a birdnose was indeed I assure you a constant source of delight and astonishment, when his solitude was not peopled and justified and beautified and even his sociability by a cold in the head, to his forefinger pad and nail, rubbing and plumbing and boring it just as for many years he polished his glasses (ecstasy of attrition!) or suffered the shakes and gracenote strangulations and enthrottlements of the Winkelmusik of Szopen or Pichon or Chopinek or Chopinetto or whoever it was embraced her heartily as sure as my name is Fred, dying all his life (thank you Mr Auber) on a sickroom talent (thank you Mr Field) and a Kleinmeister's Leidenschaftsucherei (thank you Mr Beckett), or crossed the Seine or the Tolka or the Pegnitz or the Fulda as the case might be and it never for one single solitary instant occurring to me that he was on all such and similar occasions (which we are sorry to say lack of space obliges us regretfully to exclude from this chronicle) indulging in and pandering to the vilest and basest excesses of sublimation of a certain kind. The wretched little wet rag of an upperlip, pugnozzling up and back in a kind of a duck or a cobra sneer to the nostrils, was happily to some extent mollified and compensated by the full firm undershot priapism of underlip and chin, a signal recovery to say the least and a reaffirmation of the promise of sentimental vehemence already so gothically declamatory in the wedgehead of the strapping girl. (16)

The passages are nearly identical, but the initial and concluding sentences of the "Draff" excerpt integrate it more skillfully and ironically into that story, while parenthetic comment is more frequent in "Sedendo et Quiescendo." The comic effect is heightened in "Draff" by such slight changes as "costive coryza" for "cold in the head," playing on names for their punning echoes, and an increased condensation along with greater accumulation of detail.

In these rather extensive illustrations of caricature, Beckett's elegant dexterity with language is evident, but the high and deliberate polish of his comic effects may be better appreciated after analysis into separate techniques. Bergson's linguistic breakdown is almost sufficient to explain the comic of *More Pricks.*

The very title of the volume incorporates puns and a twisted quotation. Considering each device separately, we may recall first the answer of Jesus to Saul:

I am Jesus whom thou persecutest: it is hard for thee to kick against the pricks. (*Acts* 9:5)

Other biblical reminders occur in the stories proper:

Faith, Hope, and—what was it? ("Ding-Dong," 47)

O Anthrax, where is thy pustule? ("Draff," 272)

They did not even give him a chance to cock up the other cheek. ("Draff," 274)

Twisted quotations come also from Chaucer, Shakespeare, and Milton:

Dream of Fair to Middling Women ("What a Misfortune," 203)

It would be like smiting the sledded Polacks on the ice. ("Dante and the Lobster," 27)

"Then you thought again," said Ruby.
"O yes," said Belacqua, "the usual pale cast." ("Love and Lethe," 132)

It was a case of darkness visible and no mistake. ("A Wet Night," 113)

Proverbs are hidden in:

The Professor of Bullscrit and Comparative Ovoidology was nowhere to be seen. But that was not his vocation, he was not a little boy. His function was to be heard. He was widely and distinctly heard. [Children should be seen and not heard.] ("A Wet Night," 89)

her absence was beginning to make itself heard, the mice were beginning to enjoy themselves [When the cat's away, the mice will play.] ("A Wet Night," 102)

Variations on common clichés sprinkle the pages:

The cold alloy in her hot palm ("What a Misfortune," 186)

Her bodice had laid down its life to save hers. ("What a Misfortune," 181)

You can't keep a dead mind down. ("What a Misfortune," 198)

common or garden incontinence ("Love and Lethe," 22)

no common or garden fix ("Yellow," 235)

Observe how he dots his i's and crucifies his t's. ("Yellow," 250)

This profusion of echoes contributes to the elaborate elegance of the prose, as do other Bergsonian devices.

The pun of the title, like that of *Whoroscope*, is not mentioned in the text, where paronomasia is rarely used. Standard definitions of both "prick" and "kick" involve pain, but in colloquial usage a kick is a passing pleasure, and a prick the sexual instrument for obtaining pleasure. The pun that embraces all the stories comically proclaims the dominance of desire over satisfaction, and irreverently twists the words of Jesus. Moreover, since the stories deal with only one hero in a series of amours, there is a comic inexactitude in *more* pricks than kicks.

Like the title, the hero's name is a book-long pun. Though Belacqua is never literalized to "beautiful water," he is called "ballocky." A biblical Shuah was the mother of Onan, and onanism may be related to Belacqua's solipsism.

In one story, as in the title of the collection, a pun summarizes a major theme. The Belacqua of "Dante and the Lobster" bubbles to his Italian teacher, "I recall one superb pun anyway: '*qui vive la pieta quando è ben morta. . . .*' " The combination of pity and piety in the Italian *pietà* is precisely the combination that Belacqua would wish to find, but cannot, on this earth-Hell, for he cannot reconcile God's mercy with His justice.

The other stories of the volume are not so quickly reducible to a comic essence. Beckett's main intention seems to be to establish comic detachment from person and event. "Laughter," Bergson insisted in *Le Rire,* "is incompatible with emotion." In *More Pricks,* Beckett eliminates emotion by sharpening those surgical instruments that Bergson grouped under comic techniques of language: misplaced literalism, hyperbole, litotes, irony, jargon, incongruity, parody, and paradox.

In this volume, which abounds in fanciful metaphor, misplaced literalism occurs rarely:

> But he's not here, damn it. . . . If he was he'd be here. ("Fingal," 38)

> "Our Lord—"
> "Speak for yourself." ("A Wet Night," 75)

Hyperbole and litotes usually re-enforce the comic elegance of more complex linguistic devices, and do not call for separate study. Irony, on the other hand, occurs at several levels. In its simplest guise—meaning opposite to statement—we find:

She had it from God, therefore he could rely on its being accurate in every particular. ("Dante and the Lobster," 24)

I gave him up in the end because he was not *serious*. ("Ding-Dong," 46)

Ironic litotes operates in:

He did not know the French for lobster. Fish would do very well. Fish had been good enough for Jesus Christ, Son of God, Saviour. It was good enough for Mlle Glain. ("Dante and the Lobster," 34)

"Oh," he gasped, "really I . . . really you . . ." and broke down. To construct a sentence with subject, predicate and object, Hairy required a pencil and a sheet of paper. ("What a Misfortune," 176)

Ironies of situation in *More Pricks* have already been discussed, and irony of tone is often composed of the several remaining devices in Bergson's catalogue. In the main, irony functions as merely another comic technique. Although its studied elegance is "different in kind or degree" from what is said, Beckett neither strives for nor attains "saying as little and meaning as much as possible." [11] Rather, he seems eager to exhibit the dexterity of his linguistic control.

Other than such Irishisms as "curate" for "bartender" and "motte" for "mistress," almost all of Beckett's jargon is literary and/or learned. Since this is one of the principal ingredients of his comic tone in this volume, examples might be chosen from almost any page, all of them increasing the reader's detachment from the characters.

brambles passim . . . tesserae of small fields ("Fingal," 23, 24)

He had allowed himself to get run down, but he scoffed at the idea of a sequitur from his body to his mind. ("Fingal," 32) a mind like a tattered concordance . . . listen to this clockwork Bartlett ("A Wet Night," 65)

Yet he found he could not, any more than Buridan's ass, move to right or left, backward or forward. ("Ding-Dong," 47)

A great major symphony of supply and demand, effect and cause, fulcrate on the middle C of the counter and waxing, as it proceeded, in the charming harmonics of blasphemy and broken glass and all the aliquots of fatigue and ebriety. ("Ding-Dong," 52)

She was very optative. ("A Wet Night," 91)

Justice and mercy had doubtless joined their ancient issue in the conscience of the guard, for he said nothing. Belacqua tendered his right hand, innocent of any more mercantile commodity than that "gentle peace" recommended by the immortal Shakespeare, having first wiped it clean on his sleeve. This member the Dogberry, after a brief converse with his incorruptible heart, was kind enough to invest with the office of cuspidor. ("A Wet Night," 97)

Greek and Roman reasons, Sturm and Drang reasons, reasons metaphysical, aesthetic, erotic, anterotic and chemical, Empedocles of Agrigentum and John of the Cross reasons, in short all but the true reasons, which did not exist, at least not for the purposes of conversation. ("A Wet Night," 123–124)

In one form or another, as Bergson pointed out, all comic of transposition rests upon incongruity.[12] Jargon, for example, is specialized terminology that is incongruous with the subject. Paradox is a juxtaposition of two items so incongruous as to be antonymic. Beckett's incongruity often arises from an image that is ludicrously out of key with what it describes. He mistreats the heavenly bodies:

The sun, that creature of habit ("Yellow," 241)

Bright and cheery above the strom of the Green, as though coached by the star of Bethlehem, the Bovril sign danced and danced. ("A Wet Night," 61)

"I don't see the moon," she said. Like a jack-in-the-box the satellite obliged. ("Draff," 267)

Belacqua is, ironically and incongruously, a slayer of flowers:

To kneel before them [snapdragons] in the dust and clay of the ground and throttle them gently till their tongues protruded ("What a Misfortune," 163)

When Belacqua lies in his coffin, his best friend arrives.

"Might I see him?" he whispered, like a priest asking for a book in the Trinity College Library. ("Draff," 263)

Belacqua's wife leads his friend to the death chamber.

They diverged, the body was between them on the bed like the keys between nations in Valasquez's *Lances,* like the water between Buda and Pest and so on, hyphen of reality. ("Draff," 263)

In "Dante and the Lobster" there are several examples of incongruity which are sharpened in the revised version: "to feel his fangs break through the splendid hard crust of toast into a yielding zone" becomes "to feel his teeth meet in a bathos of pith and dough" (25). Similarly, "so that the whole presented an appearance of a diamond and square with common center" is changed to "so that the whole resembled the Japanese flag" (26).

Since Beckett is a master of the off-key image, he frequently accumulates paragraphs and even scenes in which the subject clashes with the tone, itself reminiscent of some well-established style. The result is parody. But before glancing at illustrations of the comic tone involved in parody, we may note a curious and sudden introduction of relative seriousness into "Dante and the Lobster." I quote the sentences before and after the atonal paragraph, which, like several pages before and after, contain the comically meticulous details of the preparation of Belacqua's lunch.

> When the first candidate [a slice of bread for a sandwich] was done, which was only when it was black through and through, it changed places with its comrade, so that now it in its turn lay on top, done to a dead end, black and smoking, waiting till as much could be said of the other.
>
> For the tiller of the field the thing was simple, he had it from his mother. The spots were Cain with his truss of thorns, dispossessed, cursed from the earth, fugitive and vagabond. The moon was that countenance fallen and branded, seared with the first stigmata of God's pity, that an outcast might not die quickly. It was a mix-up in the mind of the tiller, but that did not matter. It had been good enough for his mother, it was good enough for him.
>
> Belacqua on his knees before the flame, poring over the grill, controlled every phase of the broiling. (26–27)

In spite of the cynical "stigmata of God's pity" and the colloquial "good enough for," Cain is treated with compassion. It is interesting, too, that this was almost the only unrevised paragraph in the story. Dante's image of Cain in the moon recurs to haunt Beckett in *Malone Dies,* but neither here nor later is it evoked in parody. Although the abrupt tonal shift may add to the comic, this paragraph seems to be a relatively sober anomaly in the volume.

The most persistent comic device of *More Pricks Than Kicks* is parody. Literary parody may mock a particular work or author; Fielding's *Shamela Andrews* after Richardson's *Pamela* is the classic example in English literature, and Joyce's "Oxen in the Sun" episode of *Ulysses,* parodying a myriad of English prose styles, is the virtuoso illustration. Beckett usually mocks a kind of literature rather than a specific work. Thus, in the following passage, "He laid his cheek against the soft of the bread, it was spongy and warm, alive.

But he would very soon take that plush feel off it, by God but he would very quickly take that fat white look off its face" ("Dante and the Lobster," 26). Beckett attacks a piece of bread as a mustachioed villain does the innocent maiden who cannot pay the rent. In the same story, the subsequent dialogue of Belacqua and a grocer is a parody of the dialogue style of all penny dreadfuls, and the misspelled sentimentalism of "The Smeraldina's Billet-Doux" parodies all man-hungry maidens.

One story in *More Pricks* is, if not a parody of another work, a variation on the same theme. Joyce's "The Dead" and Beckett's "A Wet Night" are both stories of Christmas Eve parties in Dublin. The hostesses in the one are sisters and niece, and in the other, mother and daughter. In both works there are festive tables and lingering descriptions of good food; there are free-flowing spirits both liquid and verbal; there are musical renditions, both vocal and instrumental, punctuated with lust and longing. Even Joyce's Protestant Mr. Browne finds a foil in Beckett's Jesuit priest, who justifies his faith: "The best reason that can be given for believing is that it is more amusing. Disbelief . . . is a bore. We do not count our change. We simply cannot bear to be bored" (76).

Although the milieu in both stories borders on the "arty," there are decades between them. The ultra-Irish Miss Ivors gives way to a Communist, the dancing to necking in the bedrooms, the blanket of snow over Ireland to a dismal rain upon Dublin. As artificially as Gabriel (in his speech) attempts to revive the past, the denizens of "A Wet Night" recite poems in old French, play an ancient musical instrument, the viol d'amore, or write poems about Calvary. Joyce's sympathy is pervasive for the dead and the dying; equally pervasive is Beckett's mockery. Man of faith and man of reason, poet and slut, dead and dying—no one escapes his poisonous pen. In a passage that thinly recalls the magnificent conclusion of "The Dead," Beckett's ridicule reaches out to all of dull Dublin.

But the wind had dropped, as it so often does in Dublin when all respectable men and women whom it delights to annoy have gone to bed, and the rain fell in a uniform untroubled manner. It fell upon the bay, the littoral, the mountains and the plains, and notably upon the Central Bog, it fell with a rather desolate uniformity. (112–113)

Perhaps, too, this passage contributes to Beckett's name for Belacqua's second wife, bboggs, mocking at once Irish landscape, orthography, and uniformity.

In describing the initial appearance of Thelma bboggs, Beckett parodies the omniscience of the Victorian author, making free use of hyperbole, litotes, jargon, and involved syntax.

When we say a girl of substance we mean that her promissory wad, to judge by her father's bearing in general and in particular by his respiration after song, was, so to speak, short-dated. To deny that Belacqua was alive to this circumstance would be to present him as an even greater imbecile than he was when it came to seeing the obvious; whereas to suggest that it was implied, however slightly, in his brusque obsession with the beneficiary to be, would constitute such an obloquy as we do not much care to deal in. Let us therefore put forth a minimum of charity and observe in a casual way, with eyes cast down and head averted until the phrase has ceased to vibrate, that he happened to conceive one of his Olympian fancies for a fairly young person with expectations. We can't straddle the fence nicer than that. (164)

The short parenthetical concluding sentence heightens the ludicrousness of the elaborate parody.

Beckett frequently manipulates the sudden tonal shift so as to establish, over the heads of his characters, a direct relationship with his reader. But unlike nineteenth-century novelists who speak in their fiction *in propria persona,* Beckett keeps his tongue firmly in his cheek, and one can rarely take his parenthetical intrusions at face value. In *More Pricks,* such intrusion usually presents irrelevantly comic information:

the reader is requested to notice that this sweet style is Belacqua's ("Ding-Dong," 56)

We have set it down too soon, perhaps. Still, let it bloody well stand. ("A Wet Night," 83)

(this is very deep) ("Love and Lethe," 123)

Reader, a rosiner is a drop of the hard.
Reader, a gloria is coffee laced with brandy. ("Love and Lethe," 119)

From now till the end there is something very *secco* and Punch and Judy about their proceedings. ("Love and Lethe," 131)

Here also art and love . . . were barred, or, perhaps better, unknown. The aesthetes and the impotent were far away. ("Ding-Dong," 50)

It is from this moment that he used to date in after years his crucial loss of interest in himself, as in a grape beyond his grasp. ("What a Misfortune," 212)

Poor Belacqua, he seems to be having a very dull, irksome morning, preparing for the fray in this manner. But he will make up for it later on, there is a good time coming for him later on, when the doctors have given him a new lease of apathy. ("Yellow," 234)

The cliché "good time coming" for Belacqua is, ironically, death on the operating table.

After Belacqua's death, Beckett allows himself a grotesquely comic omniscient intrusion:

Belacqua had often looked forward to meeting the girls, Lucy especially, hallowed and transfigured beyond the veil. What a hope! Death had already cured him of that naïveté. ("Draff," 264)

Perhaps the most significant personal intrusion in the volume comes at the end of "Dante and the Lobster." When Belacqua realizes that lobsters are boiled alive, he thinks with unwonted piety, "It's a quick death, God help us." Beckett's own mordant conclusion follows: "It is not"—a denial that seems to embrace human death, from McCabe to Belacqua.

Such flat contradiction is rare in *More Pricks,* where Beckett prefers the polish of paradox. Isolated examples are:

A gentlewoman of the people ("Ding-Dong," 55)

Past the worst of the best ("Walking Out," 142)

impersonal pity ("What a Misfortune," 162)

Known to his admirers as Hairy, he was so glabrous and to the ladies as Tiny, he was so enormous. ("What a Misfortune," 175)

In "Yellow" appears a commentary upon paradox and the comic mode that is relevant to all of Beckett's works. In an examination of Belacqua's mind (from an Olympian omniscience), which prefigures that minute scrutiny to which Beckett will subject the minds of later protagonists, he allows his hero to have an inspiration:

At this crucial point the good God came to his assistance with a phrase from a paradox of Donne: *Now among our wise men, I doubt not but many would be found, who would laugh at Heraclitus weeping, none which would weep at Democritus laughing.* This was a godsend and no error. Not the phrase as a judgment, but its terms, the extremes of wisdom that it tendered to Belacqua. It is true that he did not care for these black and white alternatives as a rule. Indeed he even went so far as to hazard a little paradox on his own account, to the effect that between contraries no alternation was possible. But was it the moment for a man to be nice? Belacqua snatched eagerly at the issue. Was it to be laughter or tears? It came to the same thing in the end, but which was it to be *now*? (*"Yellow,"* 235–236)

He must efface himself altogether and do the little soldier. It was this paramount consideration that made him decide in favour of Bim and Bom, Grock, Democritus, whatever you are pleased to call it, and postpone its dark converse to a less public occasion. This was an abnegation if you like, for Belacqua could not resist a lachrymose philosopher, and still less when, as was the case with Heraclitus, he was obscure at the same time. He was in his element in dingy tears, and luxuriously so when these were furnished by a pre-Socratic man of acknowledged distinction. How often had he not exclaimed, skies being grey: "Another minute of this and I consecrate the remnant of my life to Heraclitus of Ephesus, I shall be that Delian diver who, after the third or fourth submersion, returns no more to the surface!" ("Yellow," 237)

It is not, of course, permissible to equate Belacqua with Beckett, and it may be doubted whether Beckett cast a similar and sudden vote for Democritus of Abdera, "the laughing philosopher" of antiquity. But the workings of Belacqua's mind had, at some point, to be the workings of Beckett's mind, and these, in turn, bear directly upon various Existentialist ideas that were gnawing at the philosophic milieu of Paris of the thirties: that "Existence," to quote Kierkegaard, "is both pathetic and comic in the same degree"; that the world is absurd; that man becomes aware of his freedom in the face of death. "Yellow" is the story of a man who, facing death, chooses the comic response, but who dies like the figure in the punch line of Belacqua's joke, to provide an even larger joke, a cosmic joke. Like the pity-piety pun of "Dante and the Lobster," the joke of "Yellow" epitomizes the story.

Belacqua tells himself about the parson who is asked to play a bit part in an amateur production. When a revolver goes off, the parson is to declare, "By God! I'm shot!" and sham dead. Objecting to taking the name of the Lord in vain, he volunteers to perform with a milder expletive. "But the production was so amateur that the revolver went off indeed and the man of God was transfixed. "Oh!" he cried, "oh . . . !

. . . BY CHRIST! *I* AM SHOT!" In parallel fashion, Belacqua *does* die in the amateur production where he plays a role, while offstage, perhaps, some audience laughs. Like the pun in "Dante and the Lobster," the comic device summarizes the work.

The joke of "Yellow" is an extreme example of the illiberal jest, for the pain of death is inflicted upon the victim. Elsewhere in *More Pricks,* we find a child run over ("Ding-Dong"), a woman maimed ("Walking Out"), rape and arson ("Draff"). On the other hand, Beckett altered an especially cruel passage of "Dante and the Lobster." With reference to the coming execution of McCabe the murderer, Beckett writes, in the book version,

> Belacqua, tearing at the sandwich and swilling the precious stout, pondered on McCabe in his cell. (32)

Cruel as this is, it is gentle compared to Belacqua's original reaction upon hearing of the denial of McCabe's petition for mercy:

> If anything was wanted to crown that exquisite gastronomical experience, it was just such a piece of news.

In the light of this lugubrious appetite, Belacqua's mercy for the lobster is all the more grotesque. When Belacqua himself lies dead, "the unassumed grief [of his friends] giv[es] zest to their bacon and eggs."

Like Beckett's illiberal jests, his shock devices belong to one of the oldest traditions of Western comedy, and are too crude for Bergson to notice in an analysis based largely on the civilized comedy of manners. Shock laughs have always played a large role in slapstick, farce, and the coarser dirty joke. Beckett does not, as in the later works, depend upon *gros mots* to evoke laughter, but he elegantly circumnavigates their territory:

He had pleasure in referring his wife and first-born to that portion of himself which he never desired any person to kick nor volunteered to kiss in another. ("What a Misfortune," 166)

The disgusting, too, is frequently employed for evoking shock laughter:

He waddled . . . into the lowly public . . . like a bit of dirt into a Hoover. ("A Wet Night," 67)

his face a blaze of acne ("A Wet Night," 85)

a great raw châteaubriant of a woman ("Yellow," 243)

he . . . had a truly military evacuation ("Yellow," 247)

If this breakdown of *More Pricks Than Kicks* into techniques for evoking laughter seems to make hash of fiction, it may be suggested that Beckett himself wields the hatchet. The single hero and the consistently comic tone do provide a certain unity to the volume, as did Descartes and a dissimilar comic tone in *Whoroscope*. In the poem, however, theme, metaphor, and linguistic formulae give form to the whole, which otherwise diffuses into the diverse incidents in Descartes's life. In *More Pricks,* the stories are disconnected in spite of occasional cross references; Beckett's comic veneer precludes sympathy for the characters. Some of the stories—"Love and Lethe," "Walking Out," and "Draff"—are excessively sharp with cynical irony; others—"Fingal," "Ding-Dong," and "The Smeraldina's Billet-Doux"—have their points blunted by overelaboration of style; still others—"A Wet Night" and "What a Misfortune"—are social satires suffering from the lack of an implied ideal. Only "Dante and the Lobster" and "Yellow" reveal a sustained theme beneath the comic cloak, and prefigure Beckett's concern with the meaning of suffering. The unevenness of the collection suggests that Beckett was exercising his stylistic wings before a longer fictional flight.

Before turning to longer fiction, Beckett published in Paris a group of thirteen English poems, *Echo's Bones.* This volume appeared in 1935, the year after *More Pricks,* and shares a vaguely Dantesque background with the stories. Two of the thirteen poems are named after characters in the stories: Alba, Belacqua's "See-me-home" girl, and Malacoda, Belacqua's undertaker. In Alba's poem, however, her beauty evokes the melancholy image of a winding sheet, rather than comic suggestions. In his poem as in "Draff," Malacoda is an undertaker's man. As in Dante's *Inferno,* Malacoda of *Echo's Bones* seems to have a trumpet-rump, but "the expert awe/ that felts his perineum mutes his signal."[13] Malacoda's trumpet-rump made an impression on both Dante and Beckett, and its resonance is apposite in a volume entitled *Echo's Bones,* into whose thirteen poems enters an infernal mood. Ironically, Beckett substitutes lilies for Danteian pitch, but then lilies are professional accouterment for Malacoda, the "undertaker's man" in the "scutal bowler" that was to become the crown of subsequent Beckett characters.

The over-all tone of the poems differs from that of the stories, being somewhat reminiscent of the Eliot of the Preludes, or of the sadder French Symbolists such as Verlaine and Corbière. Beckett paints scenes (usually Irish) of vulgarity, meaninglessness, cruelty, with slight comic touches. Nine of the thirteen poems involve a first-person persona, but the character of this persona is never established; he might be a slow-spoken Belacqua Shuah, with comparable solipsistic tendencies ("the sky/ of my skull"). It is possible to extract examples of most of the Bergsonian linguistic devices, and yet the comic tone rarely dominates.

Twisted cliché or quotation:

good as gold now in the prime after a brief prodigality ("Sanies I")

suck is not suck that alters . . .
lo Alighieri has got off au revoir to all that ("Sanies II")

He could not serve typhoid and mammon ("Serena I")

Misplaced literalism:

The Barfrau makes a big impression with her mighty bottom ("Sanies II")

They are necking gobble-gobble ("Sanies II")

Pun: "Enueg," the title of two poems, may be a play upon the old form of "enough" and its near-homonym "ennui." A Latin pun on "world" and "clean" is contained in the brief lines" Veronica mundi/ Veronica munda," which refer to the legend of St. Veronica, who wiped Christ's face on the way to Calvary, and found His features miraculously imprinted on her handkerchief.

Jargon: There are occasional colloquial intrusions, such as "Give us a wipe for the love of Jesus," after the Latin pun just discussed. Of Beckett's more usual learned comic jargon, only the following example is noteworthy:

I see main verb at last
her whom alone in the accusative
I have dismounted to love. ("Sanies I")

Irony: Within the bitter, sometimes desperate context of the poems, most pleas to God, Lord, and Christ may be taken at face value, but the concluding lines of "Serena II" cast doubt upon the effectiveness of all prayer.

So say your prayers now and go to bed
your prayers before the lamps start to sing behind the larches
here at these knees of stone
then to bye-bye on the bones.

Incongruity: This is perhaps the single linguistic technique that Beckett continues to use with comic overtones, however harsh the laughter.

throttled with clouds . . .
a pint of nepenthe or moly ("Enueg I")

Feet in marmalade . . .
heart in marmalade ("Enueg II")

viper's curtsey ("Serena I")

tired now hair ebbing gums ebbing ebbing home ("Sanies I")

Parody would require more development than Beckett gives to any of the poems; nor is there personal intrusion, since the "I" lacks comic detachment. Paradox, too, is absent, but in connection with Belacqua's comment on Donne's paradox in "Yellow," the reappearance of Democritus, the laughing philosopher, has sardonic resonance.

Democritus
scuttling along between a crutch and a stick
his stump caught up horribly, like a claw, under his breech,
smoking [not laughing] ("Enueg I")

The horror in the lines is scarcely comic, but if they are related backward to the laughing Democritus of the Donne quotation and forward to Beckett's French heroes, whom these lines might describe, one is again reminded of Kierkegaard's insistence on the kinship between the comic and the pathetic.

The poems contain the two Beckett comic techniques that bolster the tradition of the illiberal jest. The shock effect of the obscene and the disgusting is seen in the titles, "Sanies" and "The Vulture," as well as in such lines as:

All heaven in the sphincter
The sphincter ("Sanies I")

and the stillborn evening turning a filthy green
manuring the night fungus ("Enueg I")

Cruelty is visible everywhere:

tired of my darling's red sputum ("Enueg I")

All aboard all souls/half-mast aye aye ("Malacoda")

Illiberal jests are particularly incisive in the short lyrics, the introductory "Vulture," and the concluding "Da Tagte Es" and "Echo's Bones." The last of these, which lends its title to the collection, is most cruelly comic.

asylum under my tread this day
their muffled revels as the flesh falls
breaking without fear or favour wind
the gantelope of sense and nonsense run
taken by the maggots for what they are

The title may refer to either of the two myths about Echo. According to Longus, having spurned Pan, she is torn limb from limb, but her fragments, buried in the earth, have the power of song. In the Ovidian tale, Juno, in revenge upon Echo for her chatter to conceal Jupiter's amours with the mountain nymphs, causes Echo to fall in love with the self-immersed Narcissus. Scorned, Echo pines until only her voice and bones remain.

Through the grammatical ambiguity of the fifth-line "they" and the second-line "theirs," Beckett's poem reduces human life to that process whereby the bones lose their flesh to be left with only an echo. For Beckett, this process evokes raucous response ("revels," "breaking . . . wind"). The "gantelope [gauntlet, but "gantelope" flavors the "run" with antelope suggestions] of sense and nonsense" plays upon all the meanings of "sense" which fill this life, but finally, as Hamlet says, "We fat ourselves for maggots." Wind broken is also breath stopped—the obscene death that attends us all "without fear or favour."

Thus, Echo's suffering flesh festers clean of her bones, and only the repetitive song remains, skeletal and ambiguous in its eschewal of rhyme, meter, stanza, and conventional syntax. In all the poems, extremely tight statements, almost aphorisms, combine with more leisurely city landscapes to paint the world's cruelty and pathos. Obscure references fill the lines; inserted into shifting mood and scene, they render explication difficult, and appreciation sporadic. Although comic notes intrude, they do not furnish either a dominant or a unifying tone.

Murphy the morph

for all the good that frequent departures out of Ireland had done him, he might as well have stayed there
Watt

Beckett moved permanently to Paris a year or two after the publication of *Echo's Bones,*[1] but *Murphy,* his first novel, appeared in London in 1938. It received scant attention—two paragraphs in the *Times Literary Supplement,* under "Political and Social Novels"[2]—and most of the edition was destroyed by bombs early in World War II.

Like *Echo's Bones, Murphy* is divided into thirteen parts, and M, the thirteenth letter of the alphabet, figures prominently in the novel. Except for Cork and Dublin interludes, the setting is London, and various sections of the city are specifically designated. In spite of the local scene, comparable to the Dublin of *More Pricks,* there is little social satire in the novel. Less than most of the short stories does *Murphy* belong to the comedy of manners, but Bergson's analysis of the comic can still serve this Beckett work.

Tone is the major source of the comic. The elegant, mocking omniscience of *Murphy* is a continuation of that of *More Pricks.* The taste of the Beckett of 1938 for this type of high polish is demonstrated even in this criticism. "The time is not altogether too green," he sneers in an article on Denis Devlin, "for the vile suggestion that art has nothing to do with clarity, does not dabble in the clear and does not make clear, any more than the light of day (or night) makes the subsolar, -lunar and -stellar excrement."[3]

Murphy is hardly a clear book, but it is clearly comic in its details. Situation, in particular, is developed with more concession to traditional comic plot than in any subsequent Beckett novel. The quest for Murphy (in which Murphy, after his own fashion, also participates) is the unifying thread of the book. Murphy, lifting a line from the Jacobean *Witch of Edmonton,* declares that life is "but a wandering to find home," and Murphy himself seems to represent home to Neary and Miss Counihan. As Wylie phrases it, "Our medians . . . meet in Murphy."

The meeting point of the medians of a triangle is the center of its circumscribing circle, and the circle is the perfect symbol of a self-contained cosmos. When that cosmos is the self, the circle becomes the symbol of solipsism, and indeed Murphy is explicitly designated as a "seedy solipsist," who pictures his mind as a sphere.

Murphy is the answer to love's young dream for Celia and Miss Counihan, neither of whom is so far gone in the dream, however, that she will accept an impecunious Murphy. For Wylie and Cooper, Murphy is a steppingstone to Neary's wallet, but for the ex-Academician Neary, Murphy evolves from student to rival to friend. After Murphy's death, there is no simple cruel-comic resolution, as after Belacqua's death. If Miss Counihan and Wylie take solace in each other's arms, as did the Smeraldina and Hairy Quin, Celia and Neary exit separately in more solipsistic fashion.

Murphy can scarcely be said to contain a well-made plot, but there is a certain "vulgarity of plausible concatenation" which Beckett found so happily wanting in Dostoyevsky and

Proust.[4] On the other hand, deliberate non-concatenation is one of the comic devices. Mocking the thrillers whose chapters close at a high point of suspense, *Murphy's* Chapter 5 ends, "he arrived to find . . . Celia spreadeagled on her face on the bed. A shocking thing had happened." But Celia proves to be unharmed, and the shocking thing—a suicide—is irrelevant to the main plot.

Within the chapters, there is occasional and ludicrous *non sequitur* from paragraph to paragraph. In Chapter 10, the dénouement consists of witty, learned dialogue that bears upon the philosophic substratum of the novel, but is largely irrelevant to the plot. Frequently, there is no transition between the remarks.

Beckett avoids transitions, but he makes use of book-long motifs for a laugh. Pre-eminent among these are Celia's profession (prostitution), Murphy's aggressive lack of profession, and the rocking chair in which both (separately) find bliss. The persistent echoes of Suk's horoscope (which Celia shrinks from calling by name), Mr. Kelly's obsession with his kite, Neary's with drink, Wylie's with money and sex, Miss Carridge's overpowering stink, and Cooper's inability to sit down, take off his hat, or bypass a saloon—all these weave through the plot, becoming the leitmotifs of the characters involved.

Other than Murphy, however, Beckett announces that there are no characters: "All the puppets in this book whinge sooner or later, except Murphy, who is not a puppet." However, since the different puppets respond with more or less flexibility to their strings, this remark cannot be taken at face value.

Celia arouses more affection than any of Belacqua's various women. Her need of Murphy is less egotistical than that of the others, and she seems to have spiritual resources, even though these serve her intermittently and are often evidenced through comic means. Thus, she fits with ease into Murphy's rocker; she seems to go through a catharsis when her neighbor, the Old Boy, commits suicide; she has an intuition, when Murphy goes to work, that he is leaving her forever; and, finally, she is stunned to numbness by Murphy's death. Although she returns to business afterwards, she is, perhaps, changed by having known Murphy. Not quite humanized, she is caricatured by her professional gait and her Beckett locutions.

Neary, second to Celia in complexity, remains a caricature. His academic phrases, his perennial thirst, his unappetizing appearance ("Do not be alarmed . . . the vast majority of them are mere bedsores") are exploited for gratuitous laughter. Still, he does come to think of Murphy as a friend. After Murphy's death, Neary is generosity itself to his impecunious companions.

The other people in the novel are reduced to their ridiculous motifs—Mr. Kelly to his kite, Miss Carridge to her odor, Ticklepenny to his homosexuality, Miss Rosie Dew to her duck-feet and medium, Bim and Bom to their crude brutality,[5] Dr. Killiecrankie and the Coroner to their sophisticated brutality. By comparison, the inmates of the ironically named Magdalen Mental Mercyseat are spared. Not that Beckett speaks kindly of them, for that might be to sentimentalize them, but he foregoes the mordant mockery with which he attacks their keepers. Moreover, Murphy's fellow feeling for the alienated makes for a tempering of Beckett's own authorial detachment. Mr. Endon, floating so self-sufficiently (except for the occasional need of a chess partner) through the Mercyseat, almost arouses admiration. And yet there is only an oblique implication that those in the Mercyseat are sane, those outside insane. Although such an inversion might seem ideal for the comedy of manners, it is an oversimplification that Beckett does not stress. Murphy is delightfully at ease with the alienated, is inordinately pleased to be taken as one of them; yet he is compelled to admit he is not one of them. Failing where they succeed, he is unable to live entirely in his mind.

Murphy has been discerningly interpreted as a Cartesian novel,[6] in which Murphy, conscious of his "unredeemed split self," seeks to withdraw from the physical world at large, and retire into his mind. In one of the most serious paragraphs of the novel, Beckett states this explicitly:

> The issue therefore, as lovingly simplified and perverted by Murphy, lay between nothing less fundamental than the big world and the little world, decided by the patients in favour of the former, in his own case unresolved. In fact, it was unresolved, only in fact. His vote was cast. "I am not of the big world, I am of the little world" was an old refrain with Murphy, and a conviction, two convictions, the negative first. How should he tolerate, let alone cultivate, the occasions of fiasco, having once beheld the beatific idols of his cave? In the beautiful Belgo-Latin of Arnold Geulincx: *Ubi nihil vales, ibi nihil velis.* (178)

Subsequent Beckett heroes will, like Murphy, find themselves reluctant to accept the absolute Cartesian cleavage between body and mind; instead, they too will be attracted to Arnold Geulincx, the seventeenth-century Cartesian, who emphasized the delights of the mind.

Although the Latin quotation is the only Murphy reference to Geulincx, there are several, mainly comic, reminders of Descartes. The "Dutch uncle," Mr. Quigley, who is fooled into sending Murphy his means of subsistence, moves about Holland in the way Descartes did three hundred years earlier. In striking and ironic contrast to Descartes, who refused to have his nativity cast, Murphy has blind faith in his horoscope, and Beckett takes every opportunity to comment upon the position of various heavenly bodies—beyond Celia's.

Unlike the rationalist Descartes, however, and only faintly reminiscent of Geulincx, whose domain was ethics, Murphy prefers purely esthetic contemplation. A "strict non-reader" though a former theology student, Murphy meditates best in his rocker in the stove-heated garret of the Mercyseat. That garret is specifically linked to Leibniz,[7] and the stove is a cogent Cartesian reminder. It is of the utmost importance, in this novel, that Murphy is killed by an explosion of his stove. Withdrawal into the mental microcosm results in death, however comically treated. Only the more purely physical caricatures are equipped for survival in this *quid-pro-quo* world.

Murphy, like *More Pricks Than Kicks,* is peopled with caricatures, and none is so grotesque as Cooper, whose "only visible humane characteristic was a morbid craving for alcoholic depressant. . . . He was a low-sized, clean-shaven, grey-faced, one-eyed man, triorchous and a nonsmoker. He had a curious hunted walk, like that of a destitute diabetic in a strange city. He never sat down and never took off his hat" (54). Murphy himself never wears a hat because the memories it awakens of the caul are too poignant, but Cooper's hat is particularized as a bowler, which is later destroyed by Cooper's throwing himself in the air to fall, seat on hat, when, freed presumably by Murphy's death, he regains his powers of the doff and the seat. It is Cooper who is responsible for Murphy's last resting place, on a barroom floor, and it is Cooper who, elected above the other caricatures in the book, is the physical incarnation of Beckett's French heroes.

Cooper is the only character who does not speak like Murphy, like Belacqua, or like Beckett as omniscient author. He says very little, in fact, but is a talented mime. "The skill is really extraordinary with which analphabetes, especially those of Irish education, circumvent their dread of verbal commitments. Now Cooper's face, though it did not seem to move a muscle, brought together and threw off in a single grimace the finest shades of irresolution, revulsion, doglike devotion, catlike discretion, fatigue, hunger, thirst and reserves of strength, in a very small fraction of the time that the finest oratory would require for a greatly inferior evasion, and without exposing its proprietor to misquotation" (205).

Cooper, however, is the only member of *Murphy's* company with this gift of expressive silence. All the others speak profusely, and Beckett plays linguistic tricks around them, much as he did in *More Pricks Than Kicks*. As in the polished prose of the short story collection, he is lavish of twisted cliché and quotation, more chary of misplaced literalism.

So multiple are his manipulations of familiar phrases that they may be subdivided. Cliché variants are plentiful:

It was a striking case of love requited. (16)

Scratch an old man and find a Quintillian. (17)

"Shall I bite the hand that starves me," said Murphy, "to have it throttle me?" (19)

Murphy, unable to believe his ears, opened his eyes. (29)

I enter the jaws of a job. (37)

words were inadequate to conceal what he felt (130)

Miss Carridge's pity knew no bounds but alms. (154)

he laboured . . . at his own little dungeon in Spain. (180)

Miss Counihan's hot buttered buttocks. (208)

Variations on proverbs or folk sayings are often found:

Celia spent every penny she earned and Murphy earned no pennies. (19)

It was like looking for a needle in a haystack full of vipers. (116)

He must sit down before he could lie down. (79)

The end degrades the way into a means (188)

Turf is compulsory in the Saorstat, but one need not bring a private supply to Newcastle. (197)

Women are really extraordinary, the way they want to give their cake to the cat and have it. They never quite kill the thing they think they love, lest their instinct for artificial respiration go a begging. (202–203)

man proposed, but God disposed, even in the Magdalen Mental Mercyseat. (237)

Twisted quotations, frequently echo and ridicule biblical sources:

The sun shone . . . on the nothing new. (1)

The imperturbable negligence of Providence to provide (21)

"The hireling fleeth because he is an hireling," . . . "What shall a man give in exchange for Celia?" (22)

Only the most local movements were possible, a licking of the lips, a turning of the other cheek to the dust, and so on. (28)

after many days, Miss Carridge found her bread, it came bobbing back to her in the form of free samples (132)

there will be more joy in heaven over Murphy finding a job than over the billions of leatherbums that never had anything else. (138)

Let there be Heaven in the midst of the waters, let it divide the waters from the waters. The Chaos and Waters Facilities Act. The Chaos, Light and Coke Co. Hell. Heaven. Helen. Celia. (176)[8]

Cooper experienced none of the famous difficulty in serving two employers. He neither clave nor despised. (197)

The horse-leech's daughter is a closed system. Her quantum of wantum cannot vary. (57, 200)[9]

Marlowe is comically misquoted:

Infinite riches in a w. c. (218)

Shakespeare is mangled:

The economy of care was better served . . . when they knit up the sleave by day. (239)

Misplaced literalism is combined with the pun:

The means of clinching it were lacking. Suppose he were to clinch it now, in the service of the Clinch clan? (179)

Of book-long comic importance is the combined misplaced literalism and pun, "off his rocker." In the world's eyes, Murphy is "off his rocker" when he is rocking blissfully and nakedly. But for Murphy, that is the best way of retiring into his microcosm. It is in the macrocosm, literally off his rocker, that *he* feels figuratively off it.

Purer examples of misplaced literalism are:

"I have it," she said. "Don't I know," said Murphy. (8)

"Why the black envelope?" . . . "Because this is blackmail." (31–32)

"She will sit as one might say pretty" "One might well." (60)

It was true that Cooper never sat, his acathisia was deep-seated and of long standing. (119)

An inelegant literalism, almost serious in its searching intent, describes Murphy's first day at the MMM (as the Mercyseat is abbreviated):

Murphy reported to Bom at two o'clock and entered upon that experience from which already he hoped for better things, without exactly knowing why or what things or in what way better. (170)

As in the stories and *Whoroscope,* the puns introduce comic ambiguities. "In the beginning," Beckett quips through Murphy, "was the pun" (65). And also at the end, for just as

T. S. Eliot's "Hurry up please, it's time," signifies more than the closing hour of a pub, so the Hyde Park guard's "All out" closes more than the gates.

In Celia's absence, Mr. Kelly attempts to console himself with a pun: "Celia s'il y a, Celia s'il y a (for he had excellent French)." The same Celia is not amused by a pun that causes Murphy to have a laughing fit bordering on epilepsy: "Why did the barmaid champagne? . . . Because the stout porter bitter" (139).

Murphy on the "jobpath" is likened to Bildad the Shuhite, who is "but a fragment of Job," and his suit "felt like felt"; he "remained constantly on his guard against the various threats to his Hyleg and whole person generally." Perhaps the seductive quality of the pun for Murphy who is, after all, "not a puppet" is a reflection of its attraction for Beckett, who may have charged it with a major meaning of the novel.

The name Celia, with its celestial overtones, for Murphy's prostitute-mistress is an obvious irony, and has a precedent in Belacqua's Alba, Ruby, Lucy, and Miss bboggs. The name Murphy does not derive, like Belacqua, from Dante, and yet is probably not pure Irish, but a pun upon the Greek "morphe" meaning "form," which is both what Murphy is seeking for himself and an indication of how he will serve Beckett—as the prototype of future fictions.[10]

Murphy has no first name, but Celia does have a second, Kelly, which is also the name of her paternal, kite-flying grandfather. Perhaps of purer Celtic lineage than Murphy—the word "kell" is a variant of "caul"—Beckett's Kelly would not be the first to associate the sexual drive with a search for the prenatal security of the womb. Since Mr. Kelly's Christian name is Willoughby, it is possible that he represents a return to the womb by an effort of will. Mr. Willoughby Kelly does not look a day over ninety, and nine months is, of course, the human fetal period; he is obsessed with that sport of children, flying a *kite* (an obsolete word for "belly"). In its modern meaning, the kite as well as Celia relate him to the sky, which also has its attraction for Murphy. Does form press in two directions—towards the temporally distant caul and the spatially distant sky?

In other puns, the insatiably thirsty Cooper is, ironically, a drainer rather than builder of casks. Although an "analphabete of Irish education," he may derive his name from the Greek "copr," meaning excrement. Neary, "a Newtonian," and Wylie may have English spatial and temporal meanings which pun on "near" and "while." Suk's horoscope, sucking from Celia a hard-earned sixpence, reminds one of the touch of lemon that Murphy is incongruously counseled to wear. The name of Mr. Endon, the one person besides Mr. Kelly who always merits the respectful "Mr.," is a transliteration of the Greek word meaning "within," which is the locus of his wealth and security.

As in the short stories, many of the funniest passages in *Murphy* are parodies, and again it is a particular tone rather than a particular work that Beckett ridicules.[11] Thus, Celia is introduced by listing her dimensions. Except for the incongruous "Unimportant" after Age and Instep, these statistics might present a Hollywood star to readers of a movie magazine. Murphy's horoscope plays upon the half-literate jargon of astrologers, and Miss Counihan's conversation echoes the sentimental novel: " 'Oh, if you have,' cried Miss Counihan, 'if you have news of my love, speak, speak, I adjure you.' She was an omnivorous reader" (119).

Cooper's few words are in Irish idiom, Mr. Kelly's questions are as rhetorical as a politician's, and the doctor and coroner are a mine of pretentious non-information. Although Beckett is less lavish of caricature descriptions than in *More Pricks,* Murphy's costume, Ticklepenny's gestures, Miss Rosie Dew's physique, exhibit his gift for drawing them.

In smaller doses, the parodic intent appears in ironic statements, often combined with litotes.

This rare faculty . . . he exercised frugally, reserving it for situations irksome beyond endurance, as when he wanted a drink and could not get one (3)

It really did look as though she were going, at her present rate of adjustment she would be gone in twenty minutes or half an hour. (35)

"Take my advice, mister—" He [the policeman] stopped. To devise words of advice was going to tax his ability to the utmost. When would he learn not to plunge into the labyrinths of an opinion when he had not the slightest idea of how he was to emerge? (44)

"You saved my life. Now palliate it." (57)

Sun, moon, statistics, time and place, emotions, and people are all grist for the mill of Beckett's irony:

The difference between her way of destroying them both, according to him, and his way, according to her. The gentle passion. (27)

"You cur," said Miss Counihan, getting her blow in first.
"You bitch," said Wylie.
They belonged to the same great group. (210)

Like Belacqua, Murphy adopts an elegant, mocking tone towards himself, but Beckett permits frequent perforation of his own cloak of detachment towards his hero. For both Murphy and Beckett, the body of the former is grotesquely ridiculous (he "squares the circle of his shoulders"), but in Chapter 6, which is completely devoted to Murphy's mind, the irony is so light that several Beckett critics have accepted the chapter at face value as a description of Beckett's mind.[12] In so doing, they ignore nuances of tone in a chapter whose opening notes are unmistakably ironic:

It is most unfortunate, but the point of this story has been reached where a justification of the expression "Murphy's mind" has to be attempted. Happily we need not concern ourselves with this apparatus as it really was—that would be an extravagance and an impertinence—but solely with what it felt and pictured itself to be. Murphy's mind is after all the gravamen of these informations. A short section to itself at this stage will relieve us from the necessity of apologizing for it further. (107)

Unlike his fellow Irishman, Berkeley, Murphy is not an idealist. He accepts the mental fact and the less pleasant physical fact, as he accepts "collusion" between his body and his mind, even though he feels his mind to be a closed system. Murphy has small interest in the crucial question of the seventeenth century—how mind and body communicate—and the ex-Academician Neary charges that Murphy's conarium (for Descartes the site of such communication) "has shrunk to nothing."

Beckett presents Murphy's metaphysical outlook tersely, studding it with comic examples. He carefully disclaims for his hero any concern with the "ethical yoyo," to which both Descartes and especially Geulincx were drawn. Beckett chooses "kick" and "kiss" as philosophic examples; he juxtaposes kick *in re* against kick *in intellectu*.

Towards the end of Chapter 6, there is a lyrical description of the third dark zone of Murphy's mind: "Here there was nothing but commotion and the pure forms of commotion." In this zone only, Murphy becomes a "mote in the dark of absolute freedom" (112), and in this zone only, no comic notes intrude. Yet the final peremptory sentence of the chapter is a possible caution against taking Murphy's mind too seriously: "This painful duty having now been discharged, no further bulletins will be issued" (113).

The aphorisms introducing Chapters 6 and 9 (the only introductory aphorisms) are problematical in intent. "Amor intellectualis quo Murphy se ipsum amat," leads, as we have seen, to his absurd death. The "amor" exists in all its Murphyesque absurdity, but the "intellectualis" may be ironic, since Murphy (not unlike his mentor Descartes) abjures learning for introspection. Similarly, the Malraux quotation, "Il est difficile à celui qui vit hors du monde de ne pas rechercher les siens" might be an authentic description of Murphy at the MMM, but it might equally well be an ironic commentary on alienation. However, a barroom floor as the final non-resting place for the ashes of a non-drinking solipsist is cruelly ironic.

Beckett's irony, as has been seen, is largely one of tone, often depending for comic effect upon the learned terminology that is his most usual jargon. Thus, Beckett describes the Mercyseat in terms of church architecture, the infant Murphy's first cry in terms of music. There are scattered erudite phrases—"an Aegean nightfall," "caesurae of glass," a "striking nominative," "aposiopesis," "an out-and-out preterist," a "striking use of the passive voice," the "eternal tautology (yes or no)," a "grass Dido," "Penelope's curriculum," the "systole–diastole" of a crowd, and a shroud that is folded in "folio and octavo." "Chaos" and "cretin" are derived from "gas" and "Christian," respectively. Mathematical terms characterize Murphy's heart: "For Murphy had such an irrational heart that no physician could get to the root of it" (3).

Neary, the quondam professor, exhibits his academic background. The air for him is "soughing with the bawdy innuendo of eternity." He refers to Murphy as "that long hank of Apollonian asthenia . . . that schizoidal spasmophile." He urges Miss Counihan and Wylie: "Do not despair. Remember there is no triangle, however obtuse, but the circumference of some circle passes through its wretched vertices. Remember also one thief was saved" (213).[13] By the very incongruity of their juxtaposition, Beckett derides both the rational and Christian deterrents from despair.

The following day, Miss Counihan condemns the fallen Celia in an incongruous mixture of the Christian and commercial: "One of the innumerable small retail redeemers . . . lodging her pennyworth of pique in the post-golgothian kitty" (232).

The stylistic veneer of such lines is reminiscent of *More Pricks,* but occasionally Beckett's comic incongruity is less obvious, more awkward and significant. The opening lines of the book, for example, "The sun shone having no alternative, on the nothing new," cloaks a philosophic determinism and circularism under ecclesiastical echoes. Similarly, terming Murphy's room a "cage," having him read time "from a clock in the prison tower," referring to London as a "warren," expressing his delight with the almost hermetic pads, are not incongruous enough to attract much attention, but later, when in Chapter 6 we have absorbed the "closed system" of Murphy's mind, we can appreciate each incongruity quietly functioning in philosophic context, instead of playing for the easy laugh.

Occasionally, incongruous juxtapositions are pushed to the point of paradox, such as "doomed to hope unending," "strangled into a state of respiration," "nothing to lose . . . therefore nothing to gain," "lapsed into consciousness," and, more searchingly, "Thus in spite of herself she began to understand as soon as she gave up trying to explain." A paradox of metaphysical resonance is related to that Democritus of Abdera who was such a helpful guide to Murphy's predecessor, Belacqua:

> the positive peace that comes when the somethings give way, or perhaps simply add up, to the Nothing, than which in the guffaw of the Abderite naught is more real. (246)

More than in the short story collection, Beckett intrudes *in propria persona,* so as to heighten the comic. There are such direct addresses to the reader as, "Try it sometime, gentle skimmer," "The number of seconds in one dark night is a simple calculation that the curious reader will work out for himself." There are eighteen ironic footnotes on the Murphy-Endon chess game (in which each contestant seeks to withdraw rather than attack). There are three preliminary warnings that Murphy's mind will be described in Chapter 6, and in his French translation Beckett omnisciently dispenses with a character left dangling in the English version, "Faison ici nos adieux à Madameoiselle Dew, car nous ne la reverrons peut-être plus." [14] Beckett also informs us when accounts by Celia, Neary, and Cooper are "expurgated, accelerated, improved and reduced," and when Ticklepenny's account to Murphy necessitates even greater editorial excision. He indicates when Miss Carridge lies to Celia. After mentioning the beautiful music that Murphy and Celia make together, Beckett explains that the phrase

is chosen with care, lest the filthy censors should lack an occasion to commit their filthy synecdoche. (76)

In his French translation, Beckett accents this jargon, parenthetic humor:

Cette phrase, lors de la rédaction en anglo-irlandais, fut choisie avec soin, de crainte qu'il ne manquât aux censeurs l'occasion de pratiquer leur synecdoche. (60)

And further,

Les termes du passage ci-dessus furent choisis avec soin, lors de la rédaction en anglo-irlandais, afin de corrompre le lecteur cultivé. (89)

The translation is not into English but into "Anglo-Irish," not to acknowledge the enrichments the Irish have brought to English literature but to lash out at the censorship of the Irish, even though *Murphy* was published in London. The

Irish and sex are themes that Beckett plays for laughs throughout his career. Two examples from *Murphy* combine both themes: "I say you know what women are . . . or has your entire life been spent in Cork?" (206), Wylie asks Cooper. Later, Murphy is on night duty at the MMM: "Murphy completed his round, an Irish virgin. (Finished on time a round was called a virgin; ahead of time, an Irish virgin)" (242).

Another comic theme of *Murphy* is that of the closed system. The Park, Miss Dwyer's figure, Murphy's mind, and the horse-leech's daughter are all closed systems, although it is only the latter whose quantum of wantum does not vary. In other instances, the tone is lightened by rhyme: a scarlet harlot, prime versus decline, tail and male, Nelly and Shelley, rusty and dusty, ill-concealed and ill-revealed, bliss and chess, a lifetime of dingy stingy repose, the glens and fens of Ireland. Wylie utters an inverted assonance, "Reary, Neally!" and Neary aphorizes, "Two in distress make sorrow less." Occasionally, repetition contributes to the comic: "Hell roast this," "Now I have no one except," "this native," and the reiterated "closed system."

Of the techniques that Bergson did not note, but which have already been found in Beckett's earlier work, the shock of obscenity is heard in Neary's expletives and Mr. Kelly's references to his rump. At one point, too, Celia expresses relief at being not a bailiff but a bumbailiff.

The comic of the disgusting revolves about Cooper, but Miss Rosie Dew's Duck's Disease (in which the buttocks spring directly from behind the knees), Ticklepenny's homosexual advances, Wylie's mollusc kisses, Neary's bedsores, and Miss Counihan's exceptionally anthropoid qualities, as well as variations upon Miss Carridge's body odor, allow the fun to get around.

Like *More Pricks Than Kicks, Murphy* is cruelly comic, compounded of most illiberal jests. The hero is consumed by fire, and his death, like Belacqua's, is recounted as a joke. Murphy is rocking furiously to escape his body:

> Soon his body would be quiet, soon he would be free. The gas went on in the w. c., excellent gas, superfine chaos. Soon his body was quiet. (253) [15]

Cruel, too, are many of the details upon which Beckett's wit depends:

> When her parents . . . died, which they did clinging warmly to their respective partners in the ill-fated *Morro Castle.* (12)

> [Murphy] still loved her [Celia] enough to enjoy cutting the tripes out of her occasionally. (140)

Other cruelly comic details sprinkle the novel. Neary dashes his head against the stone buttocks of Cuchulain's statue. The Old Boy cuts his throat and then expires in an ambulance, at his own expense. At the Magdalen Mental Mercyseat the patients attempt suicide, or they sleep in the frozen attitudes of the victims at Pompeii. At that same Mercyseat the sadistic attendants, Bim and Bom, are apparently named for the Russian clowns who were allowed to tell the cruel truth about the Soviet system as a joke. Bim and Bom, Ticklepenny, and Dr. Killiecrankie dispose of Murphy's remains. "The essence of all cold storage," said Dr. Killiecrankie, "is a free turnover. I need every refrigerator" (270).

In the main, the comic techniques of *Murphy* do not differ from those in the earlier Beckett works, but two new comic devices appear briefly, and are interesting for their suggestions of later comic methods: mathematical series, and fictions of Beckett's fictions.

Before entering the MMM, Murphy takes to Hyde Park a lunch of five different biscuits, and, mouth watering, gives some thought to, without specifically enumerating, the hundred and twenty possible variations upon the order of eating them, but they are finally devoured by Nelly, Miss Rosie Dew's dachshund in heat.

Some time later, on night duty at the Mercyseat, Murphy discovers Mr. Endon before the indicator light panel that registers the attendants' rounds. Murphy watches the six permutations and combinations that Mr. Endon elicits by some "amental" pattern, from the lighting, extinguishing, and indicating system.

Finally, there are two references to the presence of Belacqua in Murphy's mind, and although this Belacqua may be assigned to Dante's Antepurgatorio, whence he came originally, some of the overtones (which I italicize) seem to apply equally to the self-mocking hero of *More Pricks Than Kicks.*

> At this moment Murphy would willingly have waived his expectation of Antepurgatory for five minutes in his chair, renounced the lee of Belacqua's rock and his embryonal repose, looking down at dawn across the reeds to the trembling of the austral sea and the sun obliquing to the north as it rose, immune from expiation until he should have dreamed it all through again with the downright dreaming of an infant, from the spermarium to the crematorium. . . . This was his Belacqua *fantasy* and perhaps the most highly systematized of the whole *collection.* It belonged to *those that lay just beyond the frontiers of suffering,* it was the *first landscape of freedom.* (77–78)

Shortly before Murphy's death, he lies down naked on the grass, and attempts in vain to summon pictures to his mind.

> He tried again with his father, his mother, Celia, Wylie, Neary, Cooper, Miss Dew, Miss Carridge, Nelly, the sheep, the chandlers, even Bom and Co., even Bim, even Ticklepenny and Miss Counihan, even Mr. Quigley. He tried with the men, women, children and animals that belong to even worse stories than this. (251)

Although the last sentence may be read as comic omniscience, its close sequence upon the roster of fictional characters of *Murphy* gives an early indication of what will become Beckett's principal fictional method—an involvement with fiction that is woven into the very fabric of that fiction.

Reference to Murphy in Beckett's subsequent novels (and not to Belacqua) suggests that Beckett himself views Murphy as his first significant creation. *Murphy* was the first of Beckett's out-of-print works to be reissued, and it was the first of his works to be translated by Beckett himself. *Murphy* contains in embryo Beckett's obsessive themes; human loneliness and the limits of intellection. The style of Beckett's first novel is determinedly elegant, and so prevalent are the comic ornaments that the Cartesian substratum is often invisible. But by devoting a chapter to Murphy's mind, Beckett arouses for Murphy a sympathy that one never feels for Belacqua.

In 1938 Beckett published not only the comic novel *Murphy* but a comic poem, "Ooftish." In contrast to the elaborate embellishments of *Murphy*, shock effect, colloquialism, blasphemy, violence, disgust, compose the comic tone of "Ooftish." [16] Even the obscure commercial title suggests an obscene anagram. A colloquial offertory leads to Golgotha, mocks love and spirit, and dissolves finally in lamb's blood. By use of colloquialisms ("cough up," "stingy," "in the pot"), abrupt imperatives, ambiguous pronouns, incongruous juxtapositions, and a virtual medical catalogue, Beckett reduces human life and the things of this world to a grotesque list of diseases and afflictions. Whereas "misery diagnosed undiagnosed misdiagnosed" is not usually comic, Beckett's fierce attack, climaxed by the double meanings in the last two lines ("put it in the pot" and "it all boils down"), presages his cruelly comic treatment of cosmic irony.

Watt Knott

Until Watt realised that between Mr Knott risen and Mr Knott retired there was so to speak nothing to choose.
Watt

In Ireland when World War II broke out, Beckett returned immediately to Paris. "I preferred France in war to Ireland in peace," he is quoted.[1] Although still an Irish citizen, Beckett joined French friends in anti-Nazi activities. Upon the capture of Alfred Péron (with whom Beckett had translated into French the "Anna Livia Plurabelle" section of Joyce's *Work in Progress*), and hours before the Germans reached his own apartment, Beckett fled to the Vaucluse. There, cut off from the war and the world he knew, compelled to a condition not unlike the solipsism to which he had already assigned Murphy and Belacqua, Beckett composed *Watt,* his second novel, and his last to be written directly in English. Péron was deported, and died in 1945 in a German concentration camp. To him Beckett dedicated the French translation of *Murphy,* published in 1947. After the war, Beckett made no attempt to publish *Watt,* but American friends in Paris financed its printing by Olympia Press in 1953.[2]

Watt has been called an anti-novel, and all of Beckett's fiction lumped in the category of "a-literature."[3] One might predict that fiction provoking such classification will not be susceptible to analytic methods based on the well-made plot, and indeed, from *Watt* on, we find Bergson's analysis is less and less descriptive of Beckett's comic. *Watt* is nevertheless an extraordinarily comic novel, and its humor often lies in an astigmatic vision, which has been penetratingly analyzed by Sartre in another context: "pure beholders . . . escape the human condition and can thereby inspect it. In the eyes of these angels, the human world is a *given* reality. . . . Human ends are contingent; they are simple fact which the angels regard as we regard the ends of bees and ants."[4] And what is the reaction of the angels? Jean-Paul was sure that it was laughter: "The angel laughs at man, the archangel at the angel, and God at all of them. But perhaps He no longer laughs at anyone, for our theologies know nothing about a laughing God; since the Greeks, the gods laugh no more."[5] In *Molloy,* Father Joly declares, "Christ never laughed . . . as far as we know." In *Watt,* Mr. Knott does not laugh; Watt barely manages to smile. Arsene and Arthur, servants of Mr. Knott, laugh immoderately, but their laughter is only indirectly evoked by the unconventional plot, characters, or language of the novel.

There is almost no plot in *Watt*. Watt takes a tram, then a train to Mr. Knott's house, stays there in service for an indeterminate period, leaves when his indirect replacement arrives, and (presumably) is institutionalized at some later period.

Nor is this summary an oversimplification. If, for example, Kafka's *Castle* were said to be about a man seeking to reach a castle but never attaining his goal, one would be neglecting, on the surface alone, the functions and machinations of the other characters in the relationship of K. to the castle. In *Watt* there are no such complications. No one stands in Watt's way; no obstacle hinders his approach to or departure from Mr. Knott's house, and the journey itself, evidently compulsive, is neither questioned nor explained. Far less than in his preceding fiction can Beckett be charged with indulging in the "vulgarity of plausible concatenation," and in this respect comparison of Kafka and Beckett is instructive. Although Watt and K. move in absurd worlds, the details of the *Castle* village are plausible, K.'s actions credible, he reasons about and in events, and each of his adventures is linked to the next, even if the entire concatenation lacks coherence.

Watt, on the other hand, is sometimes the observer, sometimes the observed. Often without sequence or connective, dialogue follows event, follows reasoning, pushed to an unbearable, seemingly nonsensical limit.[6] Towards the end of the novel, continuous use of *non sequitur* conveys the final disintegration of Watt's mind, or the alogical absurdity of the cosmos, and suggests that the latter may be a reflection of the former.

Watt suffered neither from the presence of Mr Knott, nor from his absence. . . .

This ataraxy covered the entire house-room, the pleasure-garden, the vegetable-garden and of course Arthur.

So that when the time came for Watt to depart, he walked to the gate with the utmost serenity.

But he was no sooner in the public road than he burst into tears. He stood there, he remembered, with bowed head, and a bag in each hand, and his tears fell, a slow minute rain, to the ground, which had recently been repaired. He would not have believed such a thing possible, if he had not been there himself. The humidity thus lent to the road surface must, he reckoned, have survived his departure by as long as two minutes at least, if not three. Fortunately the weather was fine.

Watt's room contained no information. It was a small, dingy, and, though Watt was a man of some bodily cleanliness, fetid compartment. Its one window commanded a very fine view of a race-course. The painting, or coloured reproduction, yielded nothing further. On the contrary, as time passed, its significance diminished.

From Mr Knott's voice nothing was to be learnt. Between Mr Knott and Watt no conversation passed. From time to time, for no apparent reason, Mr Knott opened his mouth in song. (207–208)

Like Mr. Knott's song, most of the details in these few abrupt paragraphs have "no apparent reason." Watt's ataraxy is a preposterous prelude to his bursting into tears. And if Watt's tears are an understandable reaction to his failure at Mr. Knott's house, the states of road repair and of weather are wildly irrelevant, the climate in particular heralding further irrelevant insistence on Watt's persistent and ironic luck with the weather. The "thing" Watt would not have believed possible is ambiguous; irony is patent in the reference to the "cleanliness" of a man who has been vomiting and picking his nose; Watt's room may or may not be the former room of Erskine, his predecessor as Mr. Knott's servant; "a racecourse" was noted on Watt's trip to Mr. Knott's house;[7] "the painting, or colored reproduction," if it is Erskine's painting, incites Watt to his only other outburst of tears (and Watt is a singularly undemonstrative man). All these *non sequiturs* are subsidiary to the central point—that Watt and Mr. Knott do not communicate; that Watt, whose senses and mind are full of Mr. Knott, learns nothing about him. But then, some ten pages earlier, we have been told of Watt's tragedy: "Of the nature of Mr Knott himself Watt remained in particular ignorance" (199).

Like Kafka's *Castle, Watt* is a novel of the failure of a quest; Watt serves Mr. Knott, lives a metaphoric "side by side" with him, but learns nothing about him. Watt's failure implies the failure of *Homo sapiens;* Watt's situation is that of rational man in the face of an irrational presence. And we are, of course, worlds away from what Bergson understood by the comic of situation.

As Beckett broadens the concept of situation, he narrows that of character. Throughout Beckett's fiction, there is only one person of dimension, the hero; rarely are there any moral overtones in the make-up of Beckett's heroes. Even more than his predecessors, Watt is a physical grotesque. He is compared to a wall, a carpet, a paper bag, a sewer pipe. His funambulistic stagger, his roadside nausea, his taste for milk, his fumblings with Mrs. Gorman—all are viewed as habits of an amusing if repulsive insect. And indeed Beckett makes the comparison explicit: "For the only way one can speak of nothing is to speak of it as though it were something, just as the only way one can speak of God is to speak of him as though he were a man, which to be sure he was, in a sense, for a time, and as the only way one can speak of man, even our anthropologists have realized that, is to speak of him as if he were a termite" (77). This perspective on insect-man, who is so easily destroyable in the purpling of a fingernail, admits wide latitude for cruelty. It is not surprising that a termite-man should lack character—even the caricatured character of Beckett's earlier fiction.

Although he is not characterized morally, Watt is pigeonholed intellectually. Belacqua was a poet, Murphy an ex-theology student, but Watt, "probably a university man," is a latter-day Cartesian. Again and again, he attempts to impose what Descartes implied, and Hegel stated: "the real is rational and the rational real." He is therefore concerned only with external phenomena; his interest in language, which he identifies with thought, is scientific; he is obsessed with logic. Far from a poet, what he demands of words is that they name things or explain events, and what he demands of things and events is that they be subservient to the rational understanding. Yet, he inexplicably undertakes the journey to the strange establishment of the inscrutable Mr. Knott.[8]

Mr. Knott, who, unlike his house servants, merits the respectful "Mr.," is portrayed entirely by incongruity and paradox. His chameleon changes take place before Watt's senses, and yet Watt remains ignorant of the nature of that vague deity figure, replete with "fascia of white light."

Incidental characters come and go around Watt, or in the stories of the people around him, and one (Lady McCann, no more important, apparently, than any of the others) is present at both beginning and end of the book. We learn little about the characters, however, except their names, which are meticulously mentioned even if the bearers flash through only a single sentence. There is no attempt at characterization beyond a few lines of dialogue, and at times a grotesque physical, social, or professional attribute. Some of the people are present episodically—notably Mr. Knott's other servants—and some scarcely endure the length of an episode, appearing from nowhere, disappearing into nowhere. Watt is the only one who remains from almost the beginning to almost the end. If the term anti-novel be allowed for *Watt,* the term anti-character would seem suitable for the grotesques that pop up without warning or coherent function.

The term anti-language, however, would be an exaggeration for the ponderous prose of much of the novel. Some of Watt's painful reasoning revolves, in fact, about the nature and power of language. At Mr. Knott's house, reason, senses, and language all fail Watt (gradually), and by the time Watt meets the narrator, Sam, at an institution, Watt employs seven types of an ambiguity that superficially resemble an anti-language. "In the brief course of the same period," Watt successively inverts first the words within the sentence, then the letters in the word, then the sentences in the paragraph, then simultaneously the words in the sentence and the sentences in the period, then simultaneously the words in the sentence and the letters in the word, then simultaneously the letters in the word and the sentences in the period, and finally simultaneously the letters in the word, and the words in the sentence, and the sentences in the period. Examples are provided of all but the last climactic simultaneity. Watt's anti-language is a rational and systematic construction. Even in his madness, he is unable to give up that reason and that language which failed him, and it is not difficult to rearrange the anagrams into English.[9]

Interpolated into the illustrations of Watt's linguistic decline, are Sam's comments that

> though we walked face to face, [Watt's words] were devoid of significance for me. (164)
>
> though we walked breast to breast, [they] made little or no sense to me. (165)
>
> notwithstanding our proximity, [they] were not perfectly clear to me. (166)
>
> though we walked belly to belly, [they] were so much wind to me. (166)
>
> though we walked pubis to pubis, [they] seemed so much balls to me. (167)
>
> though we walked glued together, [they] were so much Irish to me. (169)

Perhaps the spoken anti-language is less susceptible than the printed of conversion into language, or, more probably, Sam (and Sam Beckett) is being ironic in order to evoke laughter at the play between anatomical part and mode of misunderstanding. The laughter, however, carries grave resonance, for, as Dan Rooney remarks in *All That Fall,* the prototypes of this face-to-face couple are Dante's damned:

> MR. ROONEY. Or you forwards and I backwards. The perfect pair. Like Dante's damned, with their faces arsy-versy. Our tears will water our bottoms. (42)

Aside from the anti-language of Part III of *Watt,* Beckett avails himself of certain Bergsonian comic linguistic tools, but with them he builds a completely idiosyncratic structure. Ironic ambiguity appears on almost every page of *Watt,* to the closing aphorism of the Addenda: "No symbols where none intended."—surely an ironic indication of their ubiquity.[10] Further, Beckett makes use of Bergson's favorite example of linguistic ambiguity, the pun.

No longer does Beckett slide paronomasia into a mellifluous, elegant paragraph; he hammers it home. Compare the Greek and subtle Murphy and Mr. Endon with the blatant English Watt and Mr. Knott.[11] There is a double pun on Knott—"not" and "knot." Watt puns at several levels; not only is it the ironic "what," the question about reality that Watt never asks, but snail-paced Watt, as opposed to the inventor of the steam engine; and faithful servant Watt as opposed to Wat Tyler, leader of the peasants' revolt. (Arsene explicitly links Watt with the latter.)

Other puns on names have hardy English roots. Mr. Hackett, the first character on scene, hacks away with questions that foreshadow Watt's insatiable thirst for knowledge. Severn, the postman, contains the ironic "sever," and indeed his letters establish no links, for he carries only bills and solicitations. Mr. Graves, the gardener, is a double pun, with neither meaning of apparent relevance to his troubles with his wife. In its Latin derivation, "grave" is weighty, important, highly serious; its Teutonic root leads to a burial place for the dead. Although Mr. Graves's uneducated Irish brogue and menial position in Mr. Knott's establishment would seem to belie the meanings of his name, it is significant that he is the only person on Mr. Knott's premises, besides the master himself, to merit the respectful "Mr." In his long, hilarious monologue, Arthur explicitly links Mr. Graves to one of his punning meanings: "you . . . let fall the seed, absent in mind, as the priest dust, or ashes, into the grave" (181).

The only strangers to appear at Mr. Knott's house (in "fugitive penetration") are the Galls, father and son.[12] Although they have come for a seemingly harmless purpose—"to choon the piano"—they leave uttering dark aphorisms:

The piano is doomed, in my opinion, said the younger.
The piano-tuner also, said the elder.
The pianist also, said the younger. (72)[13]

No mere pronouncement of doom can disturb a man of Watt's kidney, but he becomes most distraught when the meaning of this incident resists him. Already, in the case of emptying Mr. Knott's slops, Watt has distinguished between the "real reason" and the "reason offered to the understanding," but the incident of the Galls is particularly alarming because it heralds all the other incidents at Mr. Knott's house "of great formal brilliance and indeterminable import." How, to the rational Watt, could such an incident be other than bitter as gall?

After his departure from Mr. Knott's house, Watt continues to be plagued by the "indeterminable import" of events and even things. Thus, at the railroad station, "his impression was . . . that this was a waiting-room of which even the nicest degrees of strange and usual could not be affirmed" (233). Out of nowhere, a mouth appears to comment to Watt on the nature of waiting-rooms—a grotesque mouth that Watt recognizes as belonging to a presumably dead woman named, appropriately, Price, for that is what has been exacted from Watt, through his commerce with Mr. Knott.

Other puns on names are comically coupled—Cream and Berry, the hardy laurel, Rose and Cerise, Art and Con.[14] Arsene and Arthur, Watt's predecessor and successor, respectively, as Mr. Knott's servants, each contains "Art," which these two characters represent in comic fashion, for they are the only two to deliver the long monologues that foreshadow Beckett's later art of the French fiction.

A witty collection of puns sparkles through the love poem of the jailed solicitor and poisoner, Grehan. Entitled "To Nelly," the poem plays upon sex as its comic theme. Nelly is also the name of Miss Rosie Dew's dachshund in heat (*Murphy*), and Nell of *Endgame* is a bitter relic of love. The Nell-knell pun may suggest the different forms of the death of love.

To Nelly

To thee, sweet Nell, when shadows fall
Jug-jug! Jug-jug!
I here in thrall
My wanton thoughts do turn.
Walks she out yet with Byrne?
Moves Hyde his hand amid her skirts
As erst? I ask, and Echo answers: Certes.

Tis well! Tis well! Far, far be it
Pu-we! Pu-we!
From me, my tit,
Such innocent joys to chide.
Burn, burn with Byrne, from Hyde
Hide naught—hide naught save that
Is Greh'ns. IT hide from Hyde, with Byrne burn not. (11–12)

Already in *Murphy,* Beckett used flat repetition to evoke laughter. In Watt he carries repetition to (and perhaps beyond) its literary limit.[15] The unbearably explicit lists, expanded series, permutations and combinations; the dozen odd "one of the reasons for that was [with or without "perhaps"] this," "not that . . . but," "not that . . . for," the "to mention only's," "never never's," "but then it was too late's," "add to this's"—are pounded at the reader until he no longer knows whether to laugh or scream. But of course that is the ambivalent reaction that Beckett intends, towards the painstaking and painful method of Watt's mind, "whatever that might mean."

A further repetition—that of sounds—is also sprinkled comically through several of the lists. We find: cries—surprise, resented—repented, driven—riven, such off-rhymes as "dimming all, dulling all, stilling all, numbing all," and "demand nothing, ordain nothing, explain nothing, propound nothing," as well as a long series of rhymes by Arsene. Once, inversion emphasizes rhyme: "and when there was no food him for came ratatat knocking at the door, and when there was for him some food onward plod along the road" (97).

Linguistic inversion itself becomes a comic device: "ten o'cluck strock." In the parody of the academic committee appears the spoonerism: "The two figures are related . . . as the cute to its roob" (187).[16] Of more consequence are Watt's almost systematic inversions as a result of his experience at Mr. Knott's establishment. His "The question to this answer was the following" heralds an inversion of walking, dressing, and, possibly, thinking, which result from his taxing ordeal. His last words in the novel, "Three and one," inverting the price of his train ticket to the "further end" of the line (and recalling the Trinity), contrast sharply with the first direct quotation of his language, when Watt is still a neophyte at Mr. Knott's establishment. "How very fortunate for Mr Gall, said Watt, that he has his son at his command, whose manner is all devotion, and whose mere presence, when he might obviously be earning an honest penny elsewhere, attests an affliction characteristic of the best tuners, and justifies emoluments rather higher than usual" (71).

In the systematic garbling of Watt's speech in the insane asylum, inversion is the principal method. Linguistic repetition and inversion (of which Bergson offers no examples) sprinkle the pages of *Watt,* but Beckett is still faithful to some of the comic techniques that Bergson grouped under transposition: jargon, parody, paradox, incongruity, and irony. Both quantitatively and qualitatively, however, their use differs markedly from that in the earlier fiction.

Learned jargon, for example, one of the main props of Beckett's wit in *More Pricks* and *Murphy,* fades to a few references: "Galileo's cradle," "Darwin's caterpillar," "Thesus and Ariadne," "Laurel and Daphne," "Mr . . . ? I beg your pardon. Like Tyler?" "as Lachesis would have it." Mr. Spiro, Watt's companion in the train, is the only one to cite abstruse authorities.

Twisted quotation, like learned jargon, evokes the sophisticated smile, and, as we might expect, suffers a decline in *Watt*. There is only one instance of literary misquotation: "Erskine will go by your side to be your guide." Nor is the line mere display of pedantry; it is an incisive and apposite irony. In the medieval morality play, it is Knowledge who tells Everyman: "Everyman, I will go with thee, and be thy guide,/ In thy most need to go by thy side." Early in *Watt*, where the misquotation occurs, Beckett (through Arsene, who utters the words) merely suggests a relationship between Everyman-Watt and Knowledge-Erskine, but by the end of the book, we know that Erskine has contributed no knowledge to Watt, and that Watt has obtained no knowledge of Mr. Knott.

Similarly, biblical echoes only gradually appear in their ironic light. An early biblical reference, "He would literally turn the other cheek . . . if he had the energy," is comically exact, and is proved shortly after the statement is made, when Watt meekly suffers the abuse of the milk-porter and of Lady McCann. But towards the end of the book, Arthur ironically mangles two well-known biblical passages:

> if the seed is to prosper and multiply ten-fold, fifteen-fold, twenty-fold, twenty-five-fold, thirty-fold, thirty-five-fold, forty-fold, forty-five-fold, and even fifty-fold; it will do so, and . . . if it is not, it will not. (181–182)

> And now the order was reversed in which, following Mr Fitzwein, now in the eleven tram, they had set out, so that the first was last, and the last first, and the second third, and the third second (196)

These twisted biblical reminders prepare us for the most important one in the novel:

For except, one, not to need, and, two, a witness to his not needing, Knott needed nothing, as far as Watt could see. (202)

Close upon this startling omission of "Mr." for Knott, Beckett plays upon the word "witness" so as to awaken resonances of the many biblical passages in which it occurs. He puns, too, upon "no" and "know," "what" and Watt, "not" and Knott, and indicates that in his two brief conclusions, Watt *does* see far. Linked by his own need to Watt's need, Mr. Knott is momentarily reduced to Knott. And yet, Watt's need continues to be so great that "this was an anthropomorphic insolence of short duration," nevertheless subject to recurrence.

Of less interest but still meaningful is Beckett's perversion of proverbs:

if one of these things was worth doing, all were worth doing, but . . . none was worth doing, no, not one (221)

the pleasure of killing two birds with one stone (234)

Comparably pointed is Beckett's use of paradox. Mr. Spiro's friends call him DUM, anagram of MUD, because he is so bright and cheerful. Within his monologue, Arsene declares, "when you cease to seek you start to find," and he describes "the being of nothing," "the horrors of joy," "the purpose that budding withers, that withering buds"; towards the end of his quest, Watt (or Sam, for the passage is written impersonally) indulges in ironic paradox, "the darkening ease, the brightening trouble."

Far more often, however, Watt and Sam both prefer flat denial to polished paradox. Hence the many "Yes, it was not" and "Not that" constructions. Early in his stay at Mr. Knott's "fixity of mystery," Watt finds that the names of things cease to designate these things for him. He is compelled to acknowledge, "This is a pot, and yet not a pot." So absurd does this seem to him that "Watt preferred on the whole having to do with things of which he did not know the name, though this too was painful to Watt, to having to do with things of which the known name, the proven name, was not the name, any more, for him" (81). Nor can Watt affirm anything about himself "that did not seem as false as if he affirmed it of a stone."[17] Wearily, however falsely, he continues to call himself a man; "But for all the relief that this afforded him, he might just as well have thought of himself as a box, or an urn" (83), to which Beckett's French heroes will try to reduce themselves.

At first, this perpetual uncertainty seems to be another of Watt's endlessly incongruous characteristics. From our first glimpse of him, "motionless, a solitary figure, lit less and less by the receding lights, until it was scarcely to be distinguished from the dim wall behind it. Tetty was not sure whether it was a man or a woman. Mr Hackett was not sure that it was not a parcel, a carpet for example, or a roll of tarpaulin, wrapped up in dark paper and tied about the middle with a cord." (16), to our last view of "the long wet dream with the hat and bags," he is an incongruous figure. Moreover, Beckett's tight artistic structure is evident even in these apparently haphazard incongruities. The first reaction to Watt—Tetty's—becomes Watt's own last reaction to the mysterious, nameless figure on the road, for he, too, cannot tell whether it is a man or a woman. Watt's hat might symbolize his unconquerable conquered mind, the bags his mortal burden, and the long wet dream, perhaps, the sterile ejaculation of his tale.

Most of Watt's attributes are immediately incongruous: He is a seasoned traveler who once was "dying in London," "probably a university man" and certainly a "very fair linguist"; he belongs to a group of "big bony shabby seedy haggard knockkneed men with rotten teeth and big red noses"; he has queer likes (wind, rats, and raw language), dislikes (earth and sky, sun and moon), and habits, both physical (his unmatched boots, milk-drinking, nose-picking, and non-healing) and mental (he knows nothing of painting or physics, but seems to have a fair musical education; he dwells on solutions that do not prevail; he builds speculative castles about Erskine's stair-climbing and about obtaining a dog to eat Mr. Knott's leftovers). But most of Watt's incongruities bear upon his effort to relate the world of appearance to a language that will describe it.

Watt's preoccupation with Erskine's activities, leading to his entrance into Erskine's room ("Ruse, a by") is climaxed by a minute description of the picture on the wall, which is composed of a dot and a circle that is open at the bottom. Watt speculates about these incongruous items, until he breaks down weeping. Although this might seem like madness, elucidation is not difficult in the context of Beckett's work. Watt's anxiety about the dot's relationship to the circle—broken though it is—must be seen as his anxiety about himself in Mr. Knott's world, since he has voluntarily abandoned any other. Even in his first period of service, he cannot situate circle and dot on the same plane; he can establish no relationship with Mr. Knott.

By the end of Watt's service, his incongruous appearance inspires unspeakable horror in Micks, Mr. Knott's servant whose arrival impels Watt's departure. Incongruity for Beckett no longer arises from a juxtaposition of atonal images, but from images that contain, below their haphazard absurdity in our world, a comic and pathetic symbolism.

Since Watt is the hero of the novel, comic incongruity centers about him, but Arsene has his duck and his fat bottom and belly; Erskine has a bell, a painting, and a compulsion to climb stairs; [18] Sam shares with Watt a fondness for "all that limited motion, without limiting vision." Sam, who has idiosyncrasies of his own, compares Watt significantly and grotesquely with "Christ believed by Bosch." This seemingly absurd evocation is extended to Sam as well. Although ambiguously ironic when the comparison is first made, the Christ figure prepares us somewhat for the almost tragic final paragraph of Part III, in which Watt, an ungainly collection of incongruous motions, stumbles backwards out of sight—without a single comic overtone. This paragraph recalls the anomalously earnest one of "Dante and the Lobster," or the description of the third dark zone of Murphy's mind. Its preparation and climactic position in *Watt* are evidence of Beckett's increased tonal mastery.

By endowing Watt with incongruous physical attributes, Beckett invests the novel with its major meaning. Through his eccentricities, Watt is both ridiculed and highlighted in the role of hero, for his heroism is intellectual. And if his intellect, like his appearance, is incongruously comic, Watt is nevertheless heroic. Plodding instead of swashbuckling, fumbling instead of skillful, he courageously undertakes domestic service at Mr. Knott's house.

Unlike Kierkegaard's swift leap of faith, or the sudden intuition of Descartes, Watt's journey is halting; he may have intended to turn back at the facultative tram stop; he prefers to ride with his back towards his destination; he once passed the station by being unready to descend; this time he procrastinates by lying down at the side of the road. Finally, however, he arrives at Mr. Knott's house. He never knows precisely how he enters it, but he *does* enter, like a knight into the Chapel Perilous, and he volunteers for service in an enchanted order that proves to be his peril and destruction.

Watt is defeated because no magic charms are bestowed upon him. He attacks an irrational order of reality with tools of the habitual world—his senses, "his most noble faculties" and his mind "whatever that might mean." Attempting to situate things in series or families, Watt acts in diametric opposition to Proust-narrator, as described by Beckett over ten years before he wrote *Watt:* "'Enchantments of reality' has the air of a paradox. But when the object is perceived as particular and unique and not merely the member of a family, when it appears independent of any general notion and detached from the sanity of a cause, isolated and inexplicable in the light of ignorance, then and then only may it be a source of enchantment" (11). Watt bends all his efforts to assimilating person, place, thing, and event into families, but he meets with constant failure; pot, the visit of the Galls, Erskine's picture, Mr. Knott's entire establishment, are under the "enchantment of reality." But most "particular and unique" of all the establishment is Mr. Knott himself, an endless conglomeration of incongruous and changing facets of an unseizable reality.

His clothes are "very various, very very various"; however, whatever else he may wear, he never removes his nightdress. But then, he goes to bed and rises at such unpredictable hours that perhaps he wishes always to be ready to retire. Unlike his clothes, the complicated concoction of Mr. Knott's nourishment "had never varied, since its establishment, long, long before," and it is composed of a weird assortment of items edible and inedible. Mr. Knott engages in furious self-displacement within his room, and, still within that circumscribed area, he subjects his furniture to all possible permutations and arrangements. His appearance undergoes change, "from one glance to the next," and, in all male registers, he sings monotonous songs in a language incomprehensible to the linguist Watt; "the open *a* sound was predominant, and the explosives *k* and *g*."

Although Mr. Knott's speech is gibberish to Watt, the master's favorite dactylic exclamations, "Exelmans! Cavendish! Habbakuk! Ecchymose!" are open to our interpretation. In grouping a French general, a British scientist, and a Hebrew prophet before a term of pathology that may be translated as "bloody blotch," Mr. Knott is sneering at all human effort and so-called achievement.

Even more sweepingly, Mr. Knott mocks the senses and the rational intelligence, Watt's (and Western man's) major weapons in the battle for knowledge. "None of Mr Knott's gestures could be called characteristic, unless perhaps that which consisted in the simultaneous obturation of the facial cavities, the thumbs in the mouth, the forefingers in the ears, the little fingers in the nostrils, the third fingers in the eyes and the second fingers, free in a crisis to promote intellection, laid along the temples" (212). Not only does Mr. Knott deride both empirical and rational knowledge but he does so in the vulgar gesture of the street urchin.

The last we hear of Mr. Knott's habits is the incongruously absurd description of how he puts on a single shoe, boot, or slipper while "he held the other tight, lest it should escape, or put it in his pocket, or put his foot upon it, or put it in a drawer, or put it in his mouth, till he might put it on, on the other foot" (213). But he does not shoe the other foot, and we are thus brought full solipsistic circle back to our introduction to Watt, who borrowed from Mr. Nixon money for a single boot,[19] and who, at the end of the book, limps in unmatched boots to the station whence he came so long ago. Neither Watt nor Mr. Knott can plant both feet solidly on the ground.

The equation of Watt with Mr. Knott has already been made in a slip by Sam: "by Knott, I beg your pardon, by Watt." Sam's comparison of Watt to Christ must also be read in the light of Watt's own enunciation of proper names: "Knott, Christ, Gomorrha, Cork." While still on the ground floor, Watt realizes that he and Mr. Knott are the same height. In the final garbled summary of the failure of his quest, Watt reduces Mr. Knott and himself to "Two men side by side"—the very "anthropomorphic insolence" he did not commit on Mr. Knott's premises. And yet there is no final equation of the two; the circle in the painting is broken at the bottom.

Less significant, if similarly incongruous on the surface, is the coupling of Watt and hump-backed Mr. Hackett. An incidental Mr. Nixon gives us the clue, speaking to Mr. Hackett: "when I see him, or think of him, I think of you, and when I see you, or think of you, I think of him" (19). When Watt bumps into the porter, the latter swears at him, "The devil raise a hump on you."[20] Besides the grotesque appearance and agitated walk of Watt and Mr. Hackett, they both construct elaborate theories upon the barest of events. But Mr. Hackett, unlike Watt, pays small attention to names, common or proper. He does not, like Watt, seek "semantic succour," and for this reason, perhaps, can placidly admire the sky instead of undertaking Watt's perilous journey to Mr. Knott's house—a journey with which Mr. Hackett is inexplicably familiar even though he has never before heard of Watt.

The social scene in which Mr. Hackett makes his single appearance exhibits Beckett in full control of the parody he wielded wittily in *More Pricks* and *Murphy*. But we read nearly two hundred pages of *Watt* before being treated to parody of a similar kind, moving from the facultative tram stop to the railroad station. Apart from the social framework, Watt's epistemological search is enlivened by Arsene's parodic description of the maids (appropriately, one of Mr. Knott's servingmen tells to another a parodic tale of two servingwomen), by Watt's parodic recounting of the generation and degeneration of a Lynch dynasty awaiting an arithmetical millennium, and by Arthur's parody of academic committees. Even in Watt's adventures proper appear such caricatures as Mr. Spiro, the popularizer of Thomistic doctrine; "catholic and military" Lady McCann; and Watt's middle-aged paramour, Mrs. Gorman the fishwife. In the last case, the rhetorical question is posed as to why they do not consummate their love.

Was it the echo murmuring in their hearts, in Watt's heart, in Mrs Gorman's, of past passion, ancient error, warning them not to sully not to trail, in the cloaca of clonic gratification, a flower so fair, so rare, so sweet, so frail? It is not necessary to suppose so. For Watt had not the strength, and Mrs Gorman had not the time, indispensable to even the most perfunctory coalescence. The irony of life! Of life in love! That he who has the time should lack the force, that she who has the force should lack the time! That a trifling and in all probability tractable obstruction of some endocrinal Bandusia, that a mere matter of forty-five or fifty minutes by the clock, should as effectively as death itself, or as the Hellespont, separate lovers. For if Watt had had a little more vigour Mrs Gorman would have just had the time, and if Mrs Gorman had had a little more time Watt could very likely have developed, with a careful nursing of his languid tides, a breaker not unworthy of the occasion. (141–142) [21]

Some time later, when Mr. Graves complains that there is no kick left in him, Arthur suggests a remedy in a style that parodies the modern testimonial advertisement.

Have you tried Bando, Mr. Graves, said Arthur. A capsule, before and after meals, in a little warm milk, and again at night, before turning in. I had tried everything, and was thoroughly disgusted, when a friend spoke to me of Bando. Her husband was never without it, you understand. Try it, she said, and come back in five or six years. I tried it, Mr Graves, and it changed my whole outlook on life. From being a moody, listless, constipated man, covered with squames, shunned by my fellows, my breath fetid and my appetite depraved (for years I had eaten nothing but high fat rashers), I became, after four years of Bando, vivacious, restless, a popular nudist, regular in my daily health, almost a father and a lover of boiled potatoes. Bando. Spelt as pronounced. (170)

Far more than literary parody, however, *Watt* abounds in logical parody, or ridicule of the rational approach. Much has been made of *Watt's* permutations and combinations, and of its legalistic style, but mathematics and legalism meet in logic.[22] What must be stressed is that Watt's mind, in all its meticulous meandering, is not Beckett's, but a parody of the mind of someone who is consumed with his own rationalism. No one could be more aware than Beckett of the insufferable monotony and absurdity of his expanded series, but without the dullness there would be less experiential fidelity to this evocation of a hero who goes bare-brained to Mr. Knott's lair. As it is phrased in the Addenda—"das fruchtbare Bathos der Erfahrung." Moreover, the boring but savage rehearsal of detail is not always permutation and/or combination. Mathematics is mocked in Arthur's monologue about the cube rooting powers of the primitive Mr. Nackybal. The members of the Academic Committee can present each other with "x squared minus x looks if there are x members of the committee and y squared minus y if there are y" (180). Mention has already been made of lists, of the locutions demanding detail; in addition there are answers to seemingly rhetorical questions, explicit expansion of alternations, and literalism misplaced beyond what Bergson envisaged.

In the social scene of the opening section, there are misplaced literalisms similar to those in the earlier works:

as God is my witness, he had his hand upon it.
God is a witness that cannot be sworn. (9)

Larry will be forty years old next March, D.V.
That is the kind of thing Dee always vees. (13)

Poor woman, God forgive her, said Tetty.
Faith I wouldn't put it past him, said Mr Hackett. (16)

Although even these witticisms bear upon the religious satire in the novel, their polish vanishes once Watt lumbers on scene, and the literalisms we find thereafter are not so much misplaced in Bergson's sense, as comic by virtue of their labored ponderousness. Even the opening paragraph, before Watt's discharge from the tram, makes some use of the linguistic literalism that prepares for the hundreds of examples to follow: "Mr Hackett turned the corner and saw, in the failing light, at some little distance, his seat. It seemed to be occupied. This seat, the property very likely of the municipality, or of the public, was of course not his, but he thought of it as his. This was Mr Hackett's attitude towards things that pleased him. He knew they were not his, but he thought of them as his. He knew were not his, because they pleased him" (7). The literalism states a contradiction. The humpbacked Mr. Hackett, Watt's *alter ego,* mentally appropriates what pleases him, and knows nevertheless that it cannot be his, precisely because it pleases him. Thus, the literalism casts a cynical shadow on the very basis of property, pleasure, and thought.

The opening literalism soon evaporates into social satire, but even that stichomythic parody dialogue is punctuated with literalism, once Watt arrives: "Mr Hackett did not know when he had been more intrigued, nay, he did not know when he had been so intrigued. He did not know either what it was that so intrigued him. What is it that so intrigues me, he said, whom even the extraordinary, even the supernatural, intrigue so seldom, and so little. Here there is nothing in the least unusual, that I can see, and yet I burn with curiosity, and with wonder. The sensation is not disagreeable, I must say, and yet I do not think I could bear it for more than twenty minutes, or half an hour" (17). Nor does Mr. Hackett have to bear Watt for long. After various speculations as to why Watt descends where he does from the tram, and why he should borrow money for a single boot, we are without transition precipitated into Watt's journey to Mr. Knott's house.

In the train Watt meets the "neo-John-Thomist" Mr. Spiro, and while Mr. Spiro expounds on questions of doctrine, we are immersed in a first mathematical series: "But Watt heard nothing of this, because of other voices, singing, crying, stating, murmuring, things unintelligible, in his ear." Together with Watt, we are faced with the fourteen possible combinations of his voices; permutations are neglected, for the order of the frequently simultaneous voices is difficult to establish. And if only four voices are taken into account, "there were others. And sometimes Watt understood all, and sometimes he understood much, and sometimes he understood little, and sometimes he understood nothing, as now" (29).

The cumulative effect of the kind of linguistic literalism that Beckett deploys so heavily in Watt is that one can understand and accept nothing. The literalism of Watt, of Sam, perhaps of Arsene and of Arthur, is a probing tool, contributing to the hesitancy of the legalistic prose, seeking a clumsy exactitude. The meticulous accumulation of detail that may or may not be relevant, the lengthy enumeration of the ups and downs of each mental seesaw, the piling up of rhetorical questions with or without answers, the many repetitions of the formula, "The reason for that was this"—all are part of Arsene's, Arthur's, Watt's, Sam's, agonized and agonizing efforts to explain the world through language by confining that language to the most literal and inartistic level—naming phenomena, explaining them, situating them in a series.

For Watt, "to explain had always been to exorcize."

For when Watt spoke of an incident of this kind, he did not necessarily do so in terms of the unique hypothesis, or of the latest, though this at first sight seems the only possible alternative, and the reason why he did not, why it is not, is this, that when one of the series of hypotheses, with which Watt laboured to preserve his peace of mind, lost its virtue, and had to be laid aside, and another set up in its place, then it sometimes happened that the hypothesis in question, after a sufficient period of rest, recovered its virtue and could be made to serve again, in the place of another, whose usefulness had come to an end, for the time being at least. To such an extent is this true, that one is sometimes tempted to wonder, with reference to two or even three incidents related by Watt as separate and distinct, if they were not in reality the same incident, variously interpreted. As to giving an example of the second event, namely the failure, that is clearly quite out of the question. For there we have to do with events that resisted all Watt's efforts to saddle them with meaning, and a formula, so that he could neither think of them, nor speak of them, but only suffer them, when they recurred, though it seems probable that they recurred no more, at the period of Watt's revelation, *to me,* but were as though they had never been. (78–79) (my italics)

In this passage, Beckett dwells at length upon absurd hypotheses and an absurd methodology for arriving at them. By virtue of the literal and meticulous description of Watt's cosmological and epistemological preoccupations, he and we are left in comic confusion.

After about a third of the book is over, we encounter the first first-person singular pronoun, "me," although an authorial presence has been earlier suggested by unexplained footnotes, question marks, a reference to Watt's "mouthpiece," and such omniscience as "it will be a long time now before Watt smiles again unless something very unexpected turns up to upset him" (27). Poking fun at his own omniscience, the narrator informs us that, ironically, Watt smiles only when he is upset.

Similarly, when Watt is first discharged from the tram, the narrator comments omnisciently, "He [Goff Nixon] made use, with reference to Watt, of an expression that we shall not record" (17). This puritanical forbearance is particularly ironic in the light of the expressions that *are* subsequently recorded in *Watt.*

Midway through the book, close upon a detailed examination of Watt's varying reactions to words, the following passage appears:

For all that I know on the subject of Mr Knott, and of all that touched Mr Knott, and on the subject of Watt, and of all that touched Watt, came from Watt, and from Watt alone. And if I do not appear to know very much on the subject of Mr Knott and of Watt, and on the subject of all that touched them, it is because Watt did not know a great deal on these subjects, or did not care to tell. But he assured me at the time, when he began to spin his yarn, that he would tell all, and then again, some years later, when he had spun his yarn, that he had told all. And as I believed him then and then again, so I continue to believe him, long after the yarn was spun, and Watt gone. Not that there is any proof that Watt did indeed tell all he knew, on these subjects, or that he set out to do so, for how could there be, I knowing nothing on these subjects, except what Watt told me. (125)

The "I" of these lines—presumably the Sam of Part III of *Watt*—is not so convinced as Mr. Nixon that Watt is "incapable . . . of telling an untruth." And we in turn may have our doubts about Sam, who recounts the possibilities of Watt's error in what he has related, then the possibilities of his own error in transcribing what Watt told him, even though he "was most careful to note down all at that time."

Before the publication of *L'Ere de soupçon,*[23] in which the credibility of authorial witness is attacked, Beckett eliminated himself from this essentially third-person novel. In his place appears the narrator, Sam, whose persona is not sketched until Part III, although, ironically, Sam was the name of the most prolific of the Lynch clan. The creation of Sam-narrator poses a new ambiguity in *Watt*.

It is especially after Watt meets Sam at an institution that irony, as defined by contemporary critics, emerges as the primary tool of ambiguity. Sometimes the irony is as subtle as in Chapter 6 of *Murphy*, and often is as ambivalent in intent as that of Euripides, so that the reader scarcely knows what to believe, or with whom to sympathize. So harsh is Sam's portrayal of Watt, that that benighted hero appeals to our protective instinct. Aside from the moving last paragraph of Part III, Sam transmits such small sympathy for Watt, that one may toy fleetingly with the notion that Sam, not Watt, is the hero. Though he reasons similarly (compare, for example, Watt on Mr. Knott's dog and Sam on the holes in the fences), Sam does not spend years in servitude to Mr. Knott. It is Sam who claims to be writing *Watt,* who converts writing into an epistemological instrument, while Watt depends only on his mind and senses.

The presence of Sam increases at once the authenticity and ambiguity of Watt's experiences at Mr. Knott's establishment. Although Sam is not mentioned, until Part III of *Watt,* which takes place in a de luxe institution where each patient has a private mansion and garden, Sam sheds for the reader a retrospective reflection on the first two parts of the novel. By Part IV, Sam as such disappears, but various question marks, hiatuses, footnotes, as well as an Addendum of parabasic flavor, indicate his presence as narrator. At the opening of Part IV, moreover, appear some cryptic comments about the order of narration:

> As Watt told the beginning of his story, not first, but second, so not fourth, but third, now he told its end. Two, one, four, three, that was the order in which Watt told his story. Heroic quatrains are not otherwise elaborated. (215)

Aside from the ironic implication against Watt-hero in the reference to *heroic* quatrains, there is deliberate confusion as to the textual order (I, II, III, IV), the chronological one (I, II, IV, III), and what may be called the epistemological one (II, I, IV, III). To order these last numbers, one might think of II and III as the core of Watt's story, with I and IV as

Sam's frame. The cursory reader may wonder whether Watt closes his tale upon a return to society and admiration of the landscape, or upon his difficult backward progress to his mansion at the institution, from which only a wraith of kitchen smoke momentarily mingles with Sam's smoke, before disappearing.

At a more trivial level, we may note Beckett's continued use of sex and Ireland, for comic effect. The social satire of the dialogue abounds in sexual references and Irish locutions. Mr. Knott has his bed linen changed only on St. Patrick's Day. There is a lengthy mock-naturalistic description of the sexually active and aggressively Irish Lynch clan, whose only function in the novel is to supply a boy to bring a dog to eat the food that Mr. Knott occasionally left. In the long monologue of Mr. Knott's servant, Arthur, the monotonous machinations of an Irish academic committee are sparked by obscene suggestions.

Three other Beckett techniques of the comic are not unrelated: the shocking, the disgusting, and the cruel. Many shock laughs are evoked by the sudden introduction of the obscene: Watt's smiles and the Angelus are both compared to farts, Lady McCann fondly recollects a bawdy schoolgirl joke, Arsene punctuates his monologue with "An ordure. . . . An excrement. . . . A turd. . . . A cat's flux." Sam tells us that Mr. Graves said "turd" and "fart" for "third" and "fourth." Mr. Case boasts, "Let me once catch a fair glimpse of an arse, and I'll pick it out for you among a million" (242).

Of the disgusting, too, there are lively examples: Tetty's childbearing, the perennially masticating Mary of Arsene's monologue, and the filthy Mr. Nackybal of Arthur's; Mr. Knott's food and the afflictions of the Lynch clan, including dogs; and last but not least, Watt's nose-blowing, nose-picking, and final baptism by a pail of slime. Perhaps some light is cast on Beckett's absorption with both the disgusting and the cruel in a passage that illustrates both. Arsene philosophizes: "life begins to ram her fish and chips down your gullet until you puke, and then the puke down your gullet until you puke the puke, and then the puked puke until you begin to like it" (44).

But the most bitterly cruel comment in the novel belongs to Sam. Describing how fond he and Watt are of rats (they delight in feeding them frogs and fledglings, and then in feeding the fed rat to one of his numerous family, watching with glee as the lucky relatives tear him apart and devour him), Sam reflects, "It was on these occasions, we agreed, after an exchange of views, that we came nearest to God" (156). Not to Mr. Knott but to God, so that there can be no mistake about the universality of the cruelty. By the introduction of God, the cruelty becomes immanent in the cosmos. Although the reaction of Arsene to cosmic cruelty is that of laughter (hollow, bitter, or mirthless), Watt can only manage a grimace in imitation of smiles he has seen.

The hero cannot laugh, but the reader is skillfully inveigled to laugh, perhaps with Beckett. This laugh is not unrelated to "black humor," which arouses "an insulting laugh that springs from the depth of the self in revolt, that provokes and defies public opinion and the cosmos itself." [24]

Like the Surrealists, Beckett blends cruelty and laughter. But the sadistic jokes of the Surrealists were acts of defiance against bourgeois strictures; "black laughter" sounded triumphantly, heroically. In *Watt,* one never knows who laughs last. Arsene, the constant laugher at his own monologue, in contrast to the Murphy of Chapter 6 of his book, finds that in his personal system "the distinction between what was inside it and what was outside it was not at all easy to draw." Arthur, in a fit of laughter, leans "for support against a passing shrub, or bush, which joined heartily in the joke," for the bush is a laurel—the physicomorphic avatar of Daphne. But

Watt, who cannot laugh, is concerned, "not after all with what the figure was, in reality, but with what the figure appeared to be, in reality. For since when were Watt's concerns with what things were, in reality" (227)?

Difficult though it is, finally impossible, Arthur, Arsene, and Watt attempt to extract information from the cosmos, or at least from the cosmos as it appears to be. They are intrepid enough to seek service at Mr. Knott's house, which also attracts men as diverse as the silent Erskine and the happily married Micks. Hindered as Watt may be by his increasingly undependable senses, reasoning, and language, he explores, throughout his stay at Mr. Knott's, "fixity," and Beckett creates ironic comedy of that exploration.

As in the cosmic irony of Kafka, the absurdity of situation and character is stressed; human frailty is flung in the face of mysterious forces. But emphasized more finally than in the *Castle* is the unreliability of our means of perception and meditation; doubt remains doubt, and does not become, as for Descartes, a road to certainty. Watt loses the reason valued so highly by the latter. His senses fail too, and language as well. Having undertaken to serve Mr. Knott, *Homo sapiens* Watt finds that the tools of his world do not render him sapient. In the face of an irrational presence, rational questions are shattered at their epistemological base. Not only, how can Watt know Mr. Knott? But how does Watt know what he knows? And the answer comes to be that Watt knows not Mr. Knott. He knows not. Rational and sensible knowledge can lead only to solipsism. Hence the comic emphasis upon the circle, that perfect self-contained solipsistic symbol. But Watt's circle is broken. Even less than Murphy and Belacqua does Watt find solipsism possible.

In one of the last of the Addenda, Watt first hears of a Knott family: "There had been a time when they [the words *Knott family*] would have pleased him, and the thought they tendered, that Mr Knott too was serial, in a vermicular series.

But not now. For Watt was an old rose now, and indifferent to the gardener" (253).

This passage may be linked to Beckett's earlier fiction, for the Belacqua of "Dante and the Lobster" is a strong young rose, and in "Draff" we hear that in rosaceous memory no gardener dies. But after a rose has withered away in the rosy effort—the only effort a rose can make—to know its gardener, all, including the gardener named Graves, may well become a matter of indifference to him.

In examination of comic elements in Beckett's work before *Watt,* Bergson's analysis was useful, but in *Watt* Beckett's comic of situation, character, and language changes radically. Corrective and consolidating theories of comedy are irrelevant to Watt. He is never cured of his intellection; he is never reintegrated into society, and any sympathy with Watt's quest would preclude interpreting the novel as a plea for the incurious social man. Watt's rationalism leads to insanity, as Murphy's withdrawal into his mind leads to death.

In Beckett's work, however, neither death nor insanity can be considered deserved punishments for vices of the characters. On the contrary, Beckett's irony against Murphy, who faces insanity and death, is so subtle that several critics have equated Murphy with Beckett. His irony against Watt is blatant and pervasive, and yet Beckett evinces sympathy with Watt's heart-breaking, mind-breaking quest. Not only is Watt subsequently evoked with Murphy (and not Belacqua) in Beckett's fictional review of his fictions, but he plays a role in *Mercier et Camier,* Beckett's first French novel. In *More Pricks,* a mocking cloak screens the hero from sympathy. In *Murphy,* an apparent sympathy for the hero sometimes obscures the irony. In *Watt,* the pathetic is blended with the comic, as Kierkegaard claimed they were blended in existence.

5

the first burst into French

It was a different experience
from writing in English. It
was more exciting for me—
writing in French.
Quoted by Israel Shenker

Beckett has never seriously, publicly answered the question as to why he decided to change his writing language. His quip, "Pour faire remarquer moi," is plainly facetious,[1] since Beckett's French work clearly does not woo public approval, and the potential audience for books in French is far smaller than for those in English. To Niklaus Gessner, Beckett stated that he switched to French "Parce qu'en français c'est plus facile d'écrire sans style,"[2] but Beckett's French is highly styled, in its own distinctive idiom that is characterized by its strict lack of ornamentation and elaboration.

By 1939, Beckett completed a group of thirteen French poems,[3] but he turned to French for fiction only in 1945, after the war was over, and he had enjoyed a vacation in English-speaking Ireland. In quick succession, he wrote a short novel *Mercier et Camier*, and four stories, "Premier amour" ("First Love"), "L'Expulsé" ("The Expelled"), "Le Calmant" ("The Tranquilizer"), and "La Fin" ("The End").[4] Since Beckett, despite pressure from his publishers, has refused to allow the novel *Mercier et Camier,* the story "Premier amour," and the drama *Eleutheria* to appear in print, these works presumably do not meet his standards. Examination of the unpublished works reveals the extraordinary continuity of Beckett's artistic achievement.

Mercier et Camier, the first French novel, is an account of the travels of two men. Mercier is tall, gaunt, bearded, and Camier is short, pudgy, and red-faced. Having spent the night apart, they have an appointment to meet at nine in Square St. Ruth, named, sardonically, for the wife-beating Marshal of France who was killed by cannon-shot in Ireland. In brief farcical scenes, Mercier and Camier keep missing each other by five minutes, but at ten to ten, they meet, even as the hands of the clock, each claiming he was the first to appear. From that point on, for some hundred pages, they are virtually inseparable.

With no hint of plausible motivation, they traverse town and country by bicycle and train, but are finally reduced to walking, with increasing boredom, fatigue, and clashes of pace. From time to time, they stop at a bar for refreshment, and once they even spend the night at a hotel. They meet a M. Gall, now manager of a bar and no longer a piano-tuner, as in *Watt.* Imperceptibly, M. Gall dissolves into a M. Gast. M. Graves, a pastoral patriarch, observes the "pseudocouple," but they do not notice him. A M. Conaire seeks Camier, who refuses to see him.

Wherever they are, it is only a short distance to Helen's apartment, where they can sleep, have their umbrella repaired, or satisfy Camier's sexual urges. But despite Helen's accommodations, they lose umbrella, bicycle, and knapsack, and throw their raincoat away. Suddenly, Camier is alone, but Mercier soon joins him, after a long absence. Towards the end of the book, they trudge laboriously, the road between them. In a last surge of effort, Camier takes Mercier by the hand, seeking to drag him along. But by the final chapter, they are separated. Watt, suddenly emerging for the first time in the novel, introduces them to each other, begs them to *tutoyer* each other (which they have done throughout the preceding chapters), and leads them almost by force to a bar (milk-drinking Watt of his own novel!). Mercier remarks that Watt reminds him of someone he used to know, a fellow named Murphy, who died ten years ago, and whose body was never found. In spite of Watt's good offices, Mercier and Camier abandon him when he grows boisterous in the bar (mild Watt of his own novel!), and they walk part way together towards where Mercier lives. But there is nothing for Camier where Mercier lives, and he bids Mercier adieu—leaving Mercier alone in the dark and the rain.

In this novel, which approximates Murphy's description of the third dark zone of his mind, where all is a "flux of forms," Beckett meticulously and ironically lists the specific incidents at the end of each two chapters. But such detail obscures rather than reveals the main design, which is centered on the nature of the double hero, Mercier and Camier.

An ambivalent pun, *mercier* is a peddler of miscellaneous small wares. A French proverb dating from the fifteenth century, "Petit panier, petit mercier," corresponds to the English, "Don't bite off more than you can chew," but during the course of the novel, neither Mercier nor Camier seems to heed this caution. Camier is not a French word, but contains the same root as *camion,* a chariot, truck, or other carrier on wheels. Relevant, too, may be the Irish meaning of the prefix "cam," somewhat analogous to French "con,"[5] since the *conarium,* where Descartes thought mind joined body, is a favorite butt of Beckett's wit.

In *Murphy,* one of the minor characters sardonically suggests that mind and body carry each other: "Everywhere I find defiled . . . in the crass and unharmonious unison, the mind at the cart-tail of the body, and the body at the chariot-wheels of the mind" (218). In Beckett's first French novel,

Mercier only gradually parts from the more physical Camier, and Beckett is deliberately ambiguous about assigning the responsibility for their separation. Each comic, symbolic incident traces a step in the disintegration of the union, until Watt, with all the violence of his rationality, can reunite them only momentarily.

In this human adventure, as in *Watt,* animals and objects are charged with meaning. Hugh Kenner has described man on a bicycle as "the supreme Cartesian achievement"; "the intelligence guides, the mobile wonder obeys." [6] In *Mercier et Camier,* the more intelligent Mercier holds the handlebar, while Camier hangs on to the saddle. Umbrella, raincoat, and sack have protective or storage value against the onslaughts or privations of the human condition. In the bar-hotel that M. Gall manages and M. Graves favors with his patronage, a M. Conaire seeks Camier. Descartes's *conarium,* where matter meets mind, is again relevant. Murphy was charged by Neary with a conarium, "shrunk to nothing." So, Camier, by rejecting M. Conaire's company, may be performing a symbolic "conarectomy," removing any possible meeting ground for mind and body. That Conaire is phonetically close to a French obscenity suits Beckett's ironic purpose, since, in this first French novel, obscenity and vulgarity underline the philosophic frustration. Cruelty and *non sequitur* also provide comic notes, but more elegant linguistic manipulation is spurned. In mood, in alternation of dialogue and description, and above all in the combination of a surface linguistic simplicity with an ambivalent complexity of meaning, *Mercier et Camier* strongly resembles the four French stories that were written at about the same time.

This deceptively colloquial French was to become Beckett's characteristic idiom. However, it is not he but Louis-Ferdinand Céline who introduced it into French fiction. Although Beckett nowhere refers to Céline, the impact in

France of *Voyage au bout de la nuit* was so forceful that it would be incredible had Beckett not read it some time after its publication in 1932.[7]

The contrast between Academy-protected written French and slang-ridden spoken French is acute and striking. Outside of direct discourse, even the French Realists rarely wrote in the language of daily speech, with all its colloquialism and vulgarity. Although Verlaine in the nineteenth century had called for the neck of eloquence to be wrung, it was Céline who accomplished this for fiction. In *Voyage au bout de la nuit,* the vituperative vulgarity of the prose is in noisy harmony with the crude subject matter of the picaresque narrator-hero-bum. With passionate anger and sweeping cynicism, the "I" of Céline's long, rambling novel describes his life as "un pauvre."

From the opening sentence, contractions and slang establish the idiom: "Ça a débuté comme ça." Vulgarity and obscenity provide a ruthless honesty:

La grande défaite, en tout, c'est d'oublier, et surtout ce qui vous a fait crever, et de crever sans comprendre jamais jusqu'à quel point les hommes sont vaches. Quand on sera au bord du trou faudra pas faire les malins nous autres, mais faudra pas oublier non plus, faudra raconter tout sans changer un mot, de ce qu'on a vu de plus vicieux chez les hommes et puis poser sa chique et puis descendre. Ça suffit comme boulot pour une vie tout entière.

(The greatest defeat, in anything, is to forget, and above all to forget what it is that has smashed you, and to let yourself be smashed without ever realizing how thoroughly devilish men can be. When our time is up, we people mustn't bear malice, but neither must we forget: we must tell the whole thing, without altering one word—everything that we have seen of man's viciousness; and then it will be over and time to go. That is enough of a job for a whole lifetime.)

Although the bulk of Céline's novel concentrates on "man's viciousness," the opening chapters present a naïve hero, who enlists in the army, falls in love, and unwarily believes what he is told. On the war, the hero remarks: "Lui, notre colonel, savait peut-être pourquoi ces deux gens-là tiraient, les Allemands aussi peut-être qu'ils savaient, mais moi, vraiment, je savais pas" ("The colonel perhaps knew why those two fellows were firing and the Germans maybe knew it too; but as for me, quite frankly, I didn't at all"). Very soon, however, the hero loses his innocence when he is exposed to the horrors of war. By the middle of the book, a practicing physician, he is almost indifferent to death: "On n'est jamais très mécontent qu'un adulte s'en aille, ça fait toujours une vache de moins sur la terre, qu'on se dit, tandis que pour un enfant, c'est tout de même moins sûr" ("One never minds very much if an adult goes; that's always one sod less in the world, one thinks to oneself, whereas in the case of a child, the thing's not quite so certain"). By the end of the book, the cynicism is unqualified; Céline hammers out his diatribes so that emotion is submerged in its own excess.

Although Beckett is far more selective of the targets of his irony, and wields that irony more pointedly, Céline has shaped his French idiom. A few incongruous similes in *Voyage au bout de la nuit* may even have suggested to Beckett a similar tonal use for a technique that he had already mastered: "Ce déluge n'empêchait pas les animaux de se rechercher, les rossignols se mirent à faire autant de bruit que les chacals. L'anarchie partout et dans d'arche, moi Noé, gâteux" ("But it [the rain] didn't stop the animals chasing each other; after sunset the nightingales began to make as much noise as the jackals. Anarchy everywhere and inside the Ark myself, a broken-down Noah").

As Céline's hero-narrator grows older and more cynical, the incongruous if grim humor is replaced by despair. Although most of Céline's vitriolic prose is socially oriented, there is a paragraph of metaphysical resonance that chants the staccato rhythms of which Beckett was to become a master-composer.

La grande fatigue de l'existence n'est peut-être en somme que cet énorme mal qu'on se donne pour demeurer vingt ans, quarante ans, davantage, raisonnable, pour ne pas être simplement, profondément soi-même, c'est-à-dire immonde, atroce, absurde. Cauchemar d'avoir à présenter toujours comme un petit idéal universel, surhomme du matin au soir, le sous-homme claudicant qu'on nous a donné.

(The great weariness of life is maybe nothing but the vast trouble we take to remain always for twenty or forty or more years at a time reasonable beings—so as not to be merely and profoundly oneself, that is to say, obscene, ghastly, and absurd. It's the nightmare of having to present to the world from morning till night as a superman, our universal petty ideal, the grovelling sub-man we really are.)

Beckett, for all the apparent artlessness of his narrative prose, weaves his ironic diatribes more tightly into the fabric of his fiction. Céline's characters, particularly his hero, rant and rave against society, but those of Beckett well up with unexplained and inexplicable passion—itself absurd, but also reflecting upon the absurdity of the world.

The diatribes of Céline's heroes and those signed by Céline's own name are indistinguishable stylistically. The incidents of *Voyage au bout de la nuit* (as of Céline's subsequent novels) are autobiographical. Although *Voyage au bout de la nuit* is loosely plotted, the hero's encounters with his friend Robinson supply continuity and climax. The combination of recognizably autobiographical incidents, coherent chronology, consistent characterization, and antisocial cynicism differentiate Céline's fiction from that of Beckett. On the other hand, Beckett has learned from Céline a grim, comic, colloquial French.

Beckett's four French stories are written in Céline's French idiom about nameless "I's" who may or may not be the same person. Like Céline's hero, those of Beckett view our habits as though they were strangers on this planet. Thus, Céline's narrator compares the Dollar to the Holy Ghost, and each sinner confesses before the bank cashier in order to be worthy of his cash.

Beckett's satire is less specific, and his details appear to be chosen at random. In each of the four stories, an "I" conscientiously recounts what he recalls, but all four are aware of the unpredictability of their memories. As the narrator Sam casts doubt on Watt's story, so these "I's" doubt their own stories. Moreover, doubt does not, as in the *Cogito,* lead to a certainty of existence; doubt leads to more profound doubt.

In these seemingly haphazard tales, one would scarcely expect a coherent plot or a situation in Bergsonian terms, and indeed the plots are difficult to summarize.[8] In "L'Expulsé" and "La Fin," both of which open when the protagonist is evicted from a building, the "I" looks for a place to live. In "L'Expulsé" the narrator is thrown down a flight of stairs—*perron* in French. Recalling Beckett's *Whoroscope* pun on Descartes, Seigneur du Perron, we may take it that the Cartesian mind-body cleavage has evicted man from the dwelling in which he was formerly housed.

For a short time, the "I's" of "Premier amour" and "La Fin" succeed in finding homes, even to having their food brought in and their slops carried out in pots, much as Mr. Knott was served. In "Le Calmant" the narrator tries to tell himself a story. Nobody, nothing, hinders any of these "I's," and yet their efforts are unfulfilled. The comic of situation, even more than in *Watt,* depends upon *non sequitur,* confusion, and disproportion, thereby implicitly deriding the orderly tradition of the well-made plot of French literature.

The alogical immediacy of the stories has a sober as well as a comic aspect. Gone is the consistent rationalism of Watt, and in its stead is Murphy's ambient "flux of forms," in which experience resists interpretation by intellect. The critic Beckett, in his 1931 essay on Proust, opposes the reality of experience against its deformation by the mind: "The most successful evocative experiment can only project the echo of a past sensation, because, being an act of intellection, it is conditioned by the prejudices of the intelligence which abstracts from any given sensation, as being illogical and insignificant, a discordant and frivolous intruder, whatever word or gesture, sound or perfume, cannot be fitted into the puzzle of a concept. But the essence of any new experience is contained precisely in this mysterious element that the vigilant will rejects as an anachronism. It is the axis about which the sensation pivots, the centre of gravity of its coherence" (33–34). Although it is not a plea for Surrealist automatic writing, Beckett's comment on Proust's "sensual memory" praises a similar rejection of logic and intellection. Like the Surrealists, Beckett employs sardonic humor and unmotivated violence to free his narratives from those bourgeois and orderly twins—Space and Time.

In the four French stories, themes and events blend in unproportioned detail. The protagonist of "L'Expulsé" dwells upon a horse's activities. In "Le Calmant" the protagonist yarn-spinner denies knowing anything about normal time. Exploding without warning into his tale are a boy who once offered him a sticky candy, or that boy accompanied by his goat, or the goat alone. In "La Fin," the longest of the stories, the protagonist devotes a brief sentence to his son, and over six pages to the shelter he constructs from an old canoe.

If these tales are in sequent order, the chronology is difficult to follow. "Premier amour," "L'Expulsé," and "La Fin" begin with the eviction from a dwelling (the cinema has long exploited the comic, slapstick aspects of being evicted). In the interval between "L'Expulsé" and "La Fin"—perhaps "Le Calmant"—the protagonist has died. Towards the end of the final story, the protagonist of "La Fin" swallows the tranquilizer that plays no role (in its pill aspect) in the story that bears that name. A single "I" could have undergone the disconnected episodes of the tales, but it is not certain whether the "I" *is* single.

Secondary characters appear even more episodically than in *Watt*, and, like the protagonists, are often nameless. They appear as "the coachman," "his wife with extraordinary buttocks," "a policeman," "a boy," "a man," "women," "a little girl unless it was a little boy," "a priest," "a man I had known in former times"—designations that can scarcely be related to the Aristotle-to-Bergson character.

Names sometimes adorn people who do not enter the stories proper, but who inhabit the hero's memories or fictions. M. Weir of "La Fin" is an exception, for he does play a role in that story; although his language is clearer than that of Watt's Mr. Knott, he serves a comparably vague deity function. Like most of Beckett's deity variants, his name has English rather than French resonances. M. Weir suggests *weird,* both in its older meaning of "fate" and its more recent one of "fantastic." More obscure is the word "weir" itself, meaning a "dam," and related perhaps to the rain against which M. Weir provides temporary shelter for the "I" of "La Fin."

Among the characters who appear only in memories or fictions are Maître Nidder, who has given to the protagonist of "L'Expulsé" his inheritance from an unknown woman, and Mme. Maxwell, who has given a horse trough to the town of the protagonist of "La Fin." Quite fittingly, Ward is the name of the boyhood teacher who introduces the protagonist of "La Fin" to Geulincx's *Ethics.*[9] Pauline is the name of the abandoned mistress in the tale heard by the protagonist of "Le Calmant"; Joe Breen or Breem is the name of the hero in the tale the narrator of "Le Calmant" used to hear from his father. Most of these names in the French stories have, comically, an English resonance.

The animals of these stories do not bear names, but they seem no lower than humans on the zoological scale, and they do not figure instructively in the beast fable tradition. Rather, they contribute to the disproportionate absurdity of the world which imperfectly houses them and their two-legged kin. The first goal of the protagonist of "L'Expulsé" is the zoo, which he fails to reach. The coachman's horse plays a large role in that story, and the narrator sleeps in its stable, along with the rats. In the original version of "L'Expulsé" the narrator expresses a fondness for sheep and pigs. In "Le Calmant" there is a serviceable and tenderly cared-for ass, and a serviceable and ill-tempered cow. In "La Fin" the protagonist's bench is next to a horse trough; rats are no longer welcome to that protagonist, although he admits to having been fond of them once. In the first published version of "La Fin," the protagonist was afflicted with crab lice, but these were omitted in the book version.

It is in language that the stories differ most strikingly from the English fiction. Besides the important shift from English to French, Beckett achieves a tonal shift from the stylistic elegance of *Murphy,* or the labored exactitude of *Watt,* to a comic of the colloquial. The Bergsonian comic roster virtually disappears; learned allusion is drastically reduced; misquotation and erudite jargon vanish; so, too, do most of the monotonous repetitions, series, permutations, combinations, of *Watt.* There are only two parodies, the Marxist fanatic of "La Fin" and the Freudian fanatic of "Le Calmant," but then Freud and Marx were themselves generative of many intellectual parodies. The nameless Freudian almost strangles the hero of "Le Calmant" while murmuring soft words in his ear. The nameless Marxist, after haranguing a crowd on its brutality, savagely turns upon the hero of "La Fin."

Of the comic devices already considered in Beckett's other works, it is incongruity, frequently exaggerated into absurdity, that evokes most of the laughter in the stories. However, rather than juxtaposing out-of-key images as in the early works, Beckett continues, as in *Watt,* to hinge his incongruities upon the minds, bodies, and actions of his protagonists. The "I's" grow older from story to story; only the hero of the unpublished "Premier amour" is young—about twenty-five; in the original version of "L'Expulsé" the hero mentions being forty or fifty years old at the time of the story; the hero of "Le Calmant" thinks he was about ninety when he died.

The three heroes of the published stories have grotesque gaits. The protagonist of "L'Expulsé" has at least five or six posture faults and constantly falls; the protagonist of "Le Calmant" is outdistanced by those suffering from Parkinson's disease, and each step seems to be the resolution of an unprecedented problem in statodynamics; the protagonist of "La Fin" tries never to look back to a place from which he is departing.

Like other Beckett characters, the heroes of the three published stories own hats upon which they feel compelled to comment. Murphy, it will be recalled, never wore a hat, whereas the near-idiot Cooper never took his bowler off. Watt and Mr. Knott are seen with and without hats. Mercier, while Watt tries to reunite him with Camier, looks longingly at a shop window in which men's hats are displayed. The protagonist of "Premier amour" is evicted from his room, but is allowed to have the money and the hat that his father left him. The hat of the protagonist of "L'Expulsé" was purchased for him by his father, and that of the protagonist of "Le Calmant," attached to his buttonhole, is requested by Pauline's lover, in exchange for a mysterious flask; that of the protagonist of "La Fin," the hand-me-down of a corpse, is at first too small, but soon he becomes accustomed to it, and even uses it as a receptacle into which to milk a cow, before it is finally secured to his buttonhole.

It is possible that the hats of certain of Beckett's French

heroes have an Irish ancestor in that of Swift's Gulliver. While Gulliver rows toward Lilliput, he fastens his hat under his chin by means of a string. Moreover, when the Lilliputians retrieve Gulliver's hat, they bore two holes in the brim, as Moran does in Beckett's *Molloy,* in order to secure the ends of an elastic.

The "I's" of the stories are physically grotesque, and their responses tend to be incongruous—those of foreigners to our world. In "L'Expulsé" the protagonist is able, after long plotting, to have his will upon sly geraniums; he will not *tutoyer* himself even in his thoughts; he sees people making the sign of the Cross at a funeral as "un grand branle-bas de chapeaux en même temps qu'un papillottement de mille et mille doigts" (25) ("a big bustle of hats at the same time as a flickering of thousands on thousands of fingers").

The protagonist of "Le Calmant" understands none of the sexual allusions of the man he meets; he lies down to rest before the altar of a cathedral. The speech of the protagonist of "La Fin" can scarcely be understood; one of his expletives is the dactylic "Exelmans!" of Mr. Knott; he detests human company and the sea.

It is interesting to note that the first versions of "L'Expulsé" and "La Fin," published, respectively, in *Fontaine* and *Temps Modernes,* contain incongruities missing from the book versions. In "L'Expulsé" the narrator dreams of a day when all gestures of affection, which are meticulously and hilariously catalogued, will disappear. He dwells on the efficacy of his bad breath as a weapon against policemen. In the early version of "La Fin" a generous Mme. Maxwell may be looking down from Heaven, enjoying the spectacle of the horses drinking from the trough she has willed to her city. In both versions of "La Fin," after the protagonist frightens the cow he milked into his hat, he dreams of the butter he could have made; in the earlier text, he dreams as well of the fatness, healthiness, and happiness he could have acquired, so as to cut a fine figure in the world. In revising both stories, Beckett reduces the comic content without apparent reason.

As may be seen from these few examples, the incongruities add to contradictions and literalisms to create the atmosphere of absurdity that is established, primarily, by *non sequitur* of event, character, and thought. Thus, the "I" of "L'Expulsé" always combines disappointment and consolation, for he is never disappointed without feeling consolation at the same time, or an instant afterwards; this seeming absurdity comments ironically on all who view the world through rose-colored glasses.

The opening incongruity of "Le Calmant" is more ambiguous: "Je ne sais plus quand je suis mort" ("I no longer know when I died"). It never becomes clear what he means by this death, except that it is not "la vraie mort charnelle."

Like Watt, Murphy, and Belacqua, the "I's" of the stories have trouble with the police, who find them suspicious. Frequently, literalisms serve to point up the absurdity of situation or character. In the opening passage of "L'Expulsé," the protagonist, having been thrown down a flight of steps, apologizes for not being able to announce how many steps there were; he is not able to count them, because he never knows which foot to count first. When the coachman laughs, the same protagonist guesses it is because he is in the coachman's carriage; he expects to be laughed at. Later, however, he decides that the coachman may be laughing because he is wondering whether it is really his carriage, and then whether it is a carriage at all.

The protagonist of "Le Calmant" also tends to make literal interpretations of words and events; he assures Pauline's lover that he knows the meaning of *baiser*, but he appears to be unaware of its obscene overtones. He questions the meaning of *tout* in the cliché, "Tout est là." The protagonist of "La Fin," after observing the movements of the sea and the beating of the rain, remarks: "Tout céla faisait plutôt liquide" (117) ("All that composed a rather liquid world").

To a greater extent than in former works, incongruity depends upon the obscene, the physically disgusting, and the cruelty of the cosmos. Visceral and sexual parts and processes are named in both literal and expletive contexts, and we recall that a foreigner to a tongue often learns obscenities first. The emendation of *urinais* to *pissais* in "La Fin" underlines Beckett's intention. Sores, cysts, and excrement abound, and only the rats seem to feel no repugnance for the protagonists. One might pity them, were they not so full of vindictive, illogical cruelty themselves, in the fashion of the cosmos they inhabit.

The "I" of "L'Expulsé" expects to be beaten after he is thrown out on the street, but when he rises to move on, he is all for knocking down a child; he feels children should be kept off the streets with "leurs landaus, cerceaux, sucettes, patinettes, trottinettes, pépés, mémés, nounous, ballons, tout leur sale petit bonheur quoi" (23) ("their carriages, hoops, lollipops, skates, scooters, grannies, nannies, balloons—in fact their whole filthy little happiness"). The same protagonist causes an old woman to fall, and hopes fervently that she has broken a femur. He toys with the idea of setting fire to the stable where he is given refuge.

When the "I" of "La Fin" is presented with clean clothes (fumigated in the earlier version) before being dismissed from his refuge, he wonders whether there is a law that clothes be supplied. Like the "I" of "L'Expulsé," he has to sign a receipt for everything he receives. Children throw stones at him and his friend; his childhood teacher died horribly in a toilet; people steal from his beggar's box.

The "I" of "Le Calmant" says explicitly: "Je me pris à songer à la cruauté, la riante" (45) ("I began to think about cruelty, laughing at it"). To this protagonist, who begins his story not knowing when he died, nothing seems so attractive as a painless death, so long as the crows do not arrive before it is completely over; that, he reflects, is the advantage of drowning, for the crabs never arrive too soon: "Tout cela est affaire d'organisation" (45). Meeting a man on the parapet of a cathedral, he longs to fling him to the ground, or be flung himself to death. He thinks it a "chose étrange" when, momentarily, he feels no pain, but he is sure that his vulnerability will return after a box of sardines and a good nightmare. Back in his familiar torment, he finds himself before the blood-stained curtains of a horse butcher—blue and white, colors of the Virgin Mary. Falling as he walks, the "I" of "Le Calmant" is not lucky enough to lose consciousness, and somehow he finds himself walking on a road that is not his, constantly climbing, without any stars to guide him, for his own light blots out the stars, if there are any behind the clouds.[10]

As they wander through the cosmos, all the "I's" reflect mordantly on the universe. Near the end of "La Fin," the hero declares: "Se tailler un royaume, au milieu de la merde universelle, puis chier dessus, ça c'était bien de moi" (119) ("To contrive a little kingdom in the midst of the universal muck, then shit on it, ah that was me all over"). Reproaching himself for evoking images, he continues to evoke them from earth, sea, and sky, jumping back and forth from his boyhood to the present, lying on his back in the punctured canoe, waiting for the water to rise. He thinks it will take at least half an hour, swallows his tranquilizer, watches the systole and diastole of the visible world, and meditates "sans regret au récit que j'avais failli faire, récit à l'image de ma vie, je veux dire sans le courage de finir ni la force de continuer" (122–123) ("The memory came faint and cold of the story I might have told, a story in the likeness of my life, I mean without the courage to end or the strength to go on").

And yet, during the course of the story which is "La Fin," the protagonist has declared several times that it would all end soon, now that "they" had sent him from the refuge. The entire cosmos and man's place in it is controlled by this mysterious "they."

The protagonist of "Le Calmant," who opens his story already dead, thinks longingly of his physical death. Could he have returned to earth after his death? No, that would not be like him—to return to earth after his death. Tonight, he insists, his old body is to disappear "dans le fracas de ses images." Nevertheless, after his visit to the cathedral, he has a quasi-certitude of being still in the world; at the end he utters the word "reality" apologetically; he is too tired to seek the exact word, since all of his words have been wrong for their situations.

The protagonist of "L'Expulsé," like that of "La Fin," mutters about the "they" who have cast him out. He knows that his expulsion is neither the cradle nor tomb of anything, or perhaps it is so much like other cradles and tombs that he is lost between them. Concluding that he hasn't the slightest idea as to why he told this story, that he could just as well have told another, he addresses the reader directly: "Ames vives, vous verrez que cela se ressemble" (40) ("Living souls, you'll see that they're all alike").

The ironic cosmological comedy and an awareness of its irony are inalienably linked by the first-person alogical narration.[11] More fiercely than in any earlier Beckett work, authenticity and immediacy resist the interpretive intelligence. The "I's" constantly interrupt themselves; their skepticism with regard to reality, truth, knowledge, becomes an epistemological adventure, comic on the surface but cruelly ironic below, because it is foredoomed to failure. The "I" of "La Fin" shrugs: "Je savais que ce serait bientôt fini, alors je jouais la comédie" (116) ("I knew it would soon be the end, so I played the part, you know, the part of—how shall I say, I don't know").

We may recall the serious or semiserious examinations of the mind in Beckett's essays on Proust and Joyce; in "Yellow," while Belacqua prepares for his operation; in Chapter 6 of *Murphy;* and in Parts II and III of *Watt.* Now Beckett's characters examine their own minds: "C'est tuant, les souvenirs." The "I" of "L'Expulsé" affirms (as Beckett does, and says that Proust does) that the only way to bury things in the mind is to think of them conscientiously, and that the only way to remember things that are dear is not to think of them.

Senses and bodily functions fail the "I" of "La Fin": "Mes besoins . . . réduits à mes dimensions" ("My needs . . . had dwindled as it were to my dimensions"). He confuses words that come from without with those that come from within. Once, like Watt, he used to be touched by proofs that he had an existence outside of himself, but now, "C'est à demander parfois si on est sur la bonne planète. Même les mots vous lâchent, c'est tout dire" (118–119) ("It's enough to make you wonder sometimes if you're on the right planet. Even the words desert you, it's as bad as that").

But it is the "I" of "Le Calmant" who makes a relentless zigzag between the epistemological and cosmological comedies. Constantly interrupting his own "tranquilizer," in the fashion of Beckett himself, this narrator-hero casts doubt upon phenomena ("Je dis cathédrale, mais je n'en sais rien" [56]—"I say cathedral, but I know nothing about it); time ("Ah je vous foutrai des temps, salauds de votre temps"[44]—"Damn your time, your filthy time"); space ("je me retrouvais dans le même vide éblouissant" [74]—"I found myself in the same dazzling void"); life and death ("ou se peut-il que dans cette histoire je sois remonté sur terre, après ma mort?" [42]—"Or can it be that in this story I came back to earth, after my death?"); providence ("c'est de la terre plutôt que du ciel, pourtant mieux côté, que m'est venu le secours, dans les instants difficiles" [51–52]—"it's from earth rather than heaven, which is quoted at a higher rate, that help has come to me at difficult moments"); reality ("Mais la réalité, trop fatigué pour chercher le mot juste" [74]—"But reality, too tired to seek the right word"); and objective knowledge ("Je m'en voudrais d'insister sur ces antinomies, car nous sommes bien entendu dans une tête" [61]—"I reproach myself with insisting on these oppositions, for of course we are inside a head"). He pleads with his fictions to tell him where he is, what time it is, to give him light.

At the end, the "I" of "Le Calmant" possesses only these comico-pathetic fragments shored against his ruin—Pauline, the mistress of a chance encounter's story, the goat of the boy who offered him candy, the little girl on the parapet of the cathedral, and, at the very last, a fleeting recollection of Joe Breen or Breem, the boy hero in the story his father told him, now grown old himself and become "le pauvre père Breem, ou Breen." Beckett implies an epistemological conundrum: Which of the stories reflects reality, if any, if at all?

6

a trilogy of novels

This time, then once more I
think, then perhaps a
last time—
Molloy

The "New Novel" in France today is often said to date from 1951, when Jérôme Lindon of Les Editions de Minuit published *Molloy,* which had been brought to him (as to other publishers, who rejected it) by Beckett's wife. The second volume of the trilogy, *Malone meurt,* appeared that same year, and the third volume, *L'Innommable,* in 1953, the year that Beckett became famous when *En Attendant Godot* was staged in Paris.[1]

Beckett's French novels, *Molloy, Malone meurt,* and *L'Innommable,* could suitably have been called "L'Expulsé," "Le Calmant," and "La Fin." Moran of *Molloy* is "expelled" from middle-class clichés, Molloy from all repose, and they are both condemned to frenetic quests. Malone on his deathbed tries, even as the protagonist of "Le Calmant," to attain some tranquillity through his fictions. And finally, an unnamable protagonist comes to a conclusion as inconclusive as that of "La Fin"; "You must go on, I can't go on, I'll go on."

The nameless "I" who arrives at this seesaw between impotence and compulsion may previously have been called Malone, Molloy, Moran; perhaps even Watt, Murphy, Belacqua (or Victor, Mercier, Camier, in works that Beckett refuses to publish). There is a family resemblance between them. "A sinecure handed down from generation to generation," in the words of the Unnamable. As with the "I's" of the short stories, nothing is certain except that each work has an "I" who tells a story. As in the stories, plot summaries are difficult, primarily because the incidents lack all proportion.[2] However, if details are glossed over, skeletal plot outlines may be attempted.

Plot and Situation. *Molloy* is divided into two parts. In the first half, a grotesque old cripple, hat fastened to his buttonhole by a lace, having arrived mysteriously in his mother's room, indeed in her bed, writes the story of his quest for his mother. In the second part, Moran, a middle-aged bourgeois inhabitant of the town of Turdy, having returned home after seeking Molloy in Ballyba (the village of Bally and its domains), writes the story of *that* quest.[3] In the second novel, Malone, dying, attempts to pass his remaining time by telling himself stories. In the third book, the Unnamable, born like Molloy in Bally, perhaps dead now, compulsively writes words. Thus, the first two are accounts of quests in the past; in the second two the accounts *are* the quests.

When the novels are reduced in this way, it is apparent why Beckett has often been compared to Kafka, since the absurd, compulsive quest is so dominant for both writers. But Kafka imposes the absurdity of the world on his characters, who behave logically, once we grant the initial aberration—that Gregor is an insect, that hungering is an art, that Joseph K. is condemned, or that K. must seek to reach the Castle. With Beckett's protagonists, there are two levels of absurdity. One appears from the opening lines:

I am in my mother's room. It's I who live there now. I don't know how I got there. Perhaps in an ambulance, certainly a vehicle of some kind. (*Molloy*)

I shall soon be quite dead at last in spite of all. (*Malone meurt*)

Where now? Who now? When now? Unquestioning. (*L'Innommable*)

The other is discovered progressively and cumulatively, from phrase to phrase, incident to incident, and work to work.

As absurdity increases from novel to novel of the trilogy, so does the spare economy of the plots, and it becomes essential to distinguish between plot and situation. Restricting the latter to its concrete physical aspects for the moment, we note that Beckett has reduced all his protagonists to virtual immobility, and that therein lies an incisive irony, for they move us by their very inability to move.

One-eyed, toothless Molloy, in his mother's bed but still asserting that he can get up, has memories of a glorious past on crutches and bicycle. Writing in bed, Molloy declares: "And the confines of my room, of my bed, of my body, are as remote from me as were those of my region, in the days of my splendour" (88).

Two-toothed Moran at his desk, having acquired crutches for his creeping paralysis, writes of the time he was quite a walker and even runner, of vague missions he performed on an autocycle. On the other hand, he dreams ecstatically of dead limbs and dead senses.

Malone, toothless as Molloy, but with fewer memories of the life he claims to have spent walking, transmits commands to his legs, but, with the best will in the world, they, like an old dog, are no longer able to obey him. Malone can reach the objects in his room only with his stick, until, some two-thirds of the way through his book, he loses that stick. Later, when his ceiling rises and falls like a womb, he can no longer turn his head. Like the protagonist of "Le Calmant," he wonders whether his room *is* a head, though not necessarily his own.

The Unnamable, as nearly a pure mentality as has appeared in fiction, derives from the Cartesian definition of man as "a thing that thinks." Even more explicitly, a sentence in Book IV of *Le Discours de la méthode* seems to foreshadow the Unnamable: "I could suppose that I had no body, and that there was no world nor any place in which I might be." For all his lack of body, the Unnamable wonders whether he casts a shadow. He mentions Malone's "mortal liveliness" in contrast to his own state. Since there is occasional pressure on his rump and the soles of his feet, he thinks he might be seated. Uncertain of his senses of seeing and hearing, intermittently unable to close his eyes, he is positive that he sheds tears. His very illocality arouses macabre laughter. Locomotion is for none of these heroes, and yet, to quote Beckett's line from *Whoroscope:* "That's not moving, that's *moving.*"

In contrast to the narrative method of the short stories, the French novels are explicitly *written.* In their novel, Moran and Molloy look back upon their adventures. For Malone and the Unnamable, the writing is the adventure.

All the narrators seek to convey the immediacy of experience before the rational intelligence tampers with it. Humor and pathos alike depend upon a seeming senselessness of each event, and upon their utter non-concatenation; for in the large sense of situation, the human condition is increasingly pathetic in each Beckett fiction.

On the first page, Molloy tells that a mysterious man comes to collect the pages he has written, and to leave some money for them, although Molloy specifies that he does not write *for* money, and indeed it would be difficult to see how he would spend it, bedridden and isolated as he is. On the first page again, both Molloy and Malone indicate that they are awaiting, not without eagerness, an imminent death.

In all the novels, both real and fictional characters enter unexpectedly and illogically, as in the stories; but within the more expanded framework of the novels, they are developed at somewhat greater length. Place, time, and season are described irrelevantly. Day and night, light and dark, take on increasing importance, as do the buzz and words of various voices, internal and/or external. More than in Beckett's last English novel, *Watt*, more than in the shorter fiction, events happen, or have happened.

In approaching the three novels as chronologically continuous, we may gain clarity by inverting the order of the Molloy and Moran halves of the first book.[4] *Molloy* shows the making of the artist, *Malone Dies* the artist making, and *The Unnamable* the artist's reflections upon art and the artist.[5] The making of the artist seems to begin, however, with Moran and not Molloy, who is already an artist when the book opens, though he denies "being an aesthete, or an artist." He is, however, aware that his view of the world is "inordinately formal."

Moran, summoned out of his smug world to seek Molloy, and then to report on his quest, begins with the paragraphs, punctuation, and order of conventional prose. A pompous, orthodox bourgeois who teaches his son "horror of the body and its function," Moran is interrupted one Sunday morning before Mass by a messenger from their mutual employer, Youdi. Thirsty and well-dressed, Gaber the messenger delivers his orders. Except for comic overtones—Gaber's complaint that Youdi's command came at night just when he was "in position to make love to his wife"; the beer that will disqualify Moran for receiving the Eucharist; our own acquaintance with the grotesque Molloy, for whom an organized quest seems fantastic—the opening of Moran's tale is quite reasonable. "I found it painful at that period not to understand," he confesses, reminding us of Watt, the non-artist.

Slowly, the absurd intrudes. It becomes evident that there is no systematic method (as to equipment, itinerary, or schedule) for undertaking the quest. Even before his departure, rebellion against Youdi's command alternates with Moran's desire to pierce its meaning. Suddenly, Molloy "or Mollose" seems familiar to Moran—perhaps his own invention, and even Mother Molloy "or Mollose" is not completely foreign. From this point on, we enter the absurd world of Beckett's signature. There are at least five Molloys, it now seems to Moran. An acute pain shoots through Moran's knee while he is giving his son an enema. Moran chooses his clothes for their conspicuousness, and sets out with lingering, loving glances at the worldly property he leaves behind. By the time the pain in his knee recurs, and Moran sends his son to Hole for a bicycle, we are ready for his violent and absurd encounters. Moran kills the "dim man" with unmotivated cruelty, as Molloy has attacked a charcoal-burner. When, interrupting Moran's nightly guffaw in the forest, Gaber reappears—still thirsty, still dressed in his Sunday clothes—Moran has virtually become Molloy, and his prose is as disordered and intense. "Moran, Jacques, home, instanter," Gaber quotes Youdi. Unwittingly, Moran has fulfilled the quest for Molloy; slowly, he has become Molloy.[6]

When we first read Molloy's half of the novel, we are ignorant of Moran's story. Instead, as in the French stories, we are plunged into *non sequitur*. Disconnected remarks fall pell-mell—the room, pots, an arrival, a mother, a possible son, love, a messenger, writing, beginning and ending. Suddenly, we witness the meeting and separation of two men, designated only as A and C, on a bare road. Returning to himself, Molloy describes his encounters with a policeman (followed by brief incarceration), a bargeman, a shepherd and his dog, a lady, whose dog he runs over and kills (followed by a sojourn at her house), and finally a charcoal-burner whom, seventy years ago, he might have loved, but whom he beats brutally instead. Memories of other adventures, above all a love affair, interrupt his spasmodic recital, which terminates when, unable to walk or even to crawl or roll, Molloy falls into a ditch at the edge of the forest. After surveying plain, town, and the forest he has just left, Molloy sinks down in his ditch. "Molloy could stay, where he happened to be," his narrative concludes (124).

In the second novel, Malone's room resembles Molloy's, but he no longer questions how he got there—"In an ambulance perhaps, a vehicle of some kind certainly" (5)—nor recalls his pre-room past, except that he has spent most of his life walking. Once, a nameless woman cared for him, as his fictional Moll later cares for his fiction, Macmann, but now Malone merely empties one pot and fills another, much as Mr. Knott did in *Watt.* Malone knows that he will die soon, not the exact day perhaps, but he feels sure it will be soon. In the meanwhile, he will keep busy telling himself stories—of a man, a woman, an animal, and a thing (probably a stone, for he has always been fond of stones [7]). When he feels the final throes, he will hastily draw up an inventory of his possessions, taking meticulous pains to define what is his, as Mr. Hackett did in *Watt.* Malone's is the systematic mind; no questions, no memories, no comic of disorder; "Present state, three stories, inventory, there" (4).

But dying does not prove to be quite so sober or so simple. In spite of Malone's determination to be tepid, to compose only calm stories, passion bubbles to the surface. His stories, his state, and his possessions flow into one another, and all assault him. Although he reveals his own name only midway through the book, Malone earlier spawns and names his fictions. His Sapo languishes into a kind of death. The memory of a friend Jackson haunts Malone, and resolutely he invents Macmann. Shifting with increasing frenzy between his fictions and his surroundings, Malone loses then finds exercise book and pencil, but then he loses his stick, and it remains lost. He moves Macmann into a lunatic asylum and sees him through a parodic love affair with an ancient crone. Even near the end of his book, Malone desperately attempts to impose method on his thoughts: "Visit, various remarks, Macmann continued, then mixture of Macmann and agony as long as possible" (99). Frightened close to death by a visitor who strikes him on the head (as Molloy struck his mother, and Moran his victim), Malone invests his fictions with maniacal yet ludicrous sadism. Finally, Lemuel, the pot-dispenser, chops down two sailors and forces the other fictions into a boat, which drifts out to sea. Lemuel, concludes Malone incoherently at the end of the novel, will never touch anyone again "never there he will never/ never anything/ there/ any more" (120).

Various critics have claimed that *The Unnamable* begins and continues in comparable incoherence, but in both works the incoherence is carefully controlled by Beckett. Malone at the end and the Unnamable at the beginning, of their respective books, are seeking to impose the peace of non-being upon existence as they, as we, know it. Perhaps Malone achieves this feat through death, but it seems to be a temporary respite, for he is resurrected early in the third volume, to revolve about the Unnamable (once it is decided that the Unnamable does not move and therefore cannot revolve about Malone) and to plague him. Although the Unnamable is almost pure mind—"let us not be over-nice"—or, perhaps, pure cognitive process, he nevertheless wonders whether he and Malone cast a shadow, he knows he sheds tears, he seems to have certain powers of seeing, hearing, feeling. Far more grotesque than his predecessors, the Unnamable sets his adventures in a limbo between concretion and abstraction. The sentences run to pages in length, are composed of breathless, mutually interactive phrases, and render difficult all isolation of language from event. The recital of the Unnamable is an unprecedented literary tour de force, but it is more than that. By "the principle of parsimony," as the Unnamable himself phrases it, Beckett's extreme concentration of the fictional components of plot and character achieves our desperate involvement in the ambivalent quest of the nameless narrator-hero.

One might say, in an attempt to recount the plot of *The Unnamable,* that Malone's moving by is its very first event, followed closely by Molloy and "all . . . from Murphy on." From a mysterious "they" a particular face emerges—Basil, who fills the Unnamable with hatred. For some twenty-five pages, the Unnamable punctuates his meditations with the movements and clothes of Malone, Molloy, and Murphy, and with the teachings of Basil, who is rebaptized Mahood. After relating Mahood to himself, the Unnamable turns to injecting himself into Mahood. At the time of their union, Mahood is just returning from a world tour, to his wife, parents, and eight or nine offspring. His efforts at approach to an arena-like nest are watched by his family, in much the same spirit that Gregor's family watch his movements in Kafka's *Metamorphosis.* However, when Mahood, like his predecessors Malone, Molloy, and their fictions, threatens to spit back the pat lessons he has swallowed, the Unnamable introduces Worm, who, "they" hope, he half hopes, will prove different, will not be human, be born, and die in cliché formulae. It is Worm who becomes Mahood's last avatar. Armless, legless, he is planted in a jar before a restaurant. Upon his container, the menu is changed daily, as is the habit of French restaurants; his sawdust is changed only weekly. But Mahood is not destroyed as easily as Malone's Sapo. In alternation, or company, with Worm, he intrudes upon and partakes of the fears of the Unnamable—fears yet desires not only of death but of a being that can be reached only through silence, whereas from first to last the Unnamable has been condemned to words. In one of the final paroxysmic sentences, Beckett reduces the comic to the hysterical, but also to the pathetic: "I'll laugh, that's how it will end, in a chuckle, chuck chuck, ow ha, pa, I'll practise, nyum, hoo, plop, psss, nothing but emotion, bing bang, that's blows, ugh, pooh, what else, oooh, aaah, that's love, enough, it's tiring, hee hee, that's the Abderite" (170). And the mention of Democritus the Abderite recalls Donne's paradox on the intimate relationship between weeping and laughter.

Beckett has said that with *The Unnamable,* he reached a dead end beyond which he felt it impossible to go. "No 'I,' no 'have,' no 'being.' No nominative, no accusative, no verb. There's no way to go on." [8] But this negative state was arrived at through Beckett's unnamable "I," through *his* "have" and "being," through words and situation, and through creatures that, for lack of a better term, we must call characters.

Character. If we examine the characters in the French trilogy, clarification is again obtained by transposing the stories of Moran and Molloy. Whereas the incidental characters of the short fiction are nameless, Moran's account begins by naming everyone—the "I" Jacques Moran (of French-Irish tonality), his son who bears his name (but "this cannot lead to confusion"), and even the son's teddy bear Baby Jack. Also particularized are Moran's servant Martha, his master Youdi, the go-between messenger Gaber, the local priest Father Ambrose; even incidental characters are meticulously named—Verger Joly, who takes notes on those attending Mass, Mrs. Clement, who has broken her femur, Mr. Savory the lawyer, Christy the gardener, Mr. Py the dentist, the neighboring Elsner sisters, their cook Hannah, their dog Zulu. In sharp contrast to this frantic denomination of the trivial is the indefiniteness of Molloy's name. Moran confuses it with Mollose, Molone, or Molloc. Once on the Molloy quest, Moran grows hazy about names. His first encounter is with someone designated simply as "a farmer," even though Moran knows him. Similarly, the man with the club, the dim man, and the final farmer are all nameless, just as people (A and C, policemen, a bargeman, a shepherd, the charcoal-burner) tend to be to Molloy. Nor does the latter describe most people he meets, but only those he remembers, particularly his repulsive mother, Mag, and his even more repulsive mistress, variously named Ruth, Edith, and Rose.

At the outset, Moran is as loquacious as the traditional novelist; he discourses about his son's character, intelligence, appearance, his own program of tutelage, his servant's thoughts and suspicions, his priest's orientation and habits. Once embarked on the Molloy quest, however, he loses interest in character, and has the immediate and irrational reactions with which the short stories have familiarized us. He thinks that his son may kill him, or that he may kill his son. He actually kills the dim man with small motivation, just as he gives of his dwindling food supply to the man with the club.

In a perceptive article, Edith Kern has contrasted the Apollonian Moran with the Dionysian Molloy.[9] They are two facets of the same personality. Moran comes to share with Molloy an inability to sit or kneel, a tendency to confuse directions and the colors blue and green; both wear their hats fastened by an elastic, Moran's under his chin and Molloy's to a buttonhole; both temporarily own knives, and both hear an ominous gong. These idiosyncrasies are at once incongruously comic and richly suggestive. The confusion of blue and green, for example, might be the artist's confusion of the imagination and nature. Hats attach Beckett's heroes to their intellectual heritage, and the gong warns them of their doom. But for all the qualities they share, Moran and Molloy are not equated from the start. Moran has to earn his way to Molloy "to see himself preferred, to fancy himself damned, blessed, to fancy himself everyman above all others" (151). Only slowly does Moran come to realize, "For what I was doing I was doing neither for Molloy, who mattered nothing to me, nor for myself, of whom I despaired, but on behalf of a cause which, while having need of us to be accomplished, was in its essence anonymous, and would subsist, haunting the minds of men, when its miserable artisans should be no more" (156–157).

With similar compulsion, Malone embarks on creation. Only one character in his recital, and that one nameless, arrives from outside Malone's head. Deliberate parodies, his fictions are differentiated from each other by name, but lumped together by their author's sardonic attitude. Malone himself suggests, "Perhaps I shall put the man and the woman in the same story, there is so little difference between a man and a woman, between mine I mean" (3). So, Molloy, lumping his mother, mistress, and hostess together, wonders whether they were really women at all, as he thought at the time.

The characters of *The Unnamable*—all fictions—are so alike as to be interchangeable, and the hero occasionally underlines this similarity by grouping them together with himself: "I am neither, I needn't say, Murphy, nor Watt, nor Mercier, nor—no, I can't even bring myself to name them, nor any of the others whose very names I forget, who told me I was they, who I must have tried to be, under duress, or through fear, or to avoid acknowledging me, not the slightest connexion" (53). The overprotest of the superlative "not the slightest connexion" ironically highlights the indissoluble bond between creation and creator, whosever the creation may be.

As in the case of the published French stories, the middle member of the trilogy deals most fully with the protagonist's fictions, and in the novel they are savagely dramatized. In those passages of *Malone Dies* that portray the Saposcat family, the Lamberts, Macmann and entourage, we remark the comic brilliance of language for which Beckett has had only sporadic use since *Murphy*. Even dying, Malone is conscious of the comic quality: "The stories I was told, at one time! And all funny, not one not funny" (98).

Two main and complementary techniques, parody and parenthetic commentary, adorn *Malone Dies;* however, the latter belongs not to Beckett but to Malone. Every time the mocking tone of the narrator threatens to disappear, to make a connection between Saposcat and Malone, the artist revises his story:

He [Sapo] attended his classes with his mind elsewhere, or blank. (9)

He attended his classes with his mind elsewhere. He liked sums (9)

Sapo had no friends—no, that won't do. (12)

Sapo was on good terms with his little friends. (12)

But Sapo was not expelled, either then or later. I must try and discover, when I have time to think about it quietly, why Sapo was not expelled when he so richly deserved to be. For I want as little as possible of darkness in this story. A little darkness, in itself, at the time, is nothing. You think no more about it and you go on. But I know what darkness is, it accumulates, thickens, then suddenly bursts and drowns everything. (13)

With increasing insistence, Malone interrupts the Sapo-Lambert parodies which brilliantly ridicule various fictions of parvenus and primitives. Using some of Beckett's funniest techniques—incongruity, jargon, litotes, *non sequitur*—Malone eavesdrops on the worries of the Saposcat parents:

Starting from a given theme, their minds laboured in unison. They had no conversation properly speaking. They made use of the spoken word in much the same way as the guard of a train makes use of his flags, or of his lantern. Or else they said, This is where we get down. And their son once signalled, they wondered sadly if it was not the mark of superior minds to fail miserably at the written paper and cover themselves with ridicule at the viva voce. They were not always content to gape in silence at the same landscape. At least his health is good, said Mr. Saposcat. Not all that, said his wife. (11)

Malone has moments of hope that these fictional parodies will lead away from himself. "We are getting on. Nothing is less like me than this patient, reasonable child, struggling all alone for years to shed a little light upon himself, avid of the least gleam, a stranger to the joys of darkness" (17). But the hope wanes as he continues to compose. "What tedium!" he keeps reiterating. Bored by one of Beckett's funniest caricatures, which parodies the hero of the *Bildungsroman,* Malone finally does away with Sapo: "she [her daughter] decided to tell her [Mrs. Lambert] what Sapo had told her, namely that he was going away and would not come back. Then, as people do when someone even insignificant dies, they summoned up such memories as he had left them, helping one another and trying to agree. But we all know that little flame and its flickerings in the wild shadows. And agreement only comes a little later, with the forgetting" (43).

When Sapo disappears, Malone finds a green-coated figure with a hat that is too small whom he baptizes Macmann (as most critics have noted, "son of man"). After a description of Macmann, parodying the realistic novelist's concern with such externals as clothes and landscape, Malone returns to himself with cruel and comic obscenity. Looking forward to his own demise, he groups himself with Beckett's former fictions, "Then it will all be over with the Murphys, Merciers, Molloys, Morans and Malones, unless it goes on beyond the grave" (63). But the outside world intrudes even this side of the grave, as Malone looks from his window (his "umbilicus") to the window across the way, where a couple is making love.

Returning resolutely to Macmann, Malone endows him with the reason of Watt, the frenzied movements (as well as the hat "attached, by a string") of the "I" of the stories, and parodic meditations about guilt and punishment, cause and effect. The long-awaited inventory of possessions (already suggested by Molloy, with whom he shares—perhaps—a boot, a bicycle bell, a knife rest, a memory of London stars) interrupts Macmann's story. Suddenly Malone experiences panic at the loss of his stick.

In a final effort to free himself from himself, Malone "discovers" Macmann in a "kind of asylum," and immerses him in a parodic love affair such as is allowed to Molloy only in memory, to Watt without consummation. Macmann's stay in his asylum room echoes details of Molloy at Lousse's house. The asylum inmates are treated less gently than in *Murphy*, and the keepers are even more mercilessly flayed. Finally, it is Lemuel, a keeper, who forces his charges out to sea while Malone (presumably) finishes dying.

Neither Molloy, Moran, nor the Unnamable is given to Malone's systematic parody, but Moran's fondness for economical Irish stew ("All honour to the land it has brought before the world" [133]), his sanctimonious attentions to his priest, his brutality towards servant and son, satirize middle-class complacency. As he comes to resemble Molloy, Moran himself tends to view his former life with a jaundiced eye. Thus, Gaber's report that Youdi has adjudged life in Keatsian terms "a thing of beauty and a joy forever" evokes from Moran, first the question, "Do you think he meant human life?" and then the surmise, "Perhaps he didn't mean human life" (226). Moran's list of theological questions is almost as parodic as the discourse of the neo-John-Thomist Mr. Spiro of *Watt*, and he may well be damned by the quietist, "Our father who art no more in heaven than on earth or in hell, I neither want nor desire that thy name be hallowed, thou knowest best what suits thee" (229).

Molloy as writer rarely uses parody, although in the conversations he reports, Beckett's dextrous social satire shines. Molloy, hat on head, thinks furiously as he is interrogated by a policeman. "Molloy, I cried, my name is Molloy. Is that your mother's name? said the sergeant. What? I said. Your name is Molloy, said the sergeant. Yes, I said, now I remember. And your mother? said the sergeant. I didn't follow. Is your mother's name Molloy too? said the sergeant. I thought it over. Your mother, said the sergeant, is your mother's—Let me think! I cried. At least I imagine that's how it was. Take your time, said the sergeant. Was mother's name Molloy? Very likely. Her name must be Molloy too, I said" (29).

In the discourse of the Unnamable, as in that of Malone and Molloy, Beckett's gift for social satire is exhibited mainly through dialogue. The fictional Mahood, returning from abroad to the arena that houses his near and dear ones, is cheered on by such cries as "What about throwing him a few scraps?" "A few more summers and he'll be in our midst. Where am I going to put him?" "He's stopped to scratch himself" (42–43). Mahood's father is discouraged from encouraging him with, "Stick it, lad, it's your last winter" (44).

This satire on family and social goals, implicitly generalized by the name Ma(n)hood, is soon abandoned by the Unnamable. Although Worm in his jar can still evoke a parodic response to his caretaker (Marguérite or Madeleine—her name changes even as Molloy's Ruth-Edith-Rose), the interplay between fact and fiction, between the words of his fictions and the only words the Unnamable knows, is so constant, and so increasingly intense, that there is no clear boundary between pain and parody, personal and artistic anguish. The protagonist and his fictions are so closely blended that we can scarcely distinguish one from the other. The "you's" of the text may be addressed to a reader, to an *alter ego,* or to another fiction: "But it didn't happen like that, it happened like this, the way it's happening now, that is to say, I don't know, you mustn't believe what I'm saying, I'm doing as I always did, I'm going on as best I can" (154).

Comic of Language. Comic devices of language—an occasional pun, twisted cliché, paradox, and above all ironic tone—are usually turned to bitter use in the trilogy. Whereas the proper names are not exactly puns, they show similar verbal play. The stem "mol," common to Molloy and Malone (and to Malone's fiction, Moll), may bear some relation to moly, the magic with which Ulysses outwitted Circe (since fiction, too, is magic), and some to the Latin stem "mol" meaning soft, for these fictions have a fluid, malleable quality. Beckett plays on this sound in speaking of Lousse's efforts "to mollify Molloy."

Molloy and his mother call each other Da-n and Ma-g; the stems "Da" and "Ma" suggest archetypal parents, and Molloy realizes this insofar as his mother is concerned. After painfully recalling his own name and that of his mother, Molloy names no one until he comes upon Teddy, the dog of Sophie Loy or Lousse. Both "dog" and "Teddy" mock religion, for dog is an anagram of god, and Teddy is the diminutive of Theodore, which contains the Greek "theo," meaning god. The dog is buried "like a Carthusian monk." "White beards and little almost angelfaces" are seen in the bloodthirsty mob, from whose vengeance Teddy's mistress saves Molloy, even though his Cartesian bicycle killed her pet.[10] Teddy's mistress confesses that her dog has had his day; she was just taking him to the veterinary to be put out of his misery, and Molloy spared her the trouble.

Although Molloy is quite positive about Teddy's name, his mistress is variously called Sophie, Loy, and Lousse. Sophie is Greek wisdom, Loy old French for law, and Irish for spade. Indeed, a good deal is made of the spade with which Lousse or Loy buries Teddy—a burial at which Molloy, because of his paralyzed leg, is only a spectator. He recalls sadly, "I contributed my presence. As if it had been my own burial. And it was" (48). Lousse is an anagram of "soul" and the French reflexive pronoun *se*. Mocking overtones are suggested by a homonym of Lousse, English "louse."

Lousse is one of the few Beckett characters who is spared physical affliction; she is scarcely described physically, except for Molloy's remarks about her extraordinary flatness and face hair, which cause him to wonder whether she is not after all a man. A combination of wisdom, self, and soul, she apparently represents a spiritual interlude in Molloy's long life. It is at Lousse's house that Molloy recalls his considerable education, and it is at Lousse's house that Molloy abandons his Cartesian bicycle. His stay at Lousse's house is prefaced by half a page of cruel, obscene irony on the desirability of cutting off his testicles. And yet, Lousse is loosely linked to Molloy's love, an old woman whom he remembers variously as Ruth, Edith, Rose, and about whose sex he also comes to have doubts. And he confuses even his mother with these two women, "which is literally unendurable, like being crucified" (79).

Moran shares Molloy's name stem, except for a liquid consonant which is interchangeable in many languages.[11] Gaber, the messenger, is old French for "to mock or ridicule," which is what he does to Moran, by means of messages ostensibly from his employer Youdi, whose name may be a combination of "you" and "id." The latter possibility is made more probable when Moran declares that the Freudian "pleasure principle" is inscribed on the threshold of the Molloy affair. On his wanderings, Moran, for all his searching, finds no trace of one Obidil (an anagram of Libido).

Freud saw the libidinous instincts in constant struggle with the death instincts, which are particularly characterized by a repetition compulsion. Moran reduces this conflict almost to nonexistence when he comes to doubt the very reality of Obidil. Shortly afterwards, the death instinct comes to the fore; Moran characterizes his situation as "that of the turd waiting for the flush" (223). But Gaber the mocker returns to summon Moran not only to life but to explicit and ironic comments on life.

In the second volume of the French trilogy, Malone's death instincts, replete with Freudian symptoms of repetition, are more powerful than those of either Molloy or Moran, whom he resembles by virtue of hat and miscellaneous possessions.

Since "r" and "l" are almost interchangeable liquid consonants, Molloy, Moran, and Malone are roughly the same phonetically. Malone is a sophisticated and self-conscious creator of his own fictions, and in naming them, he exhibits Beckettian verbal play. Thus Saposcat, combining "wisdom" and "dung," or the slang onomotopoeia "sssscat," is instantly more vulnerable than Macmann, son of man. In a sardonic commentary upon the writer, Malone's pencil is named a Venus, and Sapo's fountain pen a Bird. The Lamberts, called the Louis in the French version, seem to come from Balzac by an ironic path, since no one is less like the nineteenth-century realist's precocious passionate youth than Beckett's brutal peasant pig-butcher.[12]

Of Malone's fictions, the most repulsive is Moll, the little old woman who has charge of Macmann in the asylum. The name is a vulgarization of Mary. At the same time, its pliable stem may be related to Molloy and Malone, and we may also recall Molloy's remarks that the syllable "Ma" means "mother" in his part of the country. Moll is also a barb at Christianity, probably at the Virgin and Mother Church. Her name vulgarizes Mary; she wears crucifix thief-earrings, and a solitary tooth is carved "to represent the celebrated sacrifice"; her employer, the asylum head who resembles Christ, constantly takes Christ's name in vain.[13] It is Moll who teaches Macmann to exalt "love . . . as a kind of lethal glue, a conception frequently to be met with in mystic texts" (92).

After Moll's death, Lemuel becomes Macmann's caretaker and hatchet man for Malone's fictions. Lemuel, besides his association with Lemuel Gulliver, whose creator wielded his own verbal hatchet, perhaps, too, is an ironic reminder of King Lemuel of Proverbs, who is taught wisdom and moderation by his mother.[14]

The Unnamable recalls Beckett's earlier fictions, and, being nameless himself, seems less in need of assigning names. Early in his story, however, appears Basil, his own first fiction, named perhaps for the plant which was supposed to be an antidote to basilisk venom. Possibly, too, there is an anagram on the French *syllabe,* just as the first three letters of "word" are contained in Worm, to which Mahood, like us all, degenerates.

Other than in names, Beckett uses puns sparingly in the trilogy. Moran learns that Condom is on the Baise. Molloy insists, "I don't like the gloom to lighten, there's something shady about it" (112). And the Unnamable in one of his gayer moments of defiance of Mahood, declares, "If he is not pleased with this panegyric I hope I may be—I nearly said hanged, but that I hope in any case, without restriction. I nearly said con, that would cut my cackle" (34).[15] Later, he declares in a pun that embraces body and mind, "I shall never get born, having failed to be conceived" (91). Much later in the discourse, there are two scatalogical puns in a single phrase: "it's like shit, there we have it at last, there it is at last, the right word, one has only to seek, seek in vain, to be sure of finding *in the end,* it's a question of *elimination*" (109) (my italics).

Whereas Beckett does not make much use of paradox in the trilogy, literal contradictions, if not as plentiful as in *Watt,* function as a tool for exploration of meaning. Paradox is a device favored not so much by Molloy, Moran, or the Unnamable, as by the suaver Malone, who writes: "incurious wondering," "concrete numbers," "Coma is for the living," "There is a limit to my impotence," "straining towards the joy of ended joy," "I have greatly groped stockstill," "I am being given . . . birth to into death," "The end of a life is always vivifying." Molloy declares, "the only way to progress, to stop." And the Unnamable, "off it goes on," "My crime is my punishment," "What I best see I see ill," "here is my only elsewhere," and "Agreed then on montony, it's more stimulating."

Comic twistings of cliché and quotation reappear in profusion in the trilogy. No longer erudite, they depend upon a biblical or quotidian frame. Molloy writes:

While still putting my best foot foremost (26)

my mother, whose charity kept me dying (28)

To him who has nothing it is forbidden not to relish filth. (30)

I first saw the murk of day (40)

Saying is inventing. (41)

I had been under the weather so long, under all weathers, that I could tell quite well between them (68)

I have always said, First learn to walk, then you can take swimming lessons. (92)

[when crawling in polygons rather than circles] perfection is not of this world (122)

Moran's pre-quest conversation is as riddled with formulae as that of his priest, who, in the same paragraph says, "we have no train to catch," and "a wink is as good as a nod" (136, 137). Moran's bourgeois piety is summed up in the phrase he attempts to use as his son's guiding principle—the phrase that drove Goethe's Faust to revolt: "Sollst entbehren."[16]

Even on his quest, Moran recalls platitudes he has always uttered:

Don't wait to be hunted to hide (156)

Conspicuousness is the A B C of my profession. (170)

The awful thing in affairs of this kind [murder] is that when you have the will you do not have the way, and vice versa. (179)

Cliché variants in *Malone Dies* tend to be more aphoristic:

Nothing is impossible, I cannot keep on denying it much longer. (8)

Live and invent. (18)

Live and cause to live. (19)

that would be no ordinary last straw. (19)

But the better late than never thanks to which true men, true links [with the species], can acknowledge the error of their ways and hasten on to the next, was beyond the power of Macmann, to whom it sometimes seemed that he could grovel and wallow in his mortality until the end of time and not have done. (68)

Sometimes Malone's monologue contains religious or biblical echoes:

I will not weigh upon the balance any more, one way or the other. (1) [17]

I would be lost in the eye of a needle (51)

for if the point pricks less than the eye, no, that's wrong, for if the point pricks more than the eye, the eye pricks too, that's wrong too. (75)

The discourse of the Unnamable also reflects the Bible:

My master then . . . in my image . . . his will is done as far as I am concerned (33)

Let there be light, it will not necessarily be disastrous. (104)

Bah, let's turn the black eye. (83)

I'm like dust, they want to make a man out of dust. (84)

Cliché variants of *The Unnamable* have popular overtones:

Where there are people, it is said, there are things. (4)

I'll fix their gibberish for them. (51)

I'll fix their jargon for them (53)

But credit where credit is due, we made a balls of it between us (58)

I have my faults, but changing my tune is not one of them. (66)

keep your mouth open and your stomach turned (67)

Thus with a single stone, when all hope seemed lost, the two rare birds. (76)

lost in the smoke, it is not real smoke, there is no fire (100)

Nothing much then in the way of sights for sore eyes. (102)

what am I doing in Mahood's story, and in Worm's, or rather what are they doing in mine, there are some irons in the fire to be going on with, let them melt. (125)

tell me what I feel and I'll tell you who I am (134)

tell me what you're doing and I'll ask you how it's possible (140–141)

on tracks as beaten as the day is long (160)

Exceptional literary echoes are:

Slough off this mortal inertia, it is out of place, in this society. (63)

That will not last for ever. For me to gather while I may. They mentioned roses. (87)

Of all Beckett's comic techniques, none is more prevalent than irony. Most of the other devices also contribute to the acrid flavor, but there are numerous passages in which the irony is one of tone alone. In contrast to the veneer of detachment of the early fiction, irony in the trilogy is often ambivalent, usually bitter, and always anguished. Irony serves, finally, to intensify the pathetic as well as the comic.

Molloy views policemen, social workers, and his fellow creatures in general with a jaundiced eye. Parenthetically, he enjoins the reader, in an ironic comment on charity and brotherly love: "Let me tell you this, when social workers offer you, free, gratis and for nothing, something to hinder you from swooning, which with them is an obsession, it is useless to recoil, they will pursue you to the ends of the earth, the vomitory in their hands" (30).

When Lousse invites him to stay at her house, Molloy directs hyperbolic irony against himself, as though he were a problem in physics: "All she asked was to feel me near her, with her, and the right to contemplate from time to time this extraordinary body both at rest and in motion" (63). Later, he couples brain and body in ironic litotes: "I was no ordinary cripple, far from it, and there were days when my legs were the best part of me, with the exception of the brain capable of forming such a judgment" (111).

Some of Molloy's most sardonic remarks have to do with his love affair with Ruth-Edith-Rose: "She gave me money after each session, to me who would have consented to know love, and probe it to the bottom, without charge. But she was an idealist. . . . I never sought to repeat the experience, having I suppose the intuition that it had been unique and perfect, of its kind, achieved and inimitable, and that it behoved me to preserve its memory, pure of all pastiche, in my heart, even if it meant my resorting from time to time to the alleged joys of so-called self-abuse" (77–78).

Dwelling with satisfaction upon his unprovoked and vicious attack on the charcoal-burner, Molloy meditates ironically upon the courage of cowards: "People imagine, because you are old, poor, crippled, terrified, that you can't stand up for yourself, and generally speaking that is so. But given favourable conditions, a feeble and awkward assailant, in your own class what, and a lonely place, and you have a good chance of showing what stuff you are made of. And it is doubtless in order to revive interest in this possibility, too often forgotten, that I have delayed over an incident of no interest in itself, like all that has a moral" (114–115).

Pondering upon his situation, Molloy records cruel phrases about his mother, and an ironic stab at the ontological questions that obsess him: "In any case, whether it was my town or not, whether somewhere under that faint haze my mother panted on or whether she poisoned the air a hundred miles away, were ludicrously idle questions for a man in my position, though of undeniable interest on the plane of pure knowledge" (123).

The first examples of Moran's irony differ from those of Molloy, in that the irony is beyond him; he is mocked not by himself but by Beckett. Thus, in his uneasy thoughts about receiving the Eucharist after half a glass of beer, the irony is one he cannot appreciate. "Would I be granted the body of Christ after a pint of Wallenstein?" (132). "The host . . . was lying heavy on my stomach. . . . And I was almost ready to suspect Father Ambrose, alive to my excesses of the forenoon, of having fobbed me off with unconsecrated bread. Or of mental reservation as he pronounced the magic words" (139).

On the quest for Molloy, Moran comes to welcome discomfort and even pain. No longer sanctimoniously pretending to love his son and be his guide, he remarks sardonically when his son declares he is all right, "He would be" (215). On his way home, deserted, derelict, almost Molloy, Moran pleads with a menacing farmer that he is on a pilgrimage to the Turdy Madonna. With irony worthy of Molloy, he reflects, "Humbly to ask a favour of people who are on the point of knocking your brains out sometimes produces good results" (238).

Malone's parodies reflect ironically upon human nature, and he is also able to mock himself. Early in his report, he declares, "The loss of consciousness for me was never any great loss," "I shall write my memoirs. That's funny, I have made a joke" (6). The loss of his stick inspires Malone to ironic meditation that derides philosophic (and particularly Cartesian) meditation: "It is thus that man distinguishes himself from the ape and rises, from discovery to discovery, ever higher, towards the light. Now that I have lost my stick I realize what it is I have lost and all it meant to me. And thence ascend, painfully, to an understanding of the Stick, shorn of all its accidents, such as I had never dreamt of" (82).

Of his memoirs, while he is writing them, he observes, "But my notes have a curious tendency, as I realize at last, to annihilate all they purport to record" (88). Both opposite and apposite, this last sentence summarizes, not only the writer's dilemma, but the impossible epistemological situation of man, condemned to language.

The Unnamable is so multifaceted and ambiguous that almost all the ironies bear upon the philosophic themes of the novel. Ironically echoing Descartes's belief that Body is divisible, and Soul indivisible, the Unnamable writes, "I may therefore perhaps legitimately suppose that the one-armed one-legged wayfarer of a moment ago and the wedge-headed trunk in which I am now marooned are simply two phases of the same carnal envelope, the soul being notoriously immune from deterioration and dismemberment" (59–60).

In the penultimate sentence of *The Unnamable,* the irony conveys the tragicomic tone of the whole: "these images at which they watered me, like a camel, before the desert, I don't know, more lies, just for the fun of it, fun, what fun we've had, what fun of it, all lies, that's soon said, you must say soon, it's the regulations" (174).

Literalism and Contradiction. Although the verbal pyrotechnics in the French trilogy of novels are not so flashy as in the early English work, they do nevertheless provide luminescence in the otherwise turbid waters of the discourse. The comic of language rests heavily upon painstaking literalism and flat self-contradiction, the one frequently re-enforcing the other.

The most obvious example is in the Moran half of *Molloy*, where contradiction is a prime lesson in the making of the writer. The book ends,

> Then I went back into the house and wrote, It is midnight. The rain is beating on the windows. It was not midnight. It was not raining.

We have come full comic circle back to the beginning:

> It is midnight. The rain is beating on the windows.

The immediate reaction is laughter, but the very flagrancy of the lie leads to an awareness that the symbolic rain and darkness of the human condition must be recorded, whatever the external climate seems to be. It is Moran, after all, who urges, "Let us be content with paradigms."

In the trilogy, as in no previous work, comic devices convey the desperate state of the writer, that obsessive liar. From the beginning literalism, contradiction, and apparent nonconcatenation of thought immerse us in Molloy's cosmological quest.

> And once again I am I will not say alone, no, that's not like me, but, how shall I say, I don't know, restored to myself, no, I never left myself, free, yes, I don't know what that means but it's the word I mean to use, free to do what, to do nothing, to know, but what, the laws of the mind perhaps, of my mind, that for example water rises in proportion as it drowns you and that you would do better, at least no worse, to obliterate texts than to blacken margins, to fill in the holes of words till all is blank and flat and the whole ghastly business looks like what it is, senseless, speechless, issueless misery. (16)

Molloy's loss of faith in intellectual reference may be a distant and ironic echo of Descartes's renunciation of book learning, for knowledge through introspection. The anguish, however, is Beckett's own.

Like Descartes, Molloy has had an excellent education, and he cannot quite hide it, even though he denies its validity. Thus, the "waves and particles" of his light result in an epistemological Uncertainty Principle, which is brilliantly compressed, as compared with Watt's laborious meditations on thing and event. "Yes, even then, when already all was fading, waves and particles, there could be no things but nameless things, no names but thingless names" (41).

An impatience with deeds that parallels his impatience with words is exemplified in a comic passage from *Molloy*, combining literalism, irony, obscenity, and a sardonic echo of Descartes's second maxim, which was "to be firm and resolute": This resolution, actually formed as I rode along, was never to be carried out, an absurd mishap prevented it. Yes, my resolutions were remarkable in this, that they were no sooner formed than something always happened to prevent their execution. That must be why I am even less resolute now than then, just as then I was even less so than I once had been. But to tell the truth (to tell the truth!) I have never been particularly resolute, I mean given to resolutions, but rather inclined to plunge headlong into the shit, without knowing who was shitting against whom or on which side I had the better chance of skulking with success" (42).

Often, the cruel abyss of the human situation is ironically contrasted with the lofty hope of Christianity. Thus, Molloy sprinkles his discourse with "Christ's" and compares his painful progress to "a veritable calvary with no limit to its stations and no hope of crucifixion" (105). The silver object he steals from Lousse—two crosses joined by a bar—in whose utter uselessness he delights, is not only the Christian Cross, but a literal double cross of betrayal.

Another passage, in which literalism is combined with contradiction in ironic exploration of meaning, epitomizes the limit of Molloy's artistic method (or seeming lack of method) and is relevant as well to Beckett's artistry:

> But I also said, Yet a little while, at the rate things are going, and I won't be able to move, but will have to stay, where I happen to be, unless someone comes and carries me. Oh I did not say it in such limpid language. And when I say I said, etc., all I mean is that I knew confusedly things were so, without knowing exactly what it was all about. And every time I say, I said this, or, I said that, or speak of a voice saying, far away inside me, Molloy, and then a fine phrase more or less clear and simple, or find myself compelled to attribute to others intelligible words, or hear my own voice uttering to others more or less articulate sounds, I am merely complying with the convention that demands you either *lie or hold your peace.* For what really happened was quite different. And I did not say, Yet a little while, at the rate things are going, etc., but that resembled perhaps what I would have said, if I had been able. In reality I said nothing at all, but I heard a murmur, *something gone wrong with the silence,* and I pricked up my ears, like an animal I imagine, which gives a start and pretends to be dead. And then sometimes there arose within me, confusedly, a kind of consciousness, which I express by saying, I said, etc., or, Don't do it Molloy, or, Is that your mother's name? said the sergeant, I quote from memory. Or which I express without sinking to the level of oratio recta, but by means of other figures quite as deceitful, as for example, It seemed to me that, etc., or, I had the impression that, etc., for it seemed to me nothing at all, and I had no impression of any kind, but simply somewhere *something had changed, so that I too had to change, or the world too had to change, in order for nothing to be changed.* (118–119) (my italics)

The italicized passages imply the metaphysics of a closed system; but the constant backtracking, the effort at exactitude, the probing for knowledge, all yield a poignant portrait of man, significantly reduced to an animal pretending to be dead, in self-defense.

As opposed to this example of "late Molloy," the literalism of the smug bourgeois, Moran, is mere pedantry, systematic torture of son and servant, before whom he tries never to change what mind he has. After receipt of Gaber's message, however, Moran's composure is shaken; self-examination and self-contradiction begin simultaneously, with the usual comic resonance. Watching his son in the bathroom, Moran remarks, "The porcelain, the mirrors, the chromium, instilled a great peace in me. At least I suppose it was they. It wasn't a great peace in any case" (162).

In looking back at the adventures of his quest for Molloy, Moran is able to summon some detachment, and, using literalism and contradiction, he searches within his cosmological situation, even venturing hesitantly upon epistemological questions. But it is evident that he is as yet an apprentice hand. After writing several times in connection with Youdi, "He'll get his report," he ponders more deeply upon his writing:

if I submit to this paltry scrivening which is not of my province, it is for reasons very different from those that might be supposed. I am still obeying orders, if you like, but no longer out of fear. No, I am still afraid, but simply from force of habit. And the voice I listen to needs no Gaber to make it heard. For it is within me and exhorts me to continue to the end the faithful servant I have always been, of a cause that is not mine, and patiently fulfil in all its bitterness my calamitous part, as it was my will, when I had a will, that others should. And this with hatred in my heart, and scorn, of my master and his designs. Yes, it is rather an ambiguous voice and not always easy to follow, in its reasonings and decrees. But I follow it none the less, more or less, I follow it in this sense, that I know what it means, and in this sense, that I do what it tells me. And I do not think there are many voices of which as much may be said. And I feel I shall follow it from this day forth, no matter what it commands. And when it ceases, leaving me in doubt and darkness, I shall wait for it to come back, and do nothing, even though the whole world through the channel of its innumerable authorities speaking with one accord, should enjoin upon me this and that, under pain of unspeakable punishments. (180–181)

Existence and expression coalesce amorphously but eternally, for this voice will never wholly leave the successive avatars of the Beckett hero.

Malone begins in sophisticated lucidity, with more conscious irony than either Molloy or Moran. On the very first page, he declares, "I could die to-day, if I wished, merely by making a little effort, if I could wish, if I could make an effort."[18] With some literalness, he formulates his future: "From now on it will be different. I shall never do anything any more from now on but play. No, I must not begin with an exaggeration. But I shall play a great part of the time, from now on, the greater part, if I can" (2–3).

Soon afterwards, he affirms, then comically denies and temporizes: "It is better to adopt the simplest explanation, even if it is not simple, even if it does not explain very much" (5).

In Malone's tales and meditations, the parodied literalness of *Watt* reappears, with more concentrated mockery. Arsene's "I regret everything" is modified to Malone's "I forgive nobody."[19] Doubts begin to assail Malone's carefully camouflaging playthings. On the face of it, nothing would seem safer than the dull, mock-naturalist descriptions of Mrs. Lambert sorting her lentils, and finally giving up impatiently, but she, like Malone's other fictions, leads back to himself, whom he half-heartedly, ironically, attempts to convert to a springboard back to fiction. "To know you can do better next time, unrecognizably better, and that there is no next time, and that it is a blessing there is not, there is a thought to be going on with" (83).

The discourse of the Unnamable depends so closely upon literalism and contradiction that examples may be taken from almost any page, all of them building the cosmo-epistemological comedy, for in the last volume of the trilogy, the two aspects blend. The Unnamable's preoccupation with self-knowledge is inseparably linked to his cosmological situation. "It would help me, since to me too I must attribute a beginning, if I could relate it to that of my abode. Did I wait somewhere for this place to be ready to receive me? Or did it wait for me to come and people it? By far the better of these hypotheses, from the point of view of usefulness, is the former, and I shall often have occasion to fall back on it. But both are distasteful. I shall say therefore that our beginnings coincide, that this place was made for me, and I for it, at the same instant" (10–11).

This arbitrary compromise cannot and does not last. On the same subject, a few pages later, literalism and contradiction stumble over each other in comic confusion: "what I say, what I shall say, if I can, relates to the place where I am, to me who am there, in spite of my inability to think of these, or to speak of them, because of the compulsion I am under to speak of them, and therefore perhaps think of them a little. Another thing. What I say, what I may say, on this subject, the subject of me and my abode, has already been said since, having always been here, I am here still" (18).

After he has created Worm, having discarded Mahood as useless in this self-exploration, in his two-front battle against complete anonymity on the one hand, and dispersion into fictions on the other, the Unnamable swears, "And I am even prepared to collaborate with him [Worm], as with Mahood and Co, to the best of my ability, being unable to do otherwise, and knowing my ability. Worm, to say he does not know what he is, where he is, what is happening, is to underestimate him. What he does not know is that there is anything to know" (82).[20]

Too soon, Worm begins to be assimilated into his creator, and the Unnamble attempts to acquiesce with *désinvolture* even to this absurd, untoward circumstance. "Of Worm, at last. Good. We must first, to begin with, go back to his beginnings, and then, to go on with, follow him patiently through the various stages, taking care to show their fatal concatenation, which have made him what I am. The whole to be tossed off with bravura. Then notes from day to day, until I collapse. And finally, to wind up with, song and dance of thanksgiving by victim, to celebrate his nativity. Please God nothing goes wrong. Mahood I couldn't die. Worm will I ever get born? It's the same problem" (90).

The situation grows increasingly desperate by its very duration, but the ironic tone is maintained in the phrasal repetition, the pronominal ambiguity, and the reduced vocabulary. No matter whose the voice, it shifts eventually to the "I," and precludes that silence so desired and feared by the nameless narrator. With progressive hysteria—itself in the comic mode by its association with laughter—the sentences lengthen, the clauses shrink, and literalism and contradiction continue to explore to the bitter hopeless endless end. Some thirty pages before the end we find the theme that is to be repeated in the concluding lines:

> Perhaps there go I after all. I can't go on in any case. But I must go on. So I'll go on. Air, air, I'll seek air, air in time, the air of time, and in space, in my head, that's how I'll go on. All very fine, but the voice is failing, it's the first time, no, I've been through that, it has even stopped, many a time, that's how it will end again, I'll go silent, for want of air, then the voice will come back and I'll begin again. My voice. The voice. I hardly hear it any more. I'm going silent. Hearing this voice no more, that's what I call going silent. That is to say I'll hear it still, if I listen hard. I'll listen hard. Listening hard, that's what I call going silent. I'll hear it still, broken, faint, unintelligible, if I listen hard. Hearing it still, without hearing what it says, that's what I call going silent. (148–149)

> it will be I, you must go on, I can't go on, you must go on, I'll go on, you must say words, as long as there are any, until they find

me, until they say me, strange pain, strange sin, you must go on, perhaps it's done already, perhaps they have said me already, perhaps they have carried me to the threshold of my story, before the door that opens my story, that would surprise me, if it opens, it will be I, it will be the silence, where I am, I don't know, I'll never know, in the silence you don't know, you must go on, I can't go on, I'll go on. (179)

Incongruity and Shock. Incongruity, obscenity, and violence proliferate as Beckett's heroes grow increasingly desperate. To a greater extent than in previous works, the specialized vocabulary of the excretory and sexual functions is sprinkled through the novels. As in the short stories, the grotesque and disgusting aspects of the protagonists and their creatures are delineated for comic effect.

Moran is toothless except for incisors; he gradually grows lame, and his clothes rot through. Molloy, completely toothless, one-eyed, partially paralyzed, without sense of smell, loses the power of locomotion as well as the toes on one foot. He rides a bicycle in the fashion Moran has envisioned, bad foot on the axle and good foot pedaling. Malone, bedridden, has useless legs, but can still employ his arms, and the Unnamable may have eyes and ears, but we are sure only of his tears, composed perhaps of "liquefied brain." Grotesque themselves, it is small wonder their fictions and memories are grotesque. The two love affairs with nonagenarians—that of Molloy with Ruth-Edith-Rose, and that of Macmann with Moll—in their emphasis upon physiological detail and sentimental dialogue, savagely ridicule all sentimental and sexual love affairs. In Beckett's French fiction, woman is portrayed in the way Joyce described her: "an animal that masturbates once a day, defecates once a week, menstruates once a month and parturates once a year." [21]

Other fictions of the narrators of the trilogy have physical characteristics as strange as those of their creators: Sapo has the colorless eyes of a gull, Mahood has one leg and the homologous arm, and Worm is limbless, enclosed in a jar, skull covered with pustules and blue-bottles. As in the shorter French fiction, disgusting and obscene details provide incongruity. All the protagonists are much concerned with defecation, as Vladimir in *Waiting for Godot* and Hamm in *Endgame* are with urination. Since the crude delight in these *gauloiseries* could hardly serve Beckett's purpose, we may explain them perhaps through a reference to a passage in which Montaigne compares his essays to "des excremens d'un vieil esprit, dur tantost, tantost láche, et toujours indigeste" ("excrement of an aged mind, sometimes hard, sometimes soft, and always undigested").[22]

For Beckett's heroes, decomposition comes to be a prime requisite of composition. Moran's conversion to literature is heralded by a pain in the knee; in *The Unnamable*, the human body is reduced to a trunk and head.

If all Beckett's French protagonists resemble each other in decrepitude and obscenity, they are distinguished in some of their incongruous habits. Molloy has the most unexpected associations, the most unfettered stream of consciousness. He imagines that he resembles Belacqua or Sordello—he can't remember exactly—crouching under a rock, but Malone recalls only Sordello. Molloy speaks of his soul leaping to the limit of its elastic. The mention of Watt in connection with a steam engine recalls Beckett's creation.[23] When asked by the policeman for his papers, he proffers bits of news (toilet) paper. Ruminating on his mother's act of giving birth to him, he realizes he had to leave her womb for "less compassionate sewers." Educated though he is, he regrets never having learned systematic decorum in his personal habits, which he describes in disgusting detail. He forgets names, places, directions; he confuses tears and laughter, induction and deduction, pedigree and bastardy. He understands a parrot better than its mistress. One of the most incongruous images —Molloy's mention of being preserved in a sealed jar, then bursting out to become part of the vegetation—takes on significance in the light of Worm's subsequent situation.

Moran's actions and thoughts become incongruous gradually, as he approaches Molloy. From the first, however, Gaber the messenger is visible only to his eyes (and probably to his son, who is, comically, born with bad teeth). Moran finds himself disliking both men and animals, and being disgusted by God. Moran's servant, Martha, has Murphy's affection for a rocking chair. Moran is meticulous about noting places—Turdy, Hole, Bally—times—especially the day he receives Gaber's message—and sums of all kinds. Moran kills a man who vaguely resembles him. After the murder, he finds his trusty keys dispersed, an ear and hat strewn on the ground. He uses his umbrella only as a cane. On his homeward voyage, Moran visualizes winter flies, and dwells delightedly on the dance of his bees.

Malone enumerates the holidays he will not live to see. Although he attempts to ignore his own incongruous and irrational fears, he fails. He is haunted by a demon lurking "like the gonoccocus in the folds of the prostate" (21). When he was young, the old awed him; now, bawling babies dumbfound him. As death approaches, he seems to expand, and to grow warmer. Aquinas, Democritus, Tiepolo, Friedrich, the goddess Maia, the embarkation for Cythera, the Colossus of Memnon, Archimedes, Sordello, terms of grammar, and Latin phrases come to his mind—all testifying to his wide culture. To him (as to Balacqua in "Dante and the Lobster") appears the vision of Cain in the moon. Like Vladimir in *Waiting for Godot,* he takes some courage in the thought that one of the two thieves was saved, and then mocks his own brief encouragement by situating the two thieves in the fictional earrings of the fictional Moll, whom he kills. As Malone's fictions move more chaotically, incongruities give way to maniacal absurdities. There is no doubt that Beckett uses both the incongruous and the absurd to symbolic purpose, but the immediate impact is weirdly comic or cruelly ironic.

In *The Unnamable* the prose is so tightly interwoven, each small clause is so immediately dependent upon its neighbor, that the wildly unexpected is almost buried in context, as in the following startling and savage example: "They hope things will change one day, it's natural. That one day on my windpipe, or some other section of the conduit, a nice little abscess will form, with an idea inside, point of departure for a general infection. This would enable me to jubilate like a normal person, knowing why. And in no time I'd be a network of fistulae, bubbling with the blessed pus of reason" (92).

The texture of the Unnamable's dialogue renders difficult the quotation of incongruities, and this is all the more true for the extended incongruity that is absurdity. One of the major meanings of the stream of meditation of the Unnamable is to be found in a double absurdity—that of the world and that of its observer. Early in the book, thc "I" describes himself as "the teller and the told." Much later, in different words, the same opposition is stressed.

on the one hand, with regard to *the noise,* that it has not been possible up to date to determine with certainty, or even approximately, what it is, in the way of noise, or how it comes to me, or by what organ it is emitted, or by what perceived, or by what intelligence apprehended, in its main drift, and on the other, that is to say with regard to *me,* this is going to take a little longer, with regard to me, nice time we're going to have now, with regard to me, that it has not yet been our good fortune to establish with any degree of accuracy what I am, where I am, whether I am words among words, or silence in the midst of silence (142) (My italics oppose the told and the teller.)

Not without importance are the explicit comments of the Unnamable on absurdity itself:

That the impossible should be asked of me, good, what else could be asked of me? But the absurd! Of me whom they have reduced to reason. (70)

To get me to be he, the anti-Mahood, and then to say, But what am I doing but living, in a kind of way, the only possible way, that's the combination. Or by the absurd prove to me that I am, the absurd of not being able. (82)

No leap is made either by Beckett or his fictions from this whirlpool of absurdity, to which the many specific absurdities of the first two volumes of the trilogy have contributed. In *Malone Dies* it is *non sequitur* of episode, reference, or phrase that is the principal means of expressing the absurd. In *Molloy* there is no motivation in such incidents as his running over Lousse's dog, her invitation for him to stay with her, his attack on the charcoal-burner. Moran's tale, except for the apparent absurdity of Youdi's command, is quite orderly, almost traditional, until he begins to ponder his quest for Molloy. Then his mental climate clouds over with contradiction and absurdity, and the rain begins to fall. Suddenly he seems to know Molloy, but in another cosmological context. "For it was only by transferring it to this atmosphere, how shall I say, of finality without end, that I could venture to consider the work I had on hand. For where Molloy could not be, nor Moran either for that matter, there Moran could bend over Molloy" (152).

Aside from the incongruous detail that has been cited with respect to both Moran and Molloy, the prime example of absurdity is Molloy's painstaking solution of how to suck sixteen stones in sequent order, given the fact that his coat has only four pockets. The seven-page description is reminiscent of the expanded permutations and combinations of *Watt,* but the irony is more clearly focused by the very isolation of the incident, the patiently correct and patently absurd reasoning of the protagonist. Like many of *Watt's* series, too, this process is pointless, for Molloy finally throws away all but one sucking stone.

Cruelty. Though Beckett's absurdities may seem to be a random series of events, their long-range and cumulative effect is to make of man the cosmic comic victim. In the three novels, the cruelty of both the cosmos and its victims is underlined. More than the former work, the trilogy is built upon cruelly illiberal jests, by way of metaphor, literalism, incident, and situation at large.

In each of the volumes, there are references to slaughterhouses, to the ways of killing animals. Molloy's mother's room —later Molloy's—is opposite the shambles. Moran's son plays with his little friends behind the slaughterhouse. Malone's Lambert buys his animals from the slaughterhouse, in order to work them to death. In *The Unnamable,* Worm is chained in his jar opposite the horse-butcher, whose apostle is Decroix.[24]

In the trilogy, the death of others is a matter of indifference; one's own painless death is desired. All the protagonists suffer, laugh at their own defeat, and are convinced that suffering is their fate, which has analogies to the biblical one of sin and death. Yet sin is largely irrelevant to Beckett's work, and death is fervently to be desired, if also feared.

Early in his novel, Molloy summarizes the encounters of this cruel world: "Until the day when, your endurance gone, in this world for you without arms, you catch up in yours the first mangy cur you meet, carry it the time needed for it to love you and you it, then throw it away" (14). Subsequently, Molloy beats his mother, kills in himself the "Aegean, thirsting for heat and light," runs over a dog, is unmoved by the death of his mistress, declares that "Day is the time for lynching," tries to slash his wrists but fears the pain, and finally takes enormous pleasure in viciously beating a stranger. Late in his voyage, he gives voice to a violent and obscene death wish for himself and his mother. All these cruelties, conveyed in Beckett's terse colloquial idiom, are exploited for a grim comic resonance.

Moran's cruelty is veiled during his hypocritical complacency, and he convinces himself that his torturing of son and servant is, of course, for their own good. As the quest for Molloy proceeds, Moran grows more openly savage until he kills the man who resembles him, hoping that Youdi will not let him "be punished for a fault committed in the execution of [his] duty" (212). Towards the end, Moran comes to a certain appreciation of his position as comic cosmic victim: "And at the thought of the punishments Youdi might inflict upon me I was seized by such a mighty fit of laughter that I shook, with mighty silent laughter and my features composed in their wonted sadness and calm. . . . Strange laughter truly, and no doubt misnamed, through indolence perhaps, or ignorance" (222). Or heroism. It is after Moran reaches the laughing stage that Gaber arrives to order him home. His quest is presumably accomplished.

Malone, stylist that he is, utters cruel aphorisms. "The end of a life is always vivifying" (37). With a vague recollection of being "stunned with a blow, on the head, in a forest perhaps" (6), a spectator of the love-making of others, Malone does not expect on All Saints Day to "hear them howling over their charnels" (61). He is disgusted with himself, "to have vagitated and not be bloody well able to rattle" (77). Generalizing on man's fate, he muses, "There is a providence for impotent old men, to the end. And when they cannot swallow any more someone rams a tube down their gullet, or up their rectum, and fills them full of vitaminized pap, so as not to be accused of murder" (81).

Malone's fictions have his own taste for cruelty. Sapo prefers a bird of prey, the hawk, to all others. Big Lambert delights in the slaughter of pigs, killing his own on Christmas Eve. His rabbits die of fright, or he allows his daughter to hold them as he wields his knife. Lemuel is more sadistic than the keepers of Beckett's previous insane asylums, bellowing, "Here is your porridge. Eat while it is boiling" (96). And yet, he is not an untortured torturer. "Flayed alive by memory, his mind crawling with cobras, not daring to dream or think and powerless not to, his cries were of two kinds, those having no other cause than moral anguish and those, similar in every respect, by means of which he hoped to forestall same" (97). Lemuel, too, reverts to Malone. Lemuel hits himself on the head with his hatchet before chopping down the two sailors. He sets the other fictions adrift, as Malone kills *his* fictions. The grotesque extravagance of these violently cruel actions tumbles them into the comic mode.

The Unnamable begins with more resignation to cosmological cruelty, even an ironic appreciation: "a certain confusion in the exordia, long enough to situate the condemned and prepare him for execution" (19), "I, of whom I know nothing, I know my eyes are open, because of the tears that pour from them unceasingly" (22), "a little hell after my own heart, not too cruel, with a few nice damned to foist my groans on" (25).

His fictions, too, combine violence and cruelty, "And let us consider what really took place, if Mahood was telling the truth when he represented me as rid at one glorious sweep of parents, wife and heirs. I've plenty of time to blow it all sky-high, this circus where it is enough to breathe to qualify for asphyxiation" (49). Anger mounts against his "loved ones," and Mahood buries his crutches in their flesh in as excessively brutal a manner as Molloy, Moran, and Malone have attacked their respective victims. In his vase, the rats are not reduced to Worm.

Gradually, the Unnamable grows more obsessed by "their" cruelty to him, victim of cosmic irony. The mysterious malevolent "they," present from Beckett's first French story, derives perhaps from Descartes's "malignant demon who . . . has employed all his artifice . . . to deceive me." But Beckett's demon (or demons) is crueler, and he laughs viciously at the sufferings of the Unnamable: "But these lights that go out hissing? Is it not more likely a great cackle of laughter, at the sight of his terror and distress? To see him flooded with light, then suddenly plunged back in darkness, must strike them as irresistibly funny" (95).

In his final, five-page sentence, in which the Unnamable despairs of knowing anything, he declares: "a culprit is indispensable . . . a victim is essential . . . I'm not suffering enough yet . . . not suffering enough to be able . . . to understand . . . it's all been done already . . . the old rigmarole . . . all words, there's nothing else" (175–177). Perhaps these last five words are the cruelest of all—that we have nothing but language, at once our only tool and our impenetrable barrier to understanding.[25]

With full awareness of our impotence, we are compelled to keep trying to know. By playing the compulsion of questions against the impossibility of answers, Beckett obtains the brilliant and excruciating tension of his work. For this compulsion towards knowledge in the face of the impossibility of knowledge defines the comic—and tragic—irony of the human situation.

The Human Situation. No longer evoking gratuitous laughter, Beckett's repertoire of comic techniques functions in the trilogy to convey cosmic irony. Even out of context as these passages were quoted, so as to illustrate literary devices, the larger meanings of his irony shine through. Beyond skillful techniques, it is the imaginative examination of cosmic and cognitive irony that determines Beckett's significant position in contemporary literature.

If, inverting the two parts of *Molloy,* we seek the cosmological viewpoint, we are instantly faced with Moran, pious Catholic. However, this orthodox believer has a private (or parallel) system of communication with a mysterious and "optative" Youdi, who uses the "prophetic present" tense as opposed to Molloy's human "mythological present." Both early and late in his quest, Moran comes to doubt the existence of Gaber the messenger, but he continues to fear Youdi to the extent that he dares not disobey the latter's command for a report on his quest, even if he is also obeying his own voice in writing that report. Quite possibly, Youdi has dissolved into an interior voice.

Molloy, like Moran, receives a messenger, but he is nameless and is sent by a nameless them. "Yes, there is more than one, apparently" (7). It is perhaps for this reason that Molloy forges no personal bond, in the manner of Moran with Youdi, but obeys only the imperatives delivered by his inner voice, all of which bear upon his relationship to his mother, as he himself is aware: "And if ever I'm reduced to looking for a meaning to my life you never can tell, it's in that old mess I'll stick my nose to begin with, the mess of that poor old uniparous whore and myself the last of my foul brood, neither man nor beast" (23).

Although Molloy's cosmological problems revolve about his mother, he forgets this at long stretches of his writing. "It came back to my mind, from nowhere, as a moment before my name, that I had set out to see my mother, at the beginning of this ending day. My reasons? I had forgotten them. But I knew them, I must have known them, I had only to find them again and I would sweep, with the clipped wings of necessity, to my mother" (35).

Much later, Molloy speculates with bitter irony about life and death: "Oh they weren't notions like yours, they were notions like mine, all spasm, sweat and trembling, without an atom of common sense or lucidity. But they were the best I had. Yes, the confusion of my ideas on the subject of death was such that I sometimes wondered, believe me or not, if it wasn't a state of being even worse than life" (91). Incapable of suicide, abandoned by his voice, Molloy sinks down in his ditch, awaiting further imperatives. The last words of his voice, "Don't fret Molloy, we're coming" (123), has a plural referent, and since Molloy, from his mother's room, *has* written his report, "they" are evidently as good as their word; "they" have come. The cosmos is absurd, arbitrary, impenetrable, but not necessarily disastrous—yet.

Malone, dying, is resolved to have no further truck with cosmological questions. He intends to devote his small remaining time—the smaller the better—not to himself, but to playing games and dying with aplomb, having no further intercourse with "them," who deliver his food and empty his slops. Through his willful invention of fictions, the aged Malone is led circuitously but inevitably back to his absurd cosmos, on the one hand, and to his absurd self, on the other. However resolutely he may close his eyes against "the sky and smoke of mankind," however outlandish he forces his stories to become, he is continually jolted back to himself and to the senseless mystery of the cosmos. His life dwindles with the dwindling length of his writing pencil.

Even at the beginning of his book, Malone bitterly and comically doubts whether he can lose himself in his creations. "And gravely I struggled to be grave no more, to live, to invent. . . . I tried to live without knowing what I was trying . . . Live and cause to live. There is no use indicting words, they are no shoddier than what they peddle. After the fiasco, the solace, the repose, I began again, to try and live, cause to live, be another, in myself, in another. How false all this is . . . no longer in order to succeed, but in order to fail. Nuance" (18–19).

When he is not caught up in the momentum of spinning his yarns, the noise and the dark frighten Malone, invading both his solitude and his fictional interludes. Like Descartes, he returns to introspection, but he refuses to recognize it as such. "Then that silence of which, knowing what I know, I shall merely say that there is nothing, how shall I merely say, nothing negative about it. And softly my little space begins to throb again. You may say it is all in my head, and indeed sometimes it seems to me I am in a head and that these eight, no, six, these six planes that enclose me are of solid bone. But thence to conclude the head is mine, no, never" (47).

Malone's ignorance and doubt lead on to further doubt and ignorance. "But what matter whether I was born or not, have lived or not, am dead or merely dying, I shall go on doing as I have always done, not knowing what it is I do, nor who I am, nor where I am, nor if I am. Yes, a little creature, I shall try and make a little creature, to hold in my arms, a little creature in my image, no matter what I say. And seeing what a poor thing I have made, or how like myself, I shall eat it. Then be alone a long time, unhappy, not knowing what my prayer should be nor to whom" (52). Thus, Malone arrives, although he cannot sustain it, at an equation of the cosmological and epistemological comedies. He can know nothing but his creation, which he will devour because it *is* his creation, and that will leave him nothing to which to pray. Out of context, the pathos and the need of tenderness submerge the irony.

Forecasting Worm, developing Molloy's reflections on reptation, Malone attempts to reduce Macmann to a reptile who can "suffer extensive mutilation." Then, improving slightly on Descartes's definition of man as a "thing that thinks," Malone causes Macmann to dream of himself as "a great cylinder endowed with the faculties of cognition and volition" (74). But it is too soon to eliminate the body and the macrocosm. The cosmos sends a representative who strikes Malone a terrible blow on the skull. Feeling that this blow is a close prelude to death, Malone is disheartened about his fictions, who have taught him nothing:

All is pretext, Sapo and the birds, Moll, the peasants, those who in the towns seek one another out and fly from one another, my doubts which do not interest me, my situation, my possessions, pretext for not coming to the point, the abandoning, the raising of the arms and going down, without further splash, even though it may annoy the bathers. Yes, there is no good pretending, it is hard to leave everything. The horror-worn eyes linger abject on all they have beseeched so long, in a last prayer, the true prayer at last, the one that asks for nothing. And it is then a little breath of fulfilment revives the dead longings and a murmur is born in the silent world, reproaching you affectionately with having despaired too late. The last word in the way of viaticum. (107)

"Affectionately" is clearly ironic, but the "viaticum" is authentic, for Malone departs only once more from his fictions, so as to invoke his death in a last obscene and violently ironic return to the first person, which he abjures—"I shall say I no more."

Here the Unnamable begins in contradiction, tentatively, "I, say I," but immediately upon this introduction of the first person singular, follows, "Unbelieving." The Unnamable's long, suffering, struggling, repetitious, probing, self-absorbed, self-denying discourse is a heroic battle against solipsism, during which he subsumes most of Beckett's themes, and terminates without an end to his anguished search for meaning. Like Descartes, the Unnamable begins in doubt—aporia. Like Descartes *and* Malone, he attempts to use method and fiction, but from the beginning he interchanges "we" and "they."

Malone is the first puppet on scene, and his brimless hat the first thing. To be sure, he might be Molloy in Malone's hat, for maybe all are here, "all . . . at least from Murphy on" (6). After posing a few questions, the Unnamable vows to pose them no more, then continues to pose them, in direct self-contradiction.

Ignorance surrounds him, but the discourse must continue, and arbitrarily he situates himself at a center rather than on some circumference. The Unnamable is not without instruction, for "they" have given him all kinds of lessons—on his mother, the light of day, God, "but what they were most determined for me to swallow was my fellow-creatures" (13).

Further, "they" gave courses in love, intelligence, counting, reasoning; one of "them," Basil, the crown of whose hat is "all worn through, like the sole of an old boot" (symbolizing the decay of mind *and* body), is soon distinguished from the amorphous others. But even he cannot lead the Unnamable to his identity. "Me, utter me, in the same foul breath as my creatures? Say of me that I see this, feel that, fear, hope, know and do not know? Yes, I will say it, and of me alone . . . I alone am man and all the rest divine" (16). But since "I" is unnamable, there is no clear distinction between human and divine.

Plunging into the literalism and contradiction of the old epistemological comedy which takes place, perhaps, in his "distant skull, where once [he] wandered, now [is] fixed," despairing that he cannot both speak and yet say nothing, the Unnamable inveighs against "all these Murphys, Molloys and Malones [that] do not fool me," against "Basil and his gang . . . invented to explain I forget what" (20, 21, 22). The Unnamable reiterates that he will speak only of himself, attempting to reduce that self to a round, hard object with a voice "that speaks, knowing that it lies[26] . . . not listening to itself but to the silence that it breaks and whence perhaps one day will come stealing the long clear sigh of advent and farewell" (26).

These fictions created "in obedience to the unintelligible terms of an incomprehensible damnation" disgust him, and yet he is again faced with Basil, who is renamed Mahood. "It was he told me stories about me, lived in my stead, issued forth from me, came back to me, entered back into me, heaped stories on my head" (29).

Mahood's stories, Mahood's voice, issue from the Unnamable, so that he becomes both "the teller and the told," not so much a lesson as a pensum, imposed, perhaps, by a master, or masters, "a whole college of tyrants." The Unnamable begins to wonder whether his masters, Mahood, and himself have any separate identity. "But thence to infer that the something required is something about me suddenly strikes me as unwarranted. Might it not rather be the praise of my master, intoned, in order to obtain his forgiveness? Or the admission that I am Mahood after all and these stories of a being whose identity he usurps, and whose voice he prevents from being heard, all lies from beginning to end? And what if Mahood were my master? I'll leave it at that, for the time being" (32).

As yet only suggesting the similarity between the cosmological and epistemological comedies, the Unnamable vents his wrath as created creature against the "paltry priests of the irrepressible ephemeral," whoever "they" may be. Compelled to words, whomever they belong to, the Unnamable, intermittently identifying himself with Mahood, tells a bitter ironic tale of the world traveler returning to his family nest. Several times the Unnamable inveighs against the "they," "my tempters," who have forced "their" words, "their" language upon him. Stalling for time and freedom in which to meditate upon himself, the Unnamable starts "another of Mahood's stories," no longer "the great traveler I had been, on my hands and knees in the later stages, then crawling on my belly or rolling on the ground," but reduced to trunk and wedge-head, planted in a deep jar near the slaughterhouse (54, 55).

Commenting with authorial omniscience, the Unnamable ascribes Beckett's earlier fictions to "them." Occasionally, the "them" seems to refer to the Unnamable's fictions;[27] occasionally, "they" are as godlike and omnipotent as Molloy's "they." Whoever "they" are, they have high hopes for the Unnamable—too high, he thinks. "It's a lot to expect of one creature, it's a lot to ask, that he should first behave as if he were not, then as if he were, before being admitted to that peace where he neither is, nor is not, and where the language dies that permits of such expressions" (65–66).

Echoing "their" voice even while denying "them," insisting on the stupidity of pupil Mahood, the Unnamable baptizes Worm. Again, he probes for fundamentals, mordantly ironic about his worm-like fate. "The essential is never to arrive anywhere, never to be anywhere, neither where Mahood is, nor where Worm is, nor where I am. . . . The essential is to go on squirming forever at the end of the line, as long as there are waters and banks and ravening in heaven a sporting God to plague his creatures per pro his chosen shits" (71).

Attempting to distinguish between Worm and Mahood (and incongruously mentioning that old fiction, Watt), the Unnamable affirms that Mahood can note things, but Worm cannot. This inspires him to reimmerse himself in the jar by the restaurant and slaughterhouse: "Here all is killing and eating" (74). But he seeks in vain—through reason, witness, and violence—evidence of his own existence. The voice returns, but there is still no knowing whose it is. More and more, this becomes the dominant comic, ironic theme—that creation and creator are indistinguishable, inseparable, irreconcilable. "Who crouches in their midst who see themselves in him and in their eyes stares his unchanging stare" (83).

The Unnamable hopes he will tire "them" finally by his need of explanations, by his "stupidity," by his "horror of silence." "Did they ever get Mahood to speak? It seems to me not. I think Murphy spoke now and then, the others too perhaps, I don't remember, but it was clumsily done, you could see the ventriloquist. And now I feel it's about to begin. They must consider me sufficiently stupefied, with all their balls about being and existing" (85).

Ruminating about his relationship with Worm, about "their" plots against him, the Unnamable seeks to believe himself in a skull. But he soon returns to Worm, then back to an ownerless voice. He shifts to the third person; "I shall not say I again, ever again, it's too farcical" (94). But the impersonal "he" turns into Worm, who hears and has, perhaps, a single lidless eye that cries "tears of mirth." Soon "I" is speaking again, and "they" causing Worm to suffer in "I."

"Their" duplicity knows no bounds: "They say they, speaking of them, to make me think it is I who am speaking. Or I say they, speaking of God knows what, to make me think it is not I who am speaking. Or rather there is silence, from the moment the messenger departs until he returns with his orders, namely, Continue" (115).

There is a brief respite, a briefer truce, and then the words come tumbling out once more, attached to a voice, to voices. Spectator and spectacle are banished, but the voice persists, and the "I" inquires, "what am I doing in Mahood's story, and in Worm's, or rather what are they doing in mine" (125)? "They" do not answer, but attempt prosaically to assimilate "I" to his photograph, his police record, his medical report. "They" refuse to leave him alone. "Their" voices and "their" words attack the Unnamable, endlessly, repetitively, hysterically, like the ballad of the dog who crawled into the kitchen, and stole a crust of bread, was killed by the cook and buried by the other dogs, who inscribe on his tombstone the ballad of the dog who crawled into the kitchen, etc.

Mercilessly, "they" continue to invade him–body and mind; "what clowns they are to keep on saying the same thing . . . they'll be there saying the same thing till they die, then perhaps a little silence, till the next gang arrives on the site, I alone am immortal, what can you expect, I can't get born" (134).

And, indeed, "it might sometimes almost be wondered if all their ballocks about life and death is not as foreign to their nature as it is to mine. The fact is they no longer know where they've got to in their affair, where they've got me to . . . if only they'd stop committing reason, on them, on me, on the purpose to be achieved, and simply go on" (136–137).

Although they accomplish nothing, "the stories go on . . .

the words are everywhere, inside me, outside me . . . I'm all these words, all these strangers, this dust of words . . . I'm something quite different . . . a wordless thing in an empty place" (139). Again, the Unnamable tries to distinguish between the teller and the told: "there is I, on the one hand, and this noise on the other" (141–142).

Interrupting his hysteria, the Unnamable makes a last attempt at method: "Equate me without pity or scruple . . . with him whose story this story had the brief ambition to be" (144). Re-enter: body, mind, microcosm, macrocosm, time, space, and even a "latest surrogate." Again the voice dominates the discourse. Wistfully, the Unnamable wishes for any path to silence—any thing, saying any thing, and by chance it might just be the right thing, the thing that is required to be said. Reviewing his past, he analyzes, "Yes, in my life, since we must call it so, there were three things, the inability to speak, the inability to be silent, and solitude" (153).

Unable to go on, he nevertheless goes on with the "wordy-gurdy," dreaming of "some little job with fluids, filling and emptying, always the same vessel," viewing places, inventing them, asking questions, aspiring; "it's screamingly sad, anything rather than laughter. What else, opinions, comparisons, anything rather than laughter" (160). Repeating himself, repeating his phrases, probing more deeply, contradicting his thrusts, backtracking, claiming and denying reason and belief, sprinkling the most abstract search with obscenities, seeking desperately to reject fictions, the Unnamable again evokes Beckett's own fictions: "he says Murphy, or Molloy, I forget, as if I were Malone, but their day is done, he wants none but himself, for me, he thinks it's his last chance, he thinks that, they taught him thinking, it's always he who speaks, Mercier never spoke, Moran never spoke, I never spoke, I seem to speak, that's because he says I as if he were I . . . I who . . . can't be found, but neither can he, he can only talk, if that much, perhaps it's not he, perhaps it's a multitude, one after another, what confusion" (163–164).

In commenting on this passage, Dan Davin wrote that this "single character spawning diversities sounds like nothing so much as an author agonizing with himself about the nature of his own identity, how far he is the creator of his own characters, something other than himself. The artist-God is no longer paring indifferent fingernails. He is chewing them and in the centre of his book."[28]

The contrast with Joyce's detached artist is apt, for in *Finnegans Wake* the shifting identities are witty and mythical; the comic mode causes them to be viewed from a distance. But Beckett's haunted "I's" are in constant anguish, even though they laugh at themselves and expect others to laugh at them. Beckett's "I's" are only incidentally Sam Beckett. Far more significantly, they are "everyman above all others." Even as Dante's fictional "I" approaches the writing sinner, Beckett's successive "I's" approach the strife-torn writer. In each case, the profound importance of the work is not autobiographical but paradigmatic. We all move through Purgatory, seeking salvation. We are all subject to physical decay and epistemological doubt. The problem is wider than that of artistic expression. Beckett questions *all* human knowledge in the questions of his fictions, for what is knowledge but a complex of words through which the individual identity can no longer be read?

The search for "I"—Everyman's "I"—begins again, or never ends. "Ah if I could laugh," sighs the Unnamable, but instead he evokes a world, and Mahood in it, then the whisper of a story. But the story points to emotion ("well well, so that's emotion"), and to reason, and to the lessons the "I" has learned from his fictions ("these nameless images . . . these imageless names"); and again all the doubting words rush in where angels, if there ever were any, duly fear to tread.

In summarizing the complex tight prose of *The Unnam-*

able, one tends to fall into the same rhythms, even into the same words "tried and trusty," or merely tried again and again, and therefore untrusty, for the words belong to a voice, which does and does not belong to the "I." Weakening towards the middle of the final five-page hysterical sentence, the Unnamable confesses, "all these stories about travellers, these stories about paralytics, all are mine, I must be extremely old, or it's memory playing tricks, if only I knew if I've lived, if I live, if I'll live, that would simplify everything, impossible to find out, that's where you're buggered, I haven't stirred, that's all I know, no, I know something else, it's not I, I always forget that . . . I'd be he, I'd be the silence, I'd be back in the silence, we'd be reunited, his story the story to be told, but he has no story, he hasn't been in story, it's not certain" (176–177). Finally, the certainty of non-identity and of non-being is just as uncertain as the uncertainty. One can know nothing within and nothing without; the cosmological and epistemological comedies are the same.

In summarizing Beckett's fictional achievement, Oliver de Magny writes, "Ses romans habillent de haillons romanesques l'impossibilité du roman; son écriture devient cette vertigineuse transparence qui épouse et révèle l'impossibilité d'écrire" ("His novels dress the impossibility of the novel in the tattered remains of the novel; his writing becomes a dizzying transparency which both reveals the impossibility of writing and couples it with the writing itself").[29]

Martin Gerard pays tribute to the philosophic profundity and to the linguistic mastery of Beckett's work. "When we look at those prose writers who have tried to solve this problem (on the one hand, silence: on the other, lies) of giving truth its being, of bringing it into existence through the medium of a fiction which should not be fictitious, we find that one and all are distinguished from the novelists of a spurious invention by the possession of a language which can, like the language of poets, comprehend and render interesting in the actual inscape of being: Melville, Joyce, Beckett, Proust for example."[30]

As early as *Molloy,* even the budding artist Moran senses that self-knowledge and self-destruction are parallel activities. He comes to wonder whether his own death will be that of Molloy as well, and asks himself, "Would we all meet again in heaven one day, I, my mother, my son, his mother, Youdi, Gaber, Molloy, his mother, Yerk, Murphy, Watt, Camier and the rest?" (230). It is possible that "heaven" is the book that contains all fictions.

Early in Molloy's account, he affirms, "What I need now is stories, it took me a long time to know that" (15). But the lucid, voluntary approach to fiction yields to an exploratory appreciation of the creative act, which is almost worthy of the Unnamable. "Not to want to say, not to know what you want to say, not to be able to say what you think you want to say, and never to stop saying, or hardly ever, that is the thing to keep in mind, even in the heat of composition" (36).

When first read, such phrases sound like nonsense that reduce vocabulary and reference, negate knowledge and meaning. That is the primitive level of Beckett's comic and of his art. But read in context, as each Beckett work must be read, in the light of the others, such passages create the comedy or irony of fictions, a comedy or irony dissolving without resolving the classical questions about the quiddity of the world and that of man, about the center of the self, if there is a self —for humankind is old now, battered and bitter, unable to go on, and going on.

Beckett's motif—if it can be reduced and abstracted from the comic concreteness of the fiction—is that words are thoughts are emotions, that fiction is our only knowledge, and all knowledge a fiction written in a foreign tongue: "that was to teach me the nature of emotion . . . it was to teach me how to reason," says the Unnamable (168). All Beckett's fictions merge, finally, into the unique, suffering artist-human, ironically probing the meaning of fiction, and the fiction of meaning. This is Beckett's unique achievement, uniquely achieved.

7

brief fiction

You would do better . . .
to obliterate texts than to
blacken margins.
Molloy

Neither the number thirteen nor the word "text" is new in Beckett's work although they first occur in combination in the thirteen *Textes pour rien.* Given Beckett's conception of cosmic irony, one can readily appreciate his fascination with the number thirteen, which is traditionally associated with misfortune. Thus, he twice groups poems in a series of thirteen, and he divides *Murphy* into thirteen chapters. The connection between his M characters—Murphy, Mercier, Moran, Molloy, Malone, Macmann, Moll, Mahood—and the fact that M is the thirteenth letter of the alphabet is scarcely fortuitous.[1]

More difficult to explain is Beckett's use of the word "text" for both poetry and prose.[2] "Text" has several possible meanings: the Latin sense of literary tissue or style, the scriptural idea of theme, or simply the wording of something written. Whatever Beckett's definition of "text," the derisive "for nothing" implies a value judgment as to the futility of the written word. Beckett himself has said that his thirteen

Textes pour rien failed to extricate him from the impasse into which *The Unnamable* drove him, and this may be why he has so far translated only one of them into English.[3] Although cosmic irony is apparent in the texts, they are such stripped fiction that Beckett extends his "principle of parsimony" even to comic devices.

Exploding into words, Texte I seems to begin where *The Unnamable* ended, barely pausing for breath: "Brusquement, non, à force, à force je n'en pus plus, je ne pus continuer" ("Suddenly, no, at last, long last, I couldn't any more, couldn't go on"). A voice, a fog, body and head, and the inevitable "they" are mentioned. Then comes a shift to "we," to questions, to the old cosmo-epistemological exploration. "Depuis quand suis-je ici? . . . Une heure, un mois, un an, cent ans, selon ce que j'entendais par ici, par moi, par être, et là-dedans je ne suis jamais allé chercher des choses extraordinaires, là-dedans je n'ai jamais beaucoup varié, il n'y avait guère que l'ici pour avoir l'air de varier" ("How long have I been here? . . . An hour, a month, a year, a hundred years, according to what I meant by here, and me, and being, and there I never much varied, only the here sometimes seemed to vary").

Landscapes, literalisms, contradictions, dissolve into "the old stories." Finally there is a fiction of a father and the memory of the father's fiction, Joe Breem or Breen, as in "Le Calmant." Beckett inserts into his own English translation of Texte I the paradoxical, "Nothing like breathing your last to put new life into you." But the life is even less lively than for the moribund Malone, for the "I" of Texte I is "tired out with so much talking, so much listening, so much toil and play."

In the second text, as in the second story "Le Calmant" and the second novel *Malone Dies,* there is still some question of light, of living beings and things, but they vanish swiftly. After the fifth text, there is barely a human situation, much less a plot. After the eighth text, no character appears, either with or without name, and even in the first eight texts the people are only brief memories—both Joe Breem or Breen and the father who told his tale; Verger Joly of Moran's half of *Molloy;* the Graves brothers, possibly from *Watt;* Molloy, Malone, and Pozzo, who have major roles in other Beckett works; the plowman Piers, a Mme. Calvet and her dog, who do not appear elsewhere. None of these characters, nor the mother and father who watch themselves growing old in a shaving mirror, is delineated in more than a line or two, with brief ironic overtones.

On the other hand, the brunt of Beckett's comic is borne by two parody characters who are created before our eyes. In the third text, the narrator, refusing to examine whose are the words, tells a story. Arbitrarily, he accepts a body, calls himself a man, or at least a "vieil enfant" whose Nanny will be responsible for everything. In spite of himself, he falls into the old philosophical brooding, and he resolves to speak only of the future. He will have a friend, an old war comrade. Together, they have only one more winter to live ("alleluia"); the friend has ear trouble, the narrator prostate trouble. As each envies the other's illness, they sit in the public park reading day-old newspapers, particularly the racing sheets and the news of the royal families: "Rien de ce qui est humain ne nous est étranger, une fois digérées les nouvelles hippiques et canines" ("Nothing human is foreign to us, once we have digested the equine and canine news"). The narrator confides that he would be better off alone, and yet Vincent remains for a few sentences—for that suddenly is the friend's name, even as it was that of one of Mr. Knott's early servants, long before Watt's time. The narrator and Vincent, veterans both, comfort each other, and the narrator begins a description of an old cripple, but breaks off suddenly, realizing that he has returned to the past. For a brief moment, he tempts himself again with the idea that he has a head and leg, practically grown together into a story. But not for long: "Les départs, les histoires, ce n'est pas pour demain. Et les voix, d'où qu'elles viennent, sont bien mortes" ("Departures, stories, are not for tomorrow. And the voices, wherever they come from, are quite dead").

In the eighth text—after the interminable debate between the "I" who is here and has never been elsewhere, and the "I" who refuses to be created; after bitter remarks about his head that was left at some bar in Ireland, and an "I" that is wandering about on the continent—the narrator perceives a white stick and an ear trumpet on Place de la République at *apéritif* time. Slowly the stick advances across the basement of a cheap department store (Magasins Réunis), and near the trumpet appears a bowler hat, near the stick a pair of worn brown shoes. The objects must be united by "le traditionnel excipient humain." How tempting it is to slip into the old crippled flesh, to go begging again. But at the very moment of pathetic gesture—of extending the hand or hat, in a café terrace or metro entrance—it will be clear that this is not *the* "I," who is begging elsewhere, other alms; "je me saurais ici, mendiant dans un autre silence, un autre noir, une autre aumône, celle d'être ou bien de cesser encore mieux, sans avoir été. Et la main vainement vieille lâcherait l'obole et les vieux pieds reprendraient, vers une mort encore plus vaine que celle de n'importe qui" ("I would know that I am here, begging in another silence, another darkness, other alms, that of being, or even better of ceasing to be, without ever having been. And the hand vainly old would drop the coin, and the old feet would set out again towards a death even more futile than that of anyone").

In this conclusion to the eighth text, Beckett implies an explanation of all his cripples and beggars. Incapacitated for this world by their lameness, deafness, and blindness, they beg no less than another world, in which being bears no relation to existence as we know it. The excerpt is symptomatic, almost symbolic of the theme and obsession of all thirteen texts—the old epistemological quest, which the fictions of our civilization no longer satisfy.

In the thirteen texts, word and deed, language and event, are even more indissoluble than in *The Unnamable,* and both are less susceptible of separate analysis. Literalism and contradiction tend towards pure negation, and yet they remain epistemological tools. But they work now in such cramped quarters that the comic is often stifled. In a virtual paean to the negative, there are only faintly comic harmonics of the desperate theme. "Non, il faut trouver . . . un nouveau non, qui annule tous les autres, tous les vieux non qui m'ont plongé ici, au fond de ce lieu qui n'en est pas un, qui n'est qu'un temps pour l'heure éternel, qui s'appelle ici, et de cet être qui s'appelle moi et n'en est pas un, et de cette voix impossible, tous les vieux non qui pendent dans le noir et se balancent comme une échelle de fumée, oui, un nouveau non, qui ne se laisse dire qu'une fois, qui ouvre sa trappe et me lampe, ombre et babil, dans une absence moins vaine que d'existence" ("No, you have to find . . . a new no, which cancels all the others, all the old no's that plunged me here, at the bottom of this place which is not one, which is only a time for eternity, which is called here, and of this being which is called I and which is not one, and of this impossible voice, all the old no's that hang in the dark and sway like a ladder of smoke, yes, a new no, which can only be said once, which opens its trap door and gulps me down, shadow and babble, in an absence less vain than existence"). (Texte XI.)

In the cosmological context of this "beauté toute négative de la parole," one would scarcely expect a comic device so polished as paradox, and the few examples pass almost unnoticed, so familiar are they in Beckett's prose: "mort comme les vivants," "assourdissant silence," "quelle variété et en même temps quelle monotonie" ("dead as the living," "deafening silence," "what variety and at the same time what monotony").

Similarly, there are only the haziest memories of other Bergsonian linguistic devices: rare but meaningful puns—"Le sujet meurt avant d'atteindre le verbe," "L'ajouter au repertoire, voilà et l'exécuter, comme je m'exécute, morceau par morceau mort" ("The subject dies before reaching the verb," "to add it to the repertoire and execute it, as I execute myself, piece by dead piece"—puns are of course untranslatable); a cliché variant—"toutes les villes ne sont pas éternelles" ("all cities are not eternal"); a biblical misquotation—"à chaque jour suffit sa peine" ("to each day its pain"). Jargon, too, is minimal at both extremes, the vulgar and the learned. In spite of scattered references to Aristotle, Catalina, Sirius, the square root of minus one, and the usual shock-troop language for sexual and excretory details, such as a description of having "fait ses humanités, dans la vespasienne à deux places Rue d'Assas," the comic echoes can scarcely arouse a Wattian smile, although the irony might well evoke Arsene's bitter, hollow, and mirthless laughter.

The narrator or voice of the thirteen texts is so self-absorbed, his *tu* and *vous* are so often intended for an *alter ego*, that authorial comment is intermittent, as in "Il raconte son histoire toutes les cinq minutes en disant que ce n'est pas la sienne, avouez que c'est malin . . . avouez que c'est fort" ("He tells his story every five minutes, saying it isn't his, admit that it's tricky . . . admit that it's clever"). Incongruities, other than those of the rare characters, are limited to such details as hearing thoughts, baring one's heart as in a salon, swallowing one's soul with sausage, memories like the spokes of a wheel, the expectation of trembling and grimaces in response to the narrator.

In a last evocation of Beckett's own fictions, in Texte IV cosmic irony is once more linked to the epistemological comedy of knowledge through fiction: "Sa vie, parlons-en, il n'aime pas ça, il a compris, de sorte que ce n'est pas la sienne, ce n'est pas lui, vous pensez, lui faire ça à lui, c'est bon pour Molloy, pour Malone, voilà les mortels, les heureux mortels, mais lui, vous n'y pensez pas, passer par là, lui qui n'a jamais bougé, lui qui est moi, toutes choses considérées, et quelles choses, et comment considérées" ("His life, let's talk about it, he doesn't like it, he understood that it isn't his, that it isn't he, just imagine doing that to him, it's all right for Molloy, for Malone, these are mortals, happy mortals, but him, don't think of putting him through that, he who has never moved, he who is I, all things considered, and what things, and how considered").

Perhaps because of the self-imposed limitations of space, perhaps because of the very paucity of fictions and events, the quest of the "I" of the thirteen texts (unless there are thirteen "I's") is even more single-minded and compulsively absurd than that of the Unnamable. In ignorance as of old, the narrator reduces the comic gamut to literalism and contradiction, shock and cruelty. Thus, the narrator, with comic literalism, attempts to situate himself: "Si j'étais là, si [la voix] avait su me faire, comme je la plaindrais, d'avoir tant parlé en vain, non, ça ne va pas, elle n'aurait pas parlé en vain, si j'étais là, et je ne la plaindrais pas, si elle m'avait fait" ("If I were there, if the voice had known how to create me, how I would pity it for having spoken so much in vain, no, that won't do, it wouldn't have spoken in vain if I were there, and I wouldn't pity it, if it had created me"). (Texte III.)

Contradiction is always self-contradiction: "J'aurais pu rester dans mon coin, au chaud, au sec, à l'abri, je ne pouvais pas. Mon coin, je vais le décrire, non, je ne peux pas" ("I could have stayed in my corner, warm, dry, protected, I couldn't. My corner, I'll describe it, no, I can't"). (Texte I.) More specifically, and shockingly, the narrator describes his surroundings, "Il fait noir comme dans une tête, avant que les vers s'y mettent" ("It is black, as it is in a head, before the worms get in it"). (Texte II.)

Quite nakedly, the problem is cosmological and epistemological, with even less distinction between them (if that is possible) than in *The Unnamable.* All the questions are old now: the meaning of being, the meaning of "I," the meaning of "here," the voice of whom, the words of whom, the effort to say simply, "I am here," the effort to believe a fiction quickly, to set it in motion without too much thought. "Se peut-il qu'il me pousse à la fin une tête à moi, où fricoter des poisons dignes de moi. . . . Rien que la tête et les deux jambes, ou une seule, au milieu, je m'en irais en sautillant. Ou rien que la tête, bien ronde, bien lisse, pas besoin de linéaments, je roulerais, je suivrais les pentes, presque un pur esprit, non ça n'irait pas, d'ici tout remonte, il faut la jambe, ou l'équivalent" ("Can it be that finally I will sprout a head in which to stew poisons worthy of me. . . . Nothing but a head and two legs, or a single leg in the middle, I would take off hopping. Or the head alone, round and smooth, don't need features, I would roll, I would follow the inclines, almost a pure mind, no, that won't do, from there everything begins all over again, the leg is needed, or the equivalent"). (Texte III.)

Starting with the head, one is in danger of re-creating the whole world, and that leads nowhere. No, the only solution is to do away with words; "qu'est-ce que c'est, cette innommable chose, que je nomme, nomme, nomme, sans l'user, et j'appelle ça des mots" ("what is it, this unnamable thing that I name, name, name, without using it up, and I call that words"). (Texte VI.)

In the seventh text, which works up to a hysterical pitch, the narrator affirms that in any case it is not a question of himself but of "X, paradigme du genre humain," with "une carcasse à l'image de Dieu et une tête contemporaine." This passionate denial of self is highly ironic in the context of the most intense search for self, and yet both denial and search are part of the human condition. The plight—cosmological and epistemological—of Molloy, Malone, and the Unnamable, searching "I's," would not be so moving and profound, were it not paradigmatic of the human species, whom avalanches of words have taught nothing.

As the torrent continues—of words and tears intermingled (for tears we have still with us)—the narrator admits to using time and space interchangeably, but, compared with the mockery of the Unnamable, there is small comic result of this coupling. The narrator comments on all the variations that words can manage, and yet they are ineffectual—"for nothing." If he could summarize them . . . but that is impossible. Again and again, he pleads for a way out at either end, womb or tomb, even though he knows there will be none.

Casting light on the violence of the earlier Beckett fiction, he sighs, "Hélas je crois qu'ils auraient pu se livrer sur moi aux plus flatteuses violences, je ne dirai pas sans que je m'en suis rendu compte, mais je dirai sans que cela m'ait aidé à me sentir là, plutôt qu'ailleurs" ("Alas I believe that they could have indulged themselves in the most flattering violence against me, I won't say without my noticing it, but I will say without its helping me feel myself there rather than elsewhere"). (Texte IX.)

Words have killed soul and body, birth and death, and yet they must find something else "qui me fera un temps, qui me fera un lieu, et une voix et un silence, une voix de silence, la voix de mon silence" ("that will make me a time, that will make me a place, and a voice and a silence, a voice of silence, the voice of my silence"). (Texte X.)

The eleventh text resumes the condemnation of words—"saletés de mots"—that have sought to make the narrator believe in an "I." By the twelfth text, the "I" is divided into three, one who speaks and questions the speaker, one who listens silently and understands nothing, and one without person or number "dont nous hantons l'être abandonné, rien" ("whose abandoned being we haunt, nothing"). But they all add up to one, which adds up to nothing; never and nothing but dead words.

With the thirteenth text, Beckett's bitter irony rises for a last comic fling. In a series of contradictions that recalls the end of *The Unnamable,* the last images are evoked of impossible shadows that never were and never will be. Lying words, will they end at last, cruelly asks the voice that is silence. Will the thirst for knowledge end in silence that is not silence? For there is no one and someone, "rien n'empêche rien" ("nothing prevents nothing"). The fading voice cannot speak, cannot be silent, and ends, "Et il y aurait un jour ici, où il n'est pas de jours, qui n'est pas un endroit, issu de l'impossible voix l'infaisable être, et un commencement de jour, que tout serait silencieux et vide et noir, comme maintenant, comme bientôt, quand tout sera fini, tout dit, dit-elle, murmure-t-elle" ("And there would be a day here where there are no days, here which is not a place, the uncreatable being evoked by the impossible voice, a beginning of day where everything would be silent and empty and black, as it is now, as it will be soon, when everything will be ended, everything said, it says, it murmurs").

The superbly ironic final words, casting the old doubt on the old words in still a new wry way, indicate that the *Textes pour rien* did not completely fail "to get out of the attitude of disintegration";[4] the final, most heart-piercingly personal plea is ironically presented as a direct quotation of a fictional voice. The spareness of these fictional texts—if they still can be called fiction (which Beckett seems to doubt by his use of the word "text")—entailing only shreds of event and character, virtually drowns the *mythos* in the *logos.*

As Beckett's "I" loses mobility and is successively robbed of all possessions but a passing fiction garbed in fewer and fewer words, Beckett reduces his own literary materials, and reduction is usually a comic process. But reduction may also be a generalizing process, as in science and philosophy, wherein the significance of a hypothesis depends upon its inclusiveness. Explicitly called "X, paradigme du genre humain" in the texts, Beckett's author-hero is reduced to the lowest of common human denominators with no distinct or distinguishing features. By use of the first person, Beckett immerses us in a paradigmatic plight that becomes our own. He denies us the detachment of the comic mode. The reduced remainder of Beckett's broad comic gamut serves to etch man's desperate state all the more incisively. The texts move in the direction of Beckett's own avowed preference for an art that expresses "that there is nothing to express, nothing with which to express, nothing from which to express, no power to express, no desire to express, together with the obligation to express." [5]

Since turning to French for most of his writing, Beckett has published only one piece of fiction in English, "From an Abandoned Work." [6] First printed in 1957, it is close to the French fiction in form and content.

As in much of Beckett's fiction, a nameless "I" relates a series of non-concatenated events. While the "I," the protagonist, is outside a house, his mother waves from a window (it is vague as to why he is outside, and why she is waving); he sees a white horse followed by a boy, or a small man or woman; suddenly, the protagonist bursts into a savage rage. After several pages of disconnected digressions, he returns to "mother in the window, the violence, rage and rain." The following day, a family or tribe of stoats attacks him; later he lies on the ground looking at the sky. On the third day, a roadman, "a ragged old brute," leers at him. Then he finds himself thrashing about in giant, woody ferns, and "just went on, my body doing its best without me."

Familiar in Beckett country are the non-paragraphed prose, the *non sequiturs* of sentence and phrase, the conclusionless conclusion, the incongruous "I," the abrupt characters, the unmotivated violence, and the first-person narration that heightens both authenticity and emotional involvement. In the nine pages of the story, there is a paucity of comic device, and yet the tale is in the ironic mode that Beckett has marked as his own.

Plot and character contribute to this mode by their illogicality and absurdity, and above all by their capacity for meaning far more than they say.[7] The "I" is again or still the nameless, paradigmatic human creature, and his adventures (separation from mother, kinship with other forms of life, slavery to fiction) are symbolic of aspects of human history.

Of all the linguistic tricks that Beckett can play, only rhyme (a *book* read in a *nook*, a *word* over*heard*, *vent* the *pent*), anagram (*over*, *vero*), and ellipsis are used. Exploratory literalism and contradiction occur, but without the painstaking insistence or the colloquial crudity of the French fiction. About his own language, the narrator says, "awful English this." About the narrative itself, the narrator complains that he does not know why he has chosen this day to describe; he does not know why he speaks, but he must speak on. As in the French stories, there is incongruous detail that is functional in context—the love of the protagonist for "still and rooted" things, his hatred of birds, his mind that is "always on the alert against itself," his strong reaction to the color white, his slow walking and rapid running, his silence since his father's death, his sudden dislike of his long coat, his love of lying face to the ground, and his inability to sustain that position. There are incongruous and ironic details, too, for anyone who is familiar with Beckett's usual protagonists: The "I" of this story has piercing sight, he regrets nothing, he utters "cursing, filthy language . . . I hope nobody heard me."

The story itself is cruelly ironic, for both cosmology and epistemology victimize man. Cruelty lies at many levels: The protagonist lacks mercy for bird, butterfly, and slug; his throat is perpetually sore; he wonders whether he killed his father as well as his mother, and hopes they are both in paradise so that he can curse them from hell—"that might take some of the shine off their bliss"; he used to be terrified of old

Balfe, who is dead and whom he resembles. All is symbol for, indication of, the cruelty of the cosmos, where meaning, if there is any, cannot be fathomed. The word play in which Beckett indulges—the protagonist's love of the words *over* and *vero*—seems to imply that truth can be known only when all is ended.

It is possible that Balfe, the only character with a proper name, is an anagram of Fable, a kind of fiction, but he may also be Baffle. For Beckett, the essence of the human condition is always to be baffled, in spite of a passing, illusory knowledge through fictions.

Although this story contains separate commentaries on the cosmos and man's impossible epistemological attack upon it, the cosmological and epistemological ironies are equated in a passage that recalls the French novels: "Then it will not be as now, day after day, out, on, round, back, in, like leaves turning, or torn out and thrown crumpled away, but a long unbroken time without before or after, light or dark, from or towards or at, the old half knowledge of when and where gone, and of what, but kinds of things still, all at once, all going, until nothing, there was never anything, never can be, life and death all nothing, that kind of thing, only a voice dreaming and droning on all around, that is something, the voice that once was in your mouth" (91).

The voice may be "in your mouth" but not necessarily yours, in spite of your sore throat. The protagonist is thus still able to make some judgment of it, repeating several times, "that is a foolish thing to say," but he never attains the comic epistemological sophistication of the narrator of the thirteenth of the *Textes pour rien,* who would wonder whether the words of the "I" did not belong to another voice commenting ironically on its own foolishness.

8
Comment c'est par le bout

Heureusement il ne s'agit pas de dire ce qui n'a pas encore été dit, mais de redire, le plus souvent possible dans l'espace le plus réduit, ce qui a été dit déjà.—"Peintres de l'empêchement"

Perhaps the initial irony concerning *Comment c'est,* published in 1961, is that it is called a novel. On the dust jacket of Beckett's first extended nondramatic writing in a decade, the designation *roman* appears between the title and the blue star-and-m of Les Editions de Minuit. Yet this work, stripping away plot and character further than ever before, is as close to poetry as to fiction; even typographically the narrative appears in irregular verses. Plot and character virtually coincide in a narrator who crawls naked through the mud, sack tied around his neck, until he meets another character who crawls naked through the mud, sack tied around *his* neck, until he in turn meets still another character who crawls naked through the mud, sack, etc., from the beginning "comment c'était" to the ending "comment c'est." This spareness of situation is paralleled by a bareness of language that even Beckett has not achieved before. With skeletal phrases, he attains the precision, control, and condensation of poetry. Rhythmic repetition, symbolic imagery, and formal structure are exploited for cosmic resonance that is constantly heightened by the comic colloquialisms of the discourse.

Not only is *Comment c'est* divided into three approximately equal parts—1. "Before Pim or the Voyage," 2. "With Pim or the Couple," 3. "After Pim or the Abandonment"—but the tripartite structure is incessantly recapitulated. Such hysterical insistence on division renders it ludicrous, whether the units be of time, place, language, or humanity. And indeed, there is frequent violation of the designated divisions. During the course of the book, nothing and no one emerges from the mud; the hero-narrator is little more than a compulsive movement in the mud, arbitrarily and absurdly imposing his trinity: "d'une seule éternité en faire trois pour plus de clarté" ("to make three eternities from a single one for greater clarity") (29).[1]

Since, like all Beckett's French fiction, *Comment c'est* takes the form of a monologue, the style is consistent in all three parts. Colloquial, unpunctuated phrases are grouped in uneven verses. Usually staccato, these phrases are sometimes linked syntactically; contrast, for example, two verses on the same page, the first choppy, the second containing a more consecutive linguistic flow achieved through participles and relative pronouns.

dans le sac donc jusqu'à présent les boîtes l'ouvre-boîte la corde mais le désir d'autre chose on ne semble pas me l'avoir donné cette fois l'image d'autres choses là avec moi dans la boue le noir dans le sac à ma portée non on ne semble pas avoir mis ça dans ma vie cette fois (15)

(in the sack up to now I recapitulate the tins the opener the cord but the wish for something else no that doesn't seem to have been given me this time the image of other things with me here in the mud in the dark in the sack within reach no that doesn't seem to have been put in my life this time) (B) qu'ayant cherchées en vain parmi les boîtes tantôt l'une tantôt l'autre suivant le désir l'image du moment que m'étant fatigué à chercher ainsi je pourrais me promettre de chercher de nouveau plus tard quand je serais moins fatigué un peu moins fatigué ou tâcher d'oublier en me disant c'est vrai n'y pense plus (15)

(which having sought in vain among the tins now one now another according to the wish the image of the moment which having thus sought till I am tired I promise myself to seek again when less tired with perhaps a little more success or to try and quite banish from my mind saying true true think no more about it) (B)

Certain word groups, permuted and combined and recombined, constitute the burdens of this narration. Never has a "novel" been built with fewer words, but the parsimonious verbal threads are woven into a tough comic texture. Conscious of the comic tone, the narrator even invokes Thalia, muse of Comedy.

The most frequent chorus in the book—whether as an integral and pithy verse line, or as part of the more usual longer verses—is "quelque chose là qui ne va pas" ("something wrong there") (B). Reflecting doubt on the matter that precedes, or follows, or both, the colloquial phrase casts its wavering, indefinite shadow over the entire monologue. Most noticeably, it appears as a complete verse in a series of complete verses, and thus comments upon the entire series:

au couple	(at the couple
en passant par l'abandon	passing by the abandonment
ou par le voyage	or by the voyage
c'est juste	it is just)
quelque chose là qui ne va pas	something wrong there (142)

In the middle of a verse, the refrain line reflects both backward and forward:

la boîte entamée remise dans le sac gardée à la main j'y pense l'appétit revenu ou n'y pense plus en ouvre une autre c'est l'un ou l'autre quelque chose là qui ne va pas c'est le début de ma vie présente rédaction (11)

(the tin broached put back in the sack or left in the hand I remember when I go to eat again or forget open another it's one or the other something wrong there it's the beginning of my life latest version) (B)

The "something wrong there" may be the cans, or forgetting where the opened can has been placed; more significantly, the "something wrong" is the beginning of the narrator's life.

Towards the end of the book, the tenses of grammar and the times of life are embraced in the summary rejection of the refrain line, this time concluding a verse.

à moins qu'elle ne me l'apprenne la voix ma vie lors de cette autre solitude qu'est le voyage c'est-à-dire au lieu d'un premier passé d'un second passé et d'un présent un passé un présent et un futur quelque chose là qui ne va pas (156)

(unless it teaches me the voice my life during that other solitude that is the voyage that is to say instead of a first past from a second past and from a present a past a present and a future something wrong there)

Within the verses, the narrator is redundantly careful to absolve himself of responsibility for the words he mouths. On almost every page he reiterates, "je cite" ("I quote") (B), or "je le dis comme je l'entends" ("I say it as I hear it") (B).[2] Impatient with words, questions, and thoughts, he lumps them together as "cette famille" ("that family"). Although the same phrases have been sporadically uttered by earlier Beckett narrators, notably the Unnamable and the "I's" of the thirteen Textes, the monologuist of *Comment c'est* is more resigned to ignorance. He scarcely seeks to know the original source of his words: "pas question" and "ça s'enchaîne," he shrugs. Vaguely but emphatically, he affirms, "on parle de." From "on," from somewhere, once without but now within him even if not his, the incessant, compulsive "murmure à la boue" ("murmur to the mud") is tantamount to breath. Perhaps there will be silence "quand ça cesse de haleter" ("when the panting stops") (B). Always there is the mud, the dark, and "un temps énorme" ("vast stretch of time") (B). Into that "temps énorme," world without end, the narrator attempts to interject his tripartite division: "comment c'était comment c'est comment ce sera" ("how it was how it is how it will be").[3] But rigid rubrics are constantly and comically flouted, since time is as continuous and pervasive as the mud.

To another time or world or life—of light up above (as in Texte II and Texte XI)—belongs all knowledge, evoked now only in self-mockery. Ironically, the narrator twists the French proverb "tout comprendre c'est tout pardonner" to "tout compris et rien su pardonner" ("to understand everything is to pardon everything"; "I understood everything and didn't know how to pardon anything"). At irregular intervals, the narrator recalls "l'anatomie" or "la géographie" or "les lettres" or "les humanités" or even "l'âme" that he used to have. By now, however, there is only the "present version" of his life, related presumably by the interminable "brefs mouvements du bas du visage" ("brief movements of the lower face") (B), frequently and cryptically summarized as "quaqua."

Other than this soundless monologue, existence consists of crawling through the slime in a straight line towards the East. Earlier Beckett heroes were unable, alternatively, to sit or to stand (Cooper and Neary of *Murphy*, Hamm and Clov of *Endgame*). Molloy, Malone, and Mahood were all reduced to reptation; Estragon of *Waiting for Godot* complains, "All my lousy life I've crawled about in the mud!" Similarly, the narrator of *Comment c'est* crawls on his belly through the mud: "dix mètres quinze mètres pied droit main droite pousse tire" ("ten yards fifteen yards right foot right hand push pull"). In different contexts, the same numbers recur; they may shift from space to time, "dix secondes quinze secondes"; to the Beckett description of thought, "dix coups quinze coups sur le crâne"; to language, "dix mots quinze mots"; to hypothetical people, "dix autres quinze autres." But whatever the temporary substantive, the numbers constantly return to the mud in which they were conceived. The movement through the mud may vary slightly: "jambe droite bras droit pousse tire dix mètres quinze mètres halte" ("right leg right arm push pull ten yards fifteen yards stop"). Occasionally, right is replaced by left, or a side or a thigh may enter the description of the motion, but the motion itself is dully repetitive, peristaltic, caricaturing man into a worm.

Obsessed as he is with the minutiae of his movements, the narrator-hero is also sporadically aware of the chaos in which he is immersed; valiantly if vainly, he persists in his attempt to trisect eternity. In the printed text, moreover, the three parts of the book are separated by half-title pages and introduced by large Arabic numbers. Within each chapter recur several phrases that lack the raucous insistence of the book-long repetitions, but that also add to the comic tone. In Part 1, "Before Pim or the Voyage," when the narrator is alone, he chants an old Beckett theme, "moi si c'est moi" ("I if it is I"); an old Beckett irony, "dans l'ordre" ("in the natural order") (B); and an old Beckett approximation, "plus ou moins" ("more or less"). In Part 2, "With Pim or the Couple," the narrator harps on the fact that Pim "n'est pas bête seulement lent" ("is not stupid merely slow"). Since Part 2 contains a kind of marriage between the narrator and Pim, happiness is comically conjugated: At intervals, we find "ce sont de bons moments"; less frequently, "c'était de bons moments"; still less frequently, "ce sera de bons moments" and "ce serait de bons moments"; more incongruously in this "temps énorme," "ce serait de bonnes secondes."

In the third, last, and most desperate part, appear references to "les jours de grande gaîté" ("days of great gaiety"). In the final chapter, a new verse refrain appears: "c'est juste" ("it is just"). But by that time, the cumulative evidence of the entire work denies both "justice" and "justesse" in the human sentence. In Part 3, too, the book-long refrains are climactically varied so as to highlight the hopeless absurdity of human fate. Thus, the "mouvements du bas du visage" that result in the compulsive monologue are modified to "mouvements pour rien du bas du visage" ("movements for nothing of the lower face") (132). "Quelque chose là qui ne va pas" is intensified to "quelque chose là qui ne va pas du tout" ("something completely wrong there") (139). The irony is patent when "comment c'était comment c'est comment ce sera" becomes "comment c'était comment c'est comment ce très certainement sera" ("how it was how it is how it most certainly will be") (163). The beat of "je cite" explodes into "qu'est-ce que ça peut bien foutre je cite" ("what the hell can it matter I quote") (159).

Having no voice, the narrator knows he speaks only when he feels his face move. With some surprise he wonders what there can be to say, but we can scarcely be surprised at the comic contradictions that tumble out of his lower face:

> on est là quelque part en vie quelque part un temps énorme puis c'est fini on n'y est plus puis de nouveau on est là de nouveau ce n'était pas fini une erreur c'est à recommencer plus ou moins au même endroit à un autre (26–27)
>
> (one is there somewhere alive somewhere a vast stretch of time then it's finished one isn't there any more then again one is there again it wasn't finished an error it's to begin again more or less in the same place in another)

Frequently, the narrator reiterates, "j'entends dire que oui puis que non" ("I hear it say yes then no"). Towards the end of Part 2, virtually every short phrase within each verse is punctuated by a "oui" or a "non" that emphasizes with comic (and pathetic) literalness the permanent contradictions of the human situation. Towards the end of Part 3, Beckett again uses the powerfully rhythmic "oui's" and "non's," but to them he adds a frequent and vituperative "de la foutaise," as well as the final Beckett answer to all questions, "pas de réponse" ("no answer").

Although it is primarily recapitulation of these phrases that establishes the distinctive comic lyricism of *Comment c'est,* Beckett also uses such lesser poetic embellishments as repetition of sound—rhyme, alliteration, and pun. The comic repercussions are evident in the play between sound and sense (which is untranslatable): "santé de fer que faire que faire," "à en avoir la peau en eau," "à quoi croire," "la fin enfin," "ils passent à pas pesants," "coi dans mon coin," "jamais vu ça sa vie ici," "il coupe court par le coup," "l'entendre dire dire l'entendre de la bouche à la boue bref baiser du bout des lèvres."

Such peripheral sound play prepares the muddy ground for the focal puns of the book, those upon the two most frequently mentioned proper names, Pim and Bom. The monosyllables *pain* and *bọn* are rich in pleasurable connotations: staff of life, bread of the Presence, central sustenance; God's world, ethical goal, practical use. But Pim and Bom, puns on *pain* and *bon,* are destitute and desperate, not knowing which of them creates the other—in the habit of Beckett's fictions. Perhaps Beckett's most bitter irony lies in his naming these cruel and dwindling solipsists "bread" and "good." Moreover, Beckett generalizes these ironic proper names, to represent the human species. Individual identity is virtually canceled in the reciprocal puns in the second of the following verses.

la même voix les mêmes choses aux noms propres près et encore deux suffisent chacun attend sans nom son Bom va sans nom vers son Pim

Bom à l'abandonné pas moi Bom toi Bom nous Bom mais moi Bom toi Pim moi à l'abandonné pas moi Pim toi Pim nous Pim mais moi Bom toi Pim quelque chose là qui ne va pas du tout (139)

(the same voice the same things with nearly the same proper names and even then two suffice each awaiting nameless his Bom goes nameless toward his Pim

Bom abandoned not I Bom you Bom but I Bom you Pim I abandoned not I Pim you Pim we Pim but I Bom you Pim something completely wrong there)

Other puns are only subtly implied through the course of the book. The reiterated title, "Comment c'est," puns on "commencer" ("to begin"). And just as "how it is" is a perpetual beginning that can never be extrapolated all the way back to point zero, so the ubiquitous mud is a perpetual end that never terminates at a given goal; "bout" ("end") is implicit in and denied by "boue" ("mud").

Part 3, "After Pim," entitled "l'abandon," contains in the single French word the solitude of English "abandonment" and the unrestrained quality of English "abandon." At a cruder level, the verbiage of the monologue is constantly summed up as "quaqua," presumably pronounced "caca."

Contributing to the ironic tone is Beckett's use of repetition to link various verses, as in the following example.

quoi sur elle ma mémoire on parle de ma mémoire peu de chose qu'elle s'améliore elle empire qu'il me revient des choses il ne me revient rien mais de là à être sûr

à être sûr que personne ne viendra plus jamais braquer sa lampe sur moi et plus jamais rien d'autres jours d'autres nuits non (18–19)

(my memory I say I quote that it is getting better it is getting worse that things are coming back to me nothing is coming back to me but to conclude from that that no one to conclude from that that no one will ever come again shine his lamp on me and nothing ever again of the old days and nights no) (B)

The repetition and climactic positions of "à être sûr" serve as ironic preparation for the final and contradictory "non." Nothing is sure in Beckett's world.

In another example, by slightly varying the linking repetition, Beckett intensifies the ironic portrayal of the narrator's predicament.

ce sera de bons moments puis de moins bons ça aussi il faut s'y attendre ce sera la nuit présente rédaction je pourrai dormir et si jamais je me réveille

et si jamais rire muet je me réveille dare-dare catastrophe Pim fin de première partie plus que la deuxième puis la troisième et dernière (40)

(there will be good moments then less good that too must be expected there will be night present version I will be able to sleep and if ever I awaken

and if ever dumb laugh I awaken sudden catastrophe Pim end of the first part only the second to go then the third only the third and last)

By the end of the book, a comic and cosmic cruelty is conveyed in the single word "bon," repeated to link the final verses.

alors ça peut changer pas de réponse finir pas de réponse je pourrais suffoquer pas de réponse m'engloutir pas de réponse plus souiller la boue pas de réponse le noir pas de réponse plus troubler le silence pas de réponse crever pas de réponse CREVER hurlements JE POURRAIS CREVER hurlements JE VAIS CREVER hurlements bon

bon bon fin de la troisième partie et dernière voilà comment c'était fin de la citation après Pim comment c'est (then it can change no answer end no answer I could suffocate no answer sink no answer no longer pollute the mud no answer the dark no answer no longer trouble the silence no answer croak no answer CROAK howls I COULD CROAK howls I AM GOING TO CROAK howls good

good good end of the third and last part there is how it was end of quotation after Pim how it is)

The entire work denies the "bon," both by virtue of the constantly repeated "mal" and the anguish that accumulates from verse to verse, and from chapter to chapter. From past to future, "un temps énorme," man grovels on his belly in the mud, with a sack tied around his neck, making brief movements of the lower face. In characterizing his condition, God's word, "Good," is cruelly ironic.

Unlike other heroes of Beckett's French fiction, the "I" of *Comment c'est* is relatively intact physically, for he lacks only a right thumb and a voice. But he is not clad in the picturesque costumes of earlier Beckett creations, for he crawls through his mud as naked as the proverbial worm. Yet he takes pride of possession, notably in a sack, which contains cans, cord, and can opener. As in other Beckett works, the very sparseness of specific objects is comic, and virtually demands symbolic interpretation.

The four objects fall at once into pairs: can and can opener, sack and cord. The first two are modern and smack of industrialization; the second two are as old as civilization—"vieux sac vieille corde vous je vous garde" ("old sack old cord I'm keeping you").[4] The can and can opener are rigid, the sack and cord pliable. Can and can opener are essentially unifunctional; sack and cord are multipurpose. But it is mainly in their linguistic connotations that the two pairs of objects differ; can and can opener are only meagerly suggestive, but sack and cord figure in many French expressions that would seem to have comic relevance to the human situation in *Comment c'est.*

Perhaps the heart of the matter is contained in "homme de sac et de corde" ("thorough scoundrel"). He may be a scoundrel, but his sentence—to be stuffed into a sack that is tied up with a cord—is crueler than his crime. So, Beckett's heroes may be scoundrels, but they are condemned to a punishment that is antecedent and irrelevant to their crimes.

Of the two objects, sack and cord, the former is of prime importance since, initially at least, it contains the other objects—perhaps, on occasion, the narrator himself. The sack is explicitly and insistently described as a fifty-kilo coalsack of wet jute. Trivially domestic though this may seem, the Coalsack is also the starless center of the Milky Way (near the Southern Cross), a black hole in the heavens. In *Murphy,* Beckett specifically links Murphy's dark center with that of our galaxy: "The sad truth was that the skylight commanded only that most dismal patch of night sky, the galactic coalsack, which would naturally look like a dirty night to any observer in Murphy's condition, cold, tired, angry, impatient and out of conceit with a system that seemed the superfluous cartoon of his own." [5] Similarly, since the coalsack is mandatory in order for the hero of *Comment c'est* to move, "sac à charbon" may be Beckett's comic shorthand for relating his crawling creature to the center of the galaxy. Of possible relevance to the dampness of the sack is the fact that amphibian life existed on a carboniferous earth a cosmic year (or 225,000,000 years) ago.

The coalsack or "sac à charbon" also suggests "sac et cendres," or sackcloth and ashes, the traditional garb of the penitent sinner. In Part 3, which is much concerned with justice, this connotation is particularly ironic. That such justice may be divine is implied in the distinction between full and empty sacks—"une histoire de grâce." A possible almighty power is characterized as "celui qui fournit les sacs" ("the one who furnishes the sacks") and "une intelligence . . . un amour qui . . . dépose nos sacs" ("an intelligence . . . a love which . . . leaves our sacks for us").

In various French phrases, the sack can stand for either belly or brain. Although the crawling hero tends to insist upon the former and to ignore the latter, Beckett paints their chaotic combination. Since "sac," as in "avoir le sac" or "être au sac" implies riches, the meager contents of the sack of *Comment c'est* are ludicrous. Nothing, during the course of the book, is acquired to fill the sack ("remplir le sac" is "to eat copiously"), and the narrator's appetite decreases to zero. As early as Part 1, the narrator's sack is literally emptied of cord, can opener, and cans. Metaphorically, "vider son sac" is to have one's say, and the phrase is entirely fitting for the way the Beckett hero spews forth his monologue.

Within the book itself, Beckett implies that the meaning of the sack is to be extended, for we read: "mon sac seul variable," "le sac premier vrai signe de vie," "le sac seul bien," "le sac ma vie," "la mort du sac," "ce sac sans quoi pas de voyage" ("my sack only variable," "the sack first real sign of life," "the sack only possession," "the sack my life," "the death of the sack," "the sack without which no voyage"). Sacks figure comically at cross-purposes: "nous laissons nos sacs à ceux qui n'en ont pas besoin nous prenons leurs sacs à ceux qui vont en avoir besoin nous partons sans sac nous en trouvons un nous pouvons voyager" ("we leave our sacks to those who don't need them we take the sacks from those who will need them we set off without sacks we find one we can voyage") (135).

When, early in the book, the narrator slips the sack over his head, we may think of "voir le fond du sac"—an effort to get to the bottom of things. Since the sack is wet, we need scarcely be astonished by the narrator's perpetual excuses; "se couvrir d'un sac mouillé" is "to be full of excuses." When the hand of the hero is seen in the sack, we recall that "prendre quelqu'un la main dans le sac" implies human guilt. Even more appropriate for the Beckett hero is "avoir la tête dans un sac" ("to be ignorant"); for this narrator belongs to the Beckett family in loudly protesting his absolute ignorance.

Less central than the sack—but then "Il ne faut point parler de corde dans la maison d'un pendu" ("one mustn't talk about rope in the house of the hanged")—the cord suggests two different lines of connotation, the one centered on poverty and the other on hanging. In the first group are such expressions as "usé jusqu'à la corde" ("thoroughly hackneyed"), "être au bout de sa corde" ("to be at the end of one's tether"), "montrer sa corde" ("to be played out"). In the second group are such locutions as "friser la corde" ("to escape danger"), and literally describing the situation of the narrator, "la corde au cou" ("condemned").

Moving from objects to people—barely distinguishable in *Comment c'est*—we note Beckett's continued comedy of names. In the French trilogy, Beckett had already indicated, by unceremoniously changing proper names, that such appellations were completely arbitrary, and did not confer identity. The last narrator of the trilogy is nameless and unnamable, but he can still name his creations Mahood and Worm. So, too, the hero of *Comment c'est* is finally nameless and unnamable, but he insists from the start upon the "beau nom de Pim" for the creature of Part 2, with whom he will form a temporary couplement. When the meeting takes place, however, the narrator suggests that he, too, may appropriate the fine name of Pim, then decides he prefers Bom, or perhaps Bim or Bem—"m à la fin et une syllabe le reste égal" ("m at the end and one syllable the rest doesn't matter"). A fleeting image of a wife becomes Pam Prim, and the phonetic similarity of Pam and Pim suggests that the narrator's partner in the Couple may be of either sex. An intermittently evoked witness and a scribe are called Krim and Kram, with suggestions of "crin," "cran," and "crâne." A maimed dog is called

Skom Skum, with a phonetic odor of "sconse." The phonetic stipulation is somewhat ridiculous, since final m is "un-French," occurring in such borrowed words as tram, macadam, and Sam.

Sam himself is not present in *Comment c'est,* as he was in *Watt,* and yet he comes inevitably to mind through the repetition of "m à la fin et une syllabe le reste égal." Phonetically "homme" and "femme" would also meet these specifications, contributing to Beckett's usual metaphysical tendency of generalizing man to Man. Moreover, Beckett's comic penchant for humanizing things—Molloy's fondness for pebbles, Malone's for his pencil, Worm for his vase—culminate in *Comment c'est,* where the voyager is inseparable from his sack. The phrase, "le sac ma vie," occurs often in *Comment c'est.* By Part 3, Beckett generalizes humanity to "une syllabe m à la fin," and phenomena to "une syllabe c à la fin." Thus, man and thing take similar form, distinguishable by a single consonant.

In contrast to the various linguistic connotations of sack and cord, can and can opener seem confined to their phenomenological aspects. The cans are plural, the can opener singular. The cans fulfill their function of containing sustenance, but the can opener does not open a single can. The cans, doing what they were designed to do, are soon thrown away in the mud; the can opener, not used for what it was intended, becomes the prime instrument in training Pim to speak. (In the one instance wherein cans are opened, it is an "outil" rather than "ouvre-boîte" that accomplishes the deed.) Once the narrator asserts "l'ouvre-boîte qui est ma vie" ("the can opener that is my life") but retracts to "mais de quoi ne puis-je en dire autant" ("but of what can't I say as much"). Can and can opener become the principals in a comedy of incongruous functions.

Within the text, it is ambivalent as to whether can opener, cans, cord, sack, and the pervasive mud are objects, metaphors, or images. Cord, comb, and can opener are specifically designated as objects, and yet their meaning can be extended. In the description of a crocus, "une main l'y maintient cette fleur jaune dans le soleil au moyen d'une corde je vois la main longue image" (25), is it the entire ridiculous still life that constitutes the image? Or the living hand? Or the condensation in this image of a longer description in "La Fin?"

In *Comment c'est,* the heralding of the first image is in comic contrast to the vagueness of the image itself:

vie dans la lumière première image un quidam quelconque je le regardais à ma manière de loin en dessous dans un miroir la nuit par la fenêtre première image (11)

(life in the light first image someone anyone I watched him after my fashion from afar stealthily in mirrors at night through windows lighted windows first image) (B)

For the heroes of Beckett's French fiction, perception becomes increasingly difficult, and the "I" of *Comment c'est* sees his first image darkly, through several glasses. Gradually, however, as the narrator warms to his narration, the images grow clearer—a parodic picture of the narrator's mother hearing his childhood prayers, brief mention of the narrator regaining consciousness in the dark in a hospital up above in the world of light, the memory of a wife in another life. Towards the middle of Part 1 occurs the most extended narration or "image" of *Comment c'est,* which was published separately under the title "L'Image." [6]

Wallowing in the slime, mouth open and tongue in the mud, the narrator takes up some mud on his tongue and rolls it around in his mouth. Gradually, he sees himself at the age of sixteen; he is with a girl in a pastoral scene of April or May. In most un-Beckettian fashion, boy and girl hold hands and swing arms, the boy carrying a pack of sandwiches in his free arm, the girl leading her little dog by the leash. But soon, characteristically ironic strokes color the picture: The hero neglects his girl friend (who is only less hideous full-face than in profile) to concentrate on himself; among his grotesque features are pimples, large stomach, gaping fly, splay feet, spindle legs, and sanctimonious smile. The pet dog trots along behind the couple, "rien à voir avec nous il a eu la même idée au même instant du Malebranche en moins rose les lettres que j'avais" ("nothing to do with us he had the same idea at the same instant Malebranche a little more pale the education I had") (37).

The only proper name in the slight narrative refers to the seventeenth-century Occasionalist philosopher, Nicolas Malebranche, who carried Cartesian dualism of mind and matter to its most extreme form, so that any action of the one upon the other was the occasion for divine intervention. In literal context—that human and canine minds should be able to act upon human and canine bodies, respectively, only by miracle—the comic depends upon incongruous disproportion. Incongruous, too, are the overtones of Malebranche's asceticism in this "love story." In its larger concern with the mind-matter dichotomy, the mention of Malebranche recalls Beckett's earliest work. Particularly apposite in this section where an image arises from mud, where a kind of matter is created by a kind of mind, the naming of Malebranche precedes the bitterest phrase in the narration, "s'il pisse il pissera sans s'arrêter je crie aucun son plaque-la là et cours t'ouvrir les veines" ("if he pees he will pee without stopping I cry no sound leave her there and run to open your veins").

Although the vulgarity attaches primarily to the dog, it looks forward metaphorically to the spurt of blood that would follow "sans s'arrêter" ("without stopping") from the opening of the veins, and this in turn would lead to silence, "aucun son." The crying also follows the "sans s'arrêter" that would make agony continuous, and it precedes the suggestions of abandonment and death. The traditional French sounds of comfort, "là, là," contrast cruelly with the suicidal final phrase.

In the next verse, the lovers are suddenly at the summit of a mountain. By the positional ambiguity of the short phrases, Beckett reduces the couple to comic animality. Like the dog, the lovers concentrate on physical pleasures. Endearments mingle with mastication: "mon amour je mords elle avale mon trésor elle mord j'avale" ("my love I bite she swallows my treasure she bites I swallow"). Although the biting and swallowing act upon the sandwich at a literal level, the movements also suggest love-making and chastising; they prefigure Part 2, "the Couple," with its sustained and deliberate ambiguity as to whether the members of the couple are lovers or victim and executioner.

Leaving the mountain, the narrator loses the scene. Still smiling, though "depuis longtemps ce n'est plus la peine" ("for a long time now it hasn't been worth the trouble"), he finds himself face down in the familiar mud. This time, when his tongue reaches out, he is no longer thirsty. Empty, the tongue re-enters his mouth, and the mouth closes.

elle doit faire une ligne droite à présent c'est fini c'est fait j'ai eu l'image (38)

(it must make a straight line at present it's done it's made I've had the image)

As originally published in three pages of unpunctuated prose, the closing words were "j'ai fait l'image." Changing the verb from *make* to *have* shifts the connotation from creation to parturition, and places the narrator at a further remove from God, who made man in His own image.

In the sixth text, Beckett had already reduced to mud the "limon" upon which God breathed on the Sixth day: [7] "la nostalgie de cette boue où souffla l'esprit de l'Eternel" ("nostalgia for that mud where the Eternal spirit breathed"). In

Comment c'est, it is the narrator who breathes into the mud, and who draws the image from mud which he rolls on his tongue. Thus, the mouth's straight line in the last verse of the image, links to the straight line towards the East, which is the human voyage in *Comment c'est.*

Who makes the voyage? Who forms the couple? Who abandons and is abandoned? As in all Beckett's French fiction, the answer is "I." This "I" is shrunk to twenty or thirty kilograms, indistinguishable from his "image," often indistinguishable from Pim, scarcely distinguishable from the mud through which he crawls. Nameless and voiceless, the "I" formulates words as compulsively as he moves towards the East, and his words are focused on his meeting with another—with Pim. It is Pim who will situate him in space and time.

At first the expectation is set up that Pim is different from "I." The constantly repeated "Before Pim, With Pim, After Pim" indicates a joining with and separation from another being. The prevision of a contact between flesh and flesh is hilarious in its abrupt physicality.

crochue pour la prise la main plonge au lieu de la fange familière une fesse sur le ventre lui aussi avant ça quoi encore ça suffit je pars (23)

(hooked for the grasp the hand plunges instead of the familiar mud a buttock on his belly he also before that what else that's enough I set out)

A few pages later, the narrator foreshadows a second meeting: "sur toi soudain une main comme sur Pim la tienne deux cris le sien muet" ("on you suddenly a hand like yours on Pim two cries his silent") (28). Virtually from the beginning, roles are interchangeable; the toucher of a buttock becomes in turn the one whose buttock is touched.

Even in Part 1, before the section that deals overtly and

explicitly with "the couple," we learn that the narrator will plunge his can opener into Pim's buttock, that Pim has a chronometer and a voice. But it is in Part 2 that the relationship between Pim and the narrator is detailed in all its comic cruelty. Making their way through the mud, hand, head, and foot of the narrator explore those of Pim, who seems to be even smaller than the narrator since he weighs twenty to thirty kilograms; Pim faces in the same direction, lies also on his belly, and either wears a wrist watch or carries a watch and chain which has announced its presence by its ticking. This creature must have been named by the narrator, and since Pim is such a fine name, the narrator indicates to Pim that he too is named Pim. Pim is momentarily confused, but the narrator is aware that at his next encounter Pim will give him the fine name of Bom. The narrator will learn his name when it is written in Roman capital letters by a fingernail across his own buttocks, precisely as he will teach Pim's name to him.

But before Pim learns to read in this fashion, he undergoes an arduous apprenticeship at the hands of the narrator. Since Pim has a voice, he is taught to speak by having the can opener plunged into his buttocks. Pim becomes a can to disgorge its contents; "c'est mécanique."

A blow on the head is the command that Pim be silent, and we may recall the blows on the head that Molloy delivered to his mother and to the charcoal-burner, that Moran dealt the dim man, that Malone's visitor used to frighten Malone, and that Malone's fiction Lemuel hammered at himself.

Pim learns other lessons besides that of silence; he learns to sing when fingernails scratch his armpit, to recite words when the can opener is plunged into his buttocks, to speak louder when the handle of the can opener strikes the small of his back; each lesson is meticulously numbered *ad infinitum* and *ad absurdum:*

cinq moins fort index dans l'anus six bravo claque à cheval sur les fesses sept mauvais même que trois huit encore même que un ou deux selon (85)

(five softer index in the anus six bravo whack on the buttocks seven bad same as three eight again same as one or two according)

As earlier fictions of Beckett's narrators teach them about love and reason, so the narrator learns by teaching Pim. Briefly recalling wife, father, and mother from the world of light, the narrator then denies that there has ever been anyone but himself: "moi on parle de moi pas Pim Pim est fini" ("me we're talking about me not Pim Pim is finished"). The intermittently evoked Krim and Kram, witness and scribe, reverse their roles, even as the narrator prepares to become the Pim of Bom or Bem. Only the maimed dog seems to contain his dualism from the start, in the double name Skom Skum. At the end of Part 2, the narrator plies Pim with his own questions, supplying the "oui's" and "non's" from the texture of his own experience.

Part 3, "the Abandonment," opens a new orgy of solitude: "cette solitude où la voix la raconte seul moyen de la vivre" ("this solitude where the voice tells it only way to live it"). Yet the narrator foresees that his solitude will be interrupted again, that he will undergo the training of Pim of Part 2. After an indefinite period, he may become the trainer again, as his trainer may become trainee. Every creature becomes, in turn, trainer and trainee, lover and loved one, a dumb and stationary executioner and a speaking, voyaging victim. The generalization of the human predicament is accomplished by an old Beckett comic device—merciless permutation, combination, and statistics, which belie the promise at the beginning of Part 2, "plus le moindre chiffre dèsormais" ("not the least little number from now on"). Similarly, although no more images were to be evoked after Part 1, the same matter continues to figure through Part 3: "le sac les bras le corps la boue le noir cheveux et ongles qui vivent tout ça" ("the sack the arms the body the mud the dark hair and nails that are living all that"). At the end, Kram and Krim dissolve into a single ear; Pim and Bem dissolve into a single "I." With verbal and numerical abandon, the narrator insists that man is abandoned.

et qu'ainsi reliés directement les uns aux autres chacun d'entre nous est en même temps Bom et Pim bourreau victime pion cancre demandeur défendeur muet et théâtre d'une parole retrouvée dans le noir la boue là rien à corriger (169)

(and that bound directly to one another each of us is at the same time Bom and Pim executioner victim schoolmaster dunce plaintiff defendant dumb and theater of a word found again in the dark the mud there nothing to correct)

Apparent opposites are only temporary aspects of a basic human substance, perpetually in the dark and the mud. "Pim Bim nom propre" ("Pim Bim proper name") are voiceless and voiced aspects of the same absurd, explosive name. (Molloy, too, confused B and P, as does Estragon in *Waiting for Godot.*)

Bim and Bom, the Russian clowns, have been haunting Beckett's work through the years from *More Pricks Than Kicks* (1935). In "Yellow," the story in which the hero dies, an unexplained Bim and Bom are grouped with Grock, the clown whose comedy depended on human failure, and with Democritus, the laughing philosopher of antiquity. In choosing to laugh at death, Beckett's first hero, Belacqua, sides with this company of comedians.[8] In *Murphy* (1938) Bim and Bom (the nicknames, respectively, of Tom and Tim Clinch) are the sadistic attendants of the Magdalen Mental Mercyseat. In the very first published version of *En Attendant Godot* (1952), the cruel and comic aspects of Bim and Bom are briefly but explicitly synthesized:

ESTRAGON.	On se croirait au spectacle.	(You'd think you were at a show.)
VLADIMIR.	Au music-hall.	(At the vaudeville.)
ESTRAGON.	Avec Bim.	(With Bim.)
VLADIMIR.	Et Bom.	(And Bom.)
ESTRAGON.	Les comiques staliniens.	(The Stalinist comedians.)

In this passage, the two friends react to the antics of Pozzo and Lucky, Beckett's most sharply delineated victim-executioner couple. But by paralleling them with Bim and Bom, Beckett levels Pozzo and Lucky, and virtually identifies them with one another as "Stalinist comedians."

Both victims and perpetrators of comic cosmic cruelty, Bim and Bom as Pim and Bom indicate the limits of "comment c'est"—victim and executioner, turn and turn about. The narrator, wallowing in slime, meeting first Pim and then Bom, perhaps creating them through his vague movements of the lower face, perhaps being each one of them in turn, finally comes to deny them both:

non jamais eu de Pim non ni de Bom non jamais eu personne non que moi pas de réponse que moi oui ça alors c'était vrai oui moi c'était vrai oui et moi je m'appelle comment pas de réponse MOI JE M'APPELLE COMMENT hurlements bon (175–176)

(no never any Pim no nor Bom no never anybody but me no answer but me yes so that was true yes me that was true yes and me my name is no answer ME MY NAME IS howls good)

Ironically, the final "bon," approval of anguished howling at namelessness, has the same sound as Bom, a name. But the human destiny is ironic, and only suffering is real. Creation and creator are conceivable, believable, only as aspects of anguish. The narrator, hearing his creation howl, utters God's judgment of his own creation: "good."

Structurally, *Comment c'est* is divided, like the Bible, into chapter and verse. The monologue of the narrator is sprinkled with casually colloquial "mon Dieu's"; the protagonist recalls praying at his mother's knee, and seeing a Bible in her hand; while crawling through the slime, he blesses or curses God. Pim believes in God (though not every day), but the narrator prays for prayer without specifying his own state of belief; in a long passage on an unnamed God occurs the phrase, "ma foi je cite toujours" ("my faith I'm still quoting"). On the other hand, the narrator frequently evokes himself on his knees, whereas this position is impossible for Pim. The narrator names Christian holidays; he is obsessed by nails in the palms of the hands; he sees traces of crosses in the mud, and leaves his arms crossed at the end of the book. The puns Pim-pain and Bom-bon have biblical resonance.

These Christian remnants rise incongruously from a crawler through primeval slime. In a verse of extraordinary comic compression, Beckett implies a contrast between his semi-amphibian hero and divine creation:

fou ou pis transformé à la Haeckel né à Potsdam où vécut également Klopstock entre autres et oeuvra quoique enterré à Altona l'ombre qu'il jette (51)

(mad or worse transformed à la Haeckel born at Potsdam where Klopstock among others also lived and worked though buried at Altona the shadow he casts)

Although Klopstock and Haeckel lived over a century apart, Beckett couples the atheist popularizer of evolution with the Romantic poet who devoted his life to writing a *Messiah.* It is Haeckel (best remembered, probably, for his capsule phrase, "Ontogeny recapitulates phylogeny") who is buried at Altona, but the ambiguity of phrasal position embraces Klopstock as well, and it is deliberately ambivalent as to which of the two men, scientist or poet, heretic or believer, is the "il" who casts his shadow over "comment c'est." The verse thus summarizes a tension between science and religion, logic and inspiration, evolution and creation, a naked worm in primeval slime and man in God's own image.

This worm-like being, the heir of Molloy who crawled like a worm, and of the Unnamable who created a fictional Worm, feeds on fish, in comic reversal of the natural order. Nibbling occasionally as he crawls, the human worm partakes mainly of sardines:

ou une boîte celeste sardines miraculeuses envoyées par Dieu à la nouvelle de mon infortune de quoi le vomir huit jours de plus (59)

(a heavenly tin miraculous sardines sent by God at the news of my misfortune so that I can vomit it for another week)

Crawling through the mud, he also eats from tins of tuna, shrimp, sprat, prawn, herring, and cod liver—all vacuum-packed and hermetically sealed in this primitive substratum.

Fish has long been a pagan fertility symbol. Since the first letters of Jesus Christ, Son of God, Saviour, spell *fish* in Greek (Ἰχθύς), fish became the symbol of Christ. In Beckett's early story, "Dante and the Lobster," there is ironic reference to this symbol: "Fish had been good enough for Jesus Christ, Son of God, Saviour. It was good enough for Mlle Glain."

The worm-like hero of *Comment c'est* nibbles at morsels of the body of Christ, taken from a vacuum-packed tabernacle, until he loses his appetite and discards his canned sustenance into the ubiquitous mud. At the end, he flings away his fictions too—Pim-pain and Bom-bon. The only Christian remainder is the compulsive journey to the East, but stars are invisible in *Comment c'est,* as in the galactic Coalsack.

As it was in the beginning, so it is in the end. The straight-line journey to the East is beset with circularity—constantly repeated phrases, gestures, and events. Life is the old, traditional, and ruthless voyage; briefly, a couple may be formed, and then the voyage continues in solitude, until there is another brief coupling, with the partners reversing their roles.

In spite of that reversal, in spite of a straight-line momentum, and although he may deny it, man keeps going round in circles, repeating a few ridiculous phrases, a few ridiculous gestures.

9

the dramatic shift to waiting

zitto! zitto! dass nur das Publikum nichts merke!
Watt

After some two decades of working in poetry and fiction, Beckett turned his hand to drama.[1] Like the fiction, his drama is concerned with man's situation in the cosmos. But given Beckett's questions about both man and cosmos, dramatic exteriorization and interaction would seem to assume the very realities he doubts. The world of the stage, shrunken and bare though it may be, is physically present before an audience, and thereby acquires metaphysical reality as well. The stage representation of phenomena, however limited, minimizes disparagement of the means of perception. Similarly, the visible concretion of *different* characters diffuses a focus on personal identity, and audible dialogue between different characters yields at least an initial illusion of communication. In turning to the theater, however, Beckett uses action to help him undermine language—an undermining that is therefore more insidious on the stage than in print.

The Paris production of *En Attendant Godot* in 1953, in a small avant-garde theater, met with unexpected success.

Since then, over a million spectators throughout the world have seen the original French production.[2] Although this extraordinary reception is scarcely proof of any widespread understanding, it bears some testimony to a breadth of appeal that cannot rest largely on mere mystification. No less a commentator than Beckett's fellow playwright, Eugène Ionesco, affirms, "C'est Beckett avec 'Fin de Partie,' 'Godot,' etc., qui est le véritable démystificateur" ("It is Beckett with *Endgame, Godot,* etc., who is the true demystifier").[3]

The spare brilliance of *Waiting for Godot* is even more remarkable when compared with the lush profusion of Beckett's unpublished play *Eleutheria.* Written in French at approximately the same time (1947 or 1948), scheduled for publication in the same year (1952), the two works are extraordinarily different.

The fierce concentration on *Godot's* four characters is dispersed over the seventeen of *Eleutheria.* The single tree and country road of *Godot* contrast with the two Parisian sets of *Eleutheria,* both in constant view of the audience. As the dialogue proceeds on one set, an action is mimed on the other. The almost eternal time of *Godot* is reduced to three successive afternoons in the three acts of *Eleutheria.* Although neither main plot nor subplots of *Eleutheria* are well made, they are scarcely more disjointed than those of the celebrated *Ubu* of Jarry, which may well have influenced them.

In the main plot, Victor, only son and heir of the Kraps, has left his family's bourgeois home for a cheap hotel room on the other side of the stage. Mme. Krap's sister, suddenly married to a Dr. Piouk, arrives from an Italian honeymoon. The absence of Victor Krap is lamented, with the father showing some sympathy for his son's deliberate withdrawal. After a disconnected dialogue between various characters, M. Krap is left alone with his valet, and he is immobile when the curtain falls.

In the second act, in Victor's hotel room, we learn that his father's immobility was that of death. Mother Krap, Aunt and Uncle Piouk, as well as friend Mme. Meck and fiancée Olga Skunk, all try in vain to lure Victor back to the family bosom, but he insists on waiting in his room. Looming larger and larger in the small room is a glazier, ostensibly there to fix a broken window.

By the third act, the glazier is running the show, governing entrances and exits, demanding that Victor mean something, listening to the advice of a Spectator who has climbed on the stage to improve the play. Dr. Piouk and Mlle. Skunk seek to tempt Victor with suicide, but after some hesitation, he refuses to succumb. Neither love, reason, nor death will seduce him from his room; waiting there is his freedom. Even the glazier finally leaves him. After gazing carefully at all parts of the audience, Victor lies down on his bed, turning his back to the public.

Most obviously comic are the names, fringing on obscenity. The young hero's family name is Krap, the heroine's Skunk. The man of letters is Henri Krap, the man of science André Piouk. Grotesque, aging women are named after flowers. Mlle. Skunk's first name, Olga, was used before by Beckett as an anagram of Logos.[4] In *Eleutheria* man of letters and man of science are both sensitive to her charms, but young Victor Krap is impervious to them. Living in complete indolence, waiting for nothing, he has perhaps achieved Victory over the Logos.

Several lines of dialogue, above all those that center on the play as a play, foreshadow Beckett's control of the dramatic medium, but the plethora of characters dulls all intensity, and much of the comic plot as well. Other than familiar Beckett themes, perhaps the only feature that *Eleutheria* shares with *Godot* is the use of vaudeville techniques in a serious drama. But in the unpublished, unproduced play, these scenes are lost among too many others. In *Waiting for*

Godot, on the other hand, they simultaneously cloak and reveal the metaphysical farce of the human condition.[5] Stale gags, shoes that pinch and stink, hats that shift from head to head—Beckett bends these worn-out techniques to his purpose.

Vaudeville comedians rather than dramatic actors played the leads in both the Paris and New York productions of *Godot.* The French playwright Jean Anouilh reviewed it felicitously as a "music-hall sketch of Pascal's *Pensées* performed by the Fratellini clowns,"[6] but perhaps a more exact description would be a "music-hall sketch of Cartesian man performed by Chaplinesque clowns."

The opening scene—a leafless tree near which a ragged man tugs at his boots, "giving up *again*" (my italics), establishes the comic ambiance before a word is spoken. The Chaplin costume prepares us for the exaggerated gestures of the silent comic: Estragon tugging at and taking off his boots; Vladimir doffing, donning, and seeking lice in his hat; the ape-stance of the two friends; their exercises; their difficulties with trousers; their imitation of the tree; their lapses from the dignified vertical; their hat-juggling routine. Moreover, the Chaplin garb suggests the hero as social victim, because Chaplin has so consistently and comically played that role. Become a symbol, Chaplin's vulnerability seems willed by fate, underwritten in the cosmic order. Relevant, too, as Jean-Jacques Mayoux points out, are Shakespeare's fools, who show how ridiculous is the conduct of their "betters."[7] In *Godot* it is we who begin as the "betters" of Vladimir and Estragon, but our "better" actions and aspirations are aped and mocked by the waiters for Godot, until we see how futile and frivolous they are.

In the tragicomedy, as in the fiction, there is an equation of plot with human situation, and the major meaning of the play lies in that equation, rather than in digressions upon God-ot.[8] The cheapest laughs are evoked by the constant repetition of the phrase "waiting for Godot," and almost every reviewer has complained that Act II merely repeats Act I. Beckett himself answered this complaint tartly, "One act would have been too little, and three would have been too much." [9]

On the surface, Act II does seem merely a comic repetition of Act I: On the same stage, two tramps, Vladimir and Estragon, make separate entrances to wait together for Godot; Pozzo and Lucky arrive together, play a comic scene, and depart together; at the approach of night, a Boy comes to announce that Godot will come not today but tomorrow. Each act closes with the words, "Yes, let's go," as the tramps remain motionless. Act I, Act II: repetition of plot, repetition of characters, static situation.

An artist of Beckett's control does not, however, simply succumb to the imitative fallacy—bore the audience in order to convince them of life's monotony. In the festering dullness of the human situation lies the first and most obvious comic level. "Boredom," Beckett wrote as early as his essay on Proust, "must be considered as the most tolerable because the most durable of human evils." In presentation, however, *Godot* conveys an almost hysterically *in*tolerable boredom, which should not obscure the comic progression, in constant tension with the surface non-action and the durable boredom of the characters. Perhaps the central focus of the comic in the tragicomedy will be more apparent if one attempts to view the drama as tragedy.

The Spanish playwright Alfonso Sastre writes the following epitaph for the two tramps: "The afternoon they died they were sad. They had come to the appointment as usual, near a tree, and they felt more alone than ever. A chilly wind was blowing, and no one came. They did not know whether it was there, but they had no other place in which to wait. They looked at each other a moment and wept sadly, with an affliction which was the summing up of their existence. They separated forever. They died—each one alone—of cold and abandonment. They cried out before dying. And then the world remained alone."[10]

Stressing the poignancy, Sastre is oblivious, in this paragraph, to Beckett's comic tone. Although it hurts Vladimir to laugh, and Estragon does not feel like laughing, they are not sad; they are bored; Pozzo and Lucky do come; Vladimir and Estragon do not separate; they do not weep. And, of course, they cannot die. They have to wait in boredom, while *we* laugh.

The seeming monotony of situation and character mocks itself. "Nothing happens," complains Estragon in Act I, even while Pozzo and Lucky are on stage, "nobody comes, nobody goes, it's awful!" In Act II, Vladimir admits, "This is becoming really insignificant." It is in the shorter Act II that the "waiting for Godot" phrase is hammered out a dozen times as opposed to three in Act I. The monotony is meant to seem cumulative and unbearable, precisely because there *are* developments in the play.

Apparently static relationships are set up in Act I: friend-friend and master-slave. The elaborate and different costumes of the one pair contrast with the Chaplinesque garb of the other, as Pozzo's chicken and bottle of wine highlight the carrots, turnips, and radishes upon which Estragon munches. The tender embraces that reunite the friends are juxtaposed against the rope and whip that bind Lucky to Pozzo. The friends' cooperative if comic efforts to pass time comment implicitly on the lack of communion between master and slave. By the end of the play, the wandering of Pozzo and Lucky is seen to be as compulsive as the waiting of Didi (Vladimir) and Gogo (Estragon).

The contrasts within each couple are most immediately obvious in Pozzo-Lucky, the indolent, garrulous master and the burdened, silent slave. The two friends, dressed alike, are nevertheless in an opposition that may be described as mental versus physical man.[11] Estragon is the first one on stage in Act

I, Vladimir in Act II, as dancing before thinking is "the natural order." Estragon's stage business bears on his boots, whereas Vladimir's is with his hat. For example, when Pozzo cracks his whip, Estragon drops his boot and Vladimir his hat. Estragon wants Lucky to dance, but Vladimir desires him to think, and it is Vladimir who triggers Lucky's thinking by placing his hat on his head. Twice Estragon mimes a scene, whereas Vladimir's tendencies are rhetorical. Estragon stinks from his feet, Vladimir from his mouth. Their very nicknames epitomize the dichotomy: Go-Go for Estragon and Di-Di (from French *dire*) for Vladimir. While Vladimir worries about their spiritual salvation, Estragon eats and sleeps on stage, and is beaten off stage. When Estragon begs for bones and alms, Vladimir berates his friend. In their stichomythic exchanges, it is Vladimir who supplies variety and Estragon the stolid repetitions. Estragon often plays straight-man to Vladimir's quips. More frequently than his friend, Estragon falls from the vertical, whereas Vladimir strides stiffly. Trapped by their common misery, Vladimir is more inventive in forcing time to pass (there are references to Vladimir's head and intelligence), but talk of suicide is initiated by Estragon. Humanitarian sentiments (pity for Lucky, and then for Pozzo), gentleness towards Godot's disappointing messenger), belong exclusively to Vladimir. It is Estragon who reiterates that life might be better if they separated, and Vladimir who insists that his friend cannot manage without him.

Although this polarity is not rigid even in Act I, it is blurred in Act II. The body-centered remarks do not all originate with Gogo, and the mind-centered ones with Didi, who claims that both of them are "in no danger of ever thinking any more." Both now engage in physical and mental exercises —equally funny in their clumsiness—to help pass the interminable wait for Godot, and Vladimir is more agile in both domains. Although Vladimir wears a different hat (Lucky's), and Estragon is bootless, both friends engage in the hat-juggling routine, and both prefer any activity to thinking. In the English text particularly, new hat business is introduced, and Estragon of Act II is "aphoristic for once." It is now Vladimir who will help Pozzo only in anticipation of some tangible reward. When Estragon hits a fallen Lucky, Vladimir shows no pity; he himself strikes a blind Pozzo, and in the French original, he also kicks Lucky. In one of the first incidents of Act I, Gogo urges Didi to button his fly, whereas in one of the last incidents of Act II, it is Didi who commands Gogo to pull up his trousers. Comic nuances result from the physical-mental contrast of Act I, but an even subtler and more pathetic humor accompanies the disintegration of the dichotomy.

The gradual diffusion of names is another comic theme in *Godot.* On the stage, Vladimir and Estragon never call each other by these names, but only Didi and Gogo. That the friends should have nicknames for each other seems natural enough, but there can be no doubt that Beckett is persistently denying the validity of subsuming man's character or identity under any name. Estragon calls himself by still another name (Catulle in the French text, and Adam in the English); in both acts, Godot's messenger addresses Vladimir as Mr. Albert; Pozzo persists in referring to Lucky as Pig, and Vladimir addresses Estragon similarly in their Act II imitation of Pozzo and Lucky; Pozzo answers to both Cain and Abel; Estragon and Vladimir engage in a name-calling duet. Above all, laughter is evoked by Estragon's mistaking Pozzo for Godot, by the assonance of Godot and Pozzo, by variants on Pozzo (Bozzo, Gozzo) and Godot (Godet, Godin).

Comically ironic, too, are the puns on those names with meaning in their respective languages: Lucky for a slave, the herb *estragon* for the solid tramp;[12] the suggestion of profundity in the use of Italian *pozzo* ("well") for the blind tyrant Pozzo.[13] Last and most obvious, the degree of divinity of the

English "God" is diminished by the French suffix, "ot," and by the suggestion, in French, of such unpleasant words as *godailler* ("to guzzle"), *godenot* ("a misshapen man"), *godichon* ("a lout")—all terms that characterize Pozzo.[14]

The assonance of Pozzo and Godot sets up an uncertainty as to whether Pozzo is Godot. The former arrives whenever the latter is expected; Pozzo is lord of the land; he says that the friends are an imperfect likeness of himself; he admits he is "not particularly human." But such suggestions are deliberately ambiguous, and should not be pushed to an equation of Pozzo and Godot.

The characters as comic types are reminiscent of the Aristotelian categories as set forth in the *Tractatus:* Alazon (boaster or imposter), Eiron (self-deprecator), and Bomolochoi (buffoon).[15] Pozzo of Act I is an Alazon, and Lucky is designated as a knook, which, as Pozzo explains in the French text, is the modern equivalent of a buffoon. Both Vladimir and Estragon, mind and body, are, at this late stage of their history, self-deprecators, and comment ironically on their status. But none of them is a mere type, a social aberration. Pozzo-Alazon is taken for Godot; he is Lucky's Godot; his boasting has metaphysical implications; his imposture is that he acts like God. Conversely, Lucky-Buffoon mocks all human achievement in his hashed monologue; he dances, he thinks, he taught Pozzo about beauty. But today the intellectual and artist is a mere buffoon. The Eirons, Vladimir and Estragon, still punctuating their transcendent waiting with pitiful play, deprecate us in deprecating themselves, for their activities mimic ours. They know the futility of their actions, and through them we become acutely aware of the futility of ours.

In the domain of comic of language, Beckett exhibits little of the more obvious virtuosity of the earlier English fiction; instead, there is an insidious undermining of language as means of communication or expression of intelligence.[16] Flat and literal repetition becomes a major comic technique.[17] Dominating all repetitions are the "waiting for Godot's." Other refrains have wider ironic implications than in their specific context—"Nothing to be done," "I'm going," "It's not certain," "It hurts?" "It's inevitable," "What'll we do now?" The very theme of repetitive monotony is symbolized by the ballad that Vladimir sings to open Act II. (A dog came in the kitchen and stole a crust of bread, whereupon he was beaten to death by the cook, then buried by the other dogs, who wrote on his tombstone, "A dog came in the kitchen," etc.[18]

Cosmic cruelty is implicit in the ballad. Similarly, after Lucky's tour de force monologue of Act I, when his audience throw themselves upon him to shut him up, the slapstick cruelty reflects that of the cosmos. The three-page, one-sentence tirade, nonsensical but not pointless, is a labyrinth of repetitive passages that summarize or parody several of the play's themes: the erosive effect of time, the relativity of facts, the futility of human activity, faith in God, proof through reason. "For reasons unknown" is opposed to "beyond all doubt"; "but time will tell" to "not so fast"; "in the light of the labors unfinished" to "in spite of the strides." A sentence can (with some difficulty) be discerned behind the cunningly combined parenthetical repetitions: "Given the existence . . . of a personal God . . . who . . . loves us dearly . . . and suffers . . . with those who . . . are plunged in torment . . . it is established beyond all doubt . . . that man . . . wastes and pines wastes and pines . . . the skull fading fading fading." These extracts, however, tend to isolate the pathos, whereas the diatribe is dazzling in its broken-record effect—the comic repetition of apparent nonsense.

In the technique of stichomythia, wherein antithesis and repetition are voiced by different characters, the comic quality depends equally upon dullness and distinction, the static and moving. Thus the dead voices are compared by Vladimir to wings and sand, by Estragon to leaves and leaves; then, after a digression, Vladimir compares them to feathers and ashes, and Estragon again to leaves and leaves. But this same Estragon does not notice that the bare stage tree of Act I has acquired a few leaves in Act II. Ironically, nature flourishes (as much as Beckett's nature can flourish) while man's situation grows increasingly hopeless.

In Act I the friends explain to each other that Godot would see about coming, would think it over, in the quiet of his home, after consulting his family,[19] his friends, his agents,[20] his correspondents, his books, and, most ironically, his bank account. Variously as Vladimir describes their activities during the wait for Godot, Estragon stubbornly repeats, "Our relaxations." And yet, from the first mention of Godot in Act I, Estragon reacts with a despairing, "Ah."[21]

Although stichomythia is reserved for the two friends, there are question and answer intervals between all the speaking characters. Estragon and Vladimir frequently introduce irony into their comments. Estragon's "I find this really most extraordinarily interesting," and "Some diversion!" and Vladimir's "How time flies when one has fun" and "This is becoming really insignificant" are detached from the action, as though Vladimir and Estragon are themselves spectators at the play. But there are even more explicit reminders that the play is a play. Estragon directs Vladimir to an unnamed Men's Room, "End of corridor, on the left," and Vladimir requests, "Keep my seat." There are of course neither seats nor corridors on stage. Vladimir cries to Estragon when he seeks to escape backstage, "Imbecile! There's no way out there." Estragon characterizes the French audience, "Aspects riants." The blind Pozzo of Act II wants to know if he is on the Board. Estragon calls Vladimir, "Crritic!"

Beckett intends both audience and actors to be aware that the play is a play. Influenced, perhaps, by Brecht's *Verfremdungseffekt,* Beckett suggested that actors in *Godot* employ the trick of "contrapuntal immobility"; lines like "I'm going" were to be accompanied by "complete stillness on the part of the speaker." [22] As Günther Anders has noted, Gogo and Didi engage in play and know they are playing, but we take similar activities seriously; "Damit sind die zwei die Ernsthaften geworden, und *wir* die Farcenspieler." [23] In the French version of *Godot*, Pozzo explains that a knook is a buffoon; traditionally, the buffoon had the ambiguous, ironic role of "break[ing] down the distinction both between folly and wisdom, and between life and art." [24]

It is mainly the two friends who wield irony, but Pozzo is not incapable of it. He describes Lucky as Atlas, himself as a liar, the world as a closed system of emotions; he urges Estragon to hurry and wipe Lucky's eyes, before he stops crying; in his declamations of Act I his exaggerated diction and involved syntax parody man as Epicurean, hypochondriac, reasoner, lyrical and prosaic declaimer. All the characters need an audience—Vladimir for the story of the two thieves, Estragon for his dreams, and even Lucky for his thoughts—but Pozzo's need is the most pressing; his very existence seems to depend upon his performance. Pozzo alone obtains an audience on stage, for any length of time.

In the fifth text of the *Textes pour rien*, the question is asked, "Pozzo pourquoi est-il parti de chez lui, il avait un château et des serviteurs" ("Why did Pozzo leave home? He had a castle and servants"). Perhaps Pozzo is comparable to Moran, who leaves his bourgeois comforts to perform an artistic function.

By Act II of *Godot*, Pozzo is bereft of castle and all servants but Lucky. Most striking, after an Act I stage business with spectacles, Pozzo is blind, just as Lucky is dumb after the uncontrolled outburst of Act I. The ethical comment is evident: a master-slave relationship blinds the master and mutes the slave.

By Act II, Pozzo has lost tangible items as well as his sight

—his pipe (with which he parodied the hypochondriac), his atomizer (with which he sprayed his throat before declaiming), and his watch (for which his heart is disgustedly mistaken). When Pozzo's comments are reduced to the violent and pragmatic, it is Vladimir of Act II who assumes some of his parodic attitudes (discussing anything and everything before coming to Pozzo's help), who echoes his phrases ("No doubt"), and who inherits his interest in time (although Pozzo of Act II inveighs hysterically against Vladimir's "When's"). In a memorable sentence that describes cosmic irony, Vladimir virtually repeats Pozzo's words: "Astride of a grave and a difficult birth. Down in the hole, lingeringly, the gravedigger puts on the forceps." Birth and death seem to be separated by a mere instant, except to those who have to live through that instant as an interminable wait for Godot.

Beckett deliberately emphasizes the duration of the waiting, in contrast to and at the expense of the action. But there *is* action, and, like much of the dialogue, it depends for its comic effect upon incongruity and absurdity. Thus, it is not Lucky's job to carry, but we see him doing little else. Estragon, less verbal than Vladimir, was once a poet, whose medium is words. Vladimir cannot laugh, and urinates torrentially. Estragon helps Vladimir only when the latter stops requesting it, and both aid Pozzo for lack of anything else to do. In Act II the friends help Pozzo to his feet, as they did Lucky in Act I. Master and slave, hat and shoe, carrot and turnip, rope and tree, goat and sheep, and above all pagan and Christian reference seem to be absurdly irrelevant to one another in the cosmos created on stage.

On the basis of Vladimir's pondering upon the thief who was saved (according to the Gospel of St. Luke), and Estragon's comparison of himself to Christ, several critics have read Christian hope into *Waiting for Godot.*[25] But Christ and thief have long been treated ironically by Beckett. In *Murphy* the puppet Neary ironically urges the other puppets to take heart, since one thief was saved; Mercier and Camier in Beckett's unpublished French novel compare themselves to the two thieves without Christ; in the French text of *Molloy* A and C are referred to as "mes deux larrons"; in *Malone Dies* Moll's crucifix earrings stand for the two thieves, and her single, cruciform yellow tooth, for Christ. Even the rationalist Watt articulates proper names "such as Knott, Christ, Gomorrha, Cork with great deliberation"; Molloy describes his misery as a mock Calvary; an Easter Chorus suggests to Malone the one "who saved me twenty centuries in advance"; the narrative of the Unnamable is punctuated with blasphemy.

In *Waiting for Godot,* as in the other works, the biblical echoes are mocking echoes, probably because Christianity (like love, another major Beckett target) seemed to promise so much to man. Vladimir thinks of the thief who was saved, only after he declares man's foot is at fault (in French, "coupable"). Of the Gospels, Estragon remembers only the map of the Holy Land, where the blue of the Dead Sea awakens his thirst. Frightened by noises he assigns to Godot, Estragon dimly echoes a verse from St. Matthew: "The wind in the reeds." Vladimir quotes with comic incompleteness from Proverbs: "Hope deferred maketh the something sick." Vladimir calls Lucky an "old and faithful servant," then accuses him of crucifying Pozzo, who, in turn, calls Lucky his "good angel"; Pozzo laughs to see that Estragon and Vladimir are of the same species as himself, "Made in God's image!" If the friends repent, it is not of sin, but of being born. Estragon's comparison of himself to Christ culminates in a bitter contrast, "And they crucified quick." Vladimir's "Christ have mercy on us" punctuates the information that Godot's beard is neither fair nor black, but white. The final promise of salvation *if* Godot comes is comically undercut by the dialogue about Estragon's fallen trousers.

Greek deities also find their way into *Godot,* since Pozzo

refers to Atlas and Pan. Estragon, tired of supporting Pozzo, informs the blind tyrant that he and his friend are not caryatids. Thus, true to Beckett's habit, he mocks the whole classico-Christian tradition in *Godot.*

Again true to his habit, Beckett evokes explosive as well as subtle laughter. Copious urination, possible lice, and obscenities provide a comic shock effect. As in the fiction, details of cruelty, comically conveyed, delineate man's metaphysical situation. Early in the play, man's position is succinctly summarized. While waiting for Godot, Estragon asks, "Where do we come in?" "Come in?" Vladimir snorts, "On our hands and knees." In each act, Estragon enters after "they" have beaten him; occasionally, he speaks of his unhappiness. The two friends sporadically entertain the idea of suicide. Estragon mentions that Vladimir has killed "the other" and "billions of others." Pozzo treats Lucky brutally; he finds it a "good sign" when Estragon's leg bleeds after he has been assaulted by Lucky. Estragon does not hesitate to seize an opportunity for revenge. The two friends impersonally discuss the possibility of Lucky's being dead. Lucky's heavy burden is revealed to be sand. In Act II when Estragon pleads for God to pity him, Pozzo arrives, seeking help and pity for himself. At the end, the two friends wistfully renounce their hope of hanging themselves, for the only cord they have, Estragon's belt—similar in length to the cord that binds a dumb Lucky to a blind Pozzo—binds Vladimir to Estragon to this life and the absurd, compulsive wait for Godot.[26]

It is not surprising that most people who came to know Beckett by way of *Waiting for Godot* compared him to Kafka, since both are impressive creators of a cruel cosmological comedy, revealing man's awkward situation in an absurd universe. For those who examine the play in the context of Beckett's other works, there are also hints of the more epistemological comedy of the fiction. The hat remains a symbol of knowledge, and the identical bowlers worn by the four characters suggest that they all belong in the same play, in the same comic context. It is significant, too, that Vladimir, the mental bum, harps on his hat, and that Lucky cannot think without his hat on his head. On the other hand, Lucky's hat on Estragon's head, or even Vladimir's, does not produce the same flow of discourse.

In the process of self-discovery through narration (of dreams, parables, jokes, or parodies) each monologuist needs an audience. In the stichomythic dialogue of the two friends, there is a subtle transfer from their inexhaustible "we" to "dead voices" who talk about "their" lives, because merely to have lived is not enough, and to be dead is not enough. "They" are compelled to speech, to pass the endless wait for Godot in discourse, in words of indeterminate origin, shifting significance, and dubious communicability.

If language is the primary level of doubt, close upon it follows doubt of events, and of their coordinates in time and space. Implicitly mocking Descartes, the friends exist because they wait, whereas their pervasive doubt includes a doubt of their very existence. Whistling in the dark, Estragon asks pathetically, "We always find something, eh Didi, to give us the impression we exist?" But the impression is fleeting, as doubt insinuates itself again.

Specific doubt begins with conversation about the scheduled rendezvous with Godot: "He said by the tree. Do you see any others?" Vladimir worries, "What are you insinuating? That we've come to the wrong place?" A moment later, "You recognize the place?" But Estragon bridles, "I didn't say that." Places are not meant to be recognized; the friends are "not from these parts." References to Ireland and France (sometimes to nonexistent places that merely sound as though they are in these countries) give a veneer of locality, but the references to the Board and the physical confines of the theater cast doubt on larger spaces.

Even more pointedly, time is called into question. Vladimir attempts to schedule their appointment with Godot: "He said Saturday. (*Pause.*) I think." But Estragon gnaws at the date, "But what Saturday? And is it Saturday? Is it not rather Sunday? (*Pause.*) Or Monday? (*Pause.*) Or Friday?" Vladimir looks *"wildly about him as though the date was inscribed in the landscape."* By Act II Vladimir can scarcely tell the morning from the evening. In the play, time is mentioned in conventional units (hours, days, seasons, years), and the very plethora of units serves to belittle and abstract it, as does the hysterical insistence on past, present, and future in *Comment c'est.* Like Pozzo's watch, time is almost perceptible, then lost from perceptibility, and even mistaken for Pozzo's heart. In Lucky's speech, God is "outside time, without extension."

Doubt of time and space leads to doubt of human memory. At the beginning of Act I, the fallibility of witness is implied, since only one of the four Evangelists reports that a thief was saved. A little later, it is Vladimir who cannot remember that the friends have already waited for Godot by this tree; it is Estragon who comments, "Off we go *again*" (my italics), when Godot's Boy arrives. In Act II, it is first Estragon's memory that is deficient, but this is followed by a similar defection on Pozzo's part. By the end of Act II it is Vladimir who comments, "Off we go again," when Godot's Boy arrives again; Estragon, asleep, does not even see him. Vladimir supposes that someone watches him as he watches Estragon, equally sure he is asleep and oblivious to what is happening.

The comedy of failing memories sets up an expectation that the Boy will not recollect appearing before, seeing Pozzo and Lucky before, meeting Vladimir and Estragon before. More certainly now, Godot will not come, and yet the tragicomedy lacks absolute certainty; for doubt exists to the degree that word, thing, and event have been undermined. In *Waiting for Godot,* Beckett contrives to approach the classical unities, only to leave us more aware of the monotonous infinitude of time, the repetitive indeterminacy of place, and the absurd discontinuity of action.

Waiting for Godot, written while Beckett was at work on the trilogy of novels, was called by him (in translation) a "tragicomedy." One cannot be sure what Beckett means by the word, but it seems likely that the New English Dictionary definition of "a play mainly of tragic character but with a happy ending" was less his intention than Sir Philip Sidney's "mungrell Tragy-comedie" as described in his *Defense of Poesie.*[27] Sidney decried the Elizabethan plays which were, in his classical view, "neither right Tragedies, nor right Comedies mingling Kings and Clownes, not because the matter so carrieth it, but thrust in Clownes by head and shoulders to play a part in majesticall matters, with neither decencie nor discretion."

"Majesticall matters" are dim and undependable memories to Beckett's bums. In Godot's continued absence, man becomes a king of shreds and patches, of blindness and dumbness, fit only to play the clown and feed the worms, "with neither decencie nor discretion." Fallen too low to be a subject for "right Tragedy," feeling too much anguish to be capable of "right Comedy," Beckett's man, while waiting for Godot, plays a part in a tragicomedy—a slapstick part of victim in a world that he did not make, and that resists his efforts to make sense of it.

10

Endgame

Or pondering Christ's
parthian shaft:
It is finished.
Murphy

When he translated *Fin de Partie* into *Endgame,* Beckett classified it as a "play."[1] Johan Huizinga defines play as "an activity which proceeds within certain limits of time and space, in a visible order, according to rules freely accepted, and outside the sphere of necessity or material utility."[2] In *Godot,* the tramps invent games to play while they wait for Godot to come. In *Endgame* there is no longer a hope that anyone may come; games are at an end, and nobody feels like playing. Yet the show goes on.

In *Endgame* the physical situation on stage is instantly grimmer than that of *Godot.* From the country road suggesting far-off space, and the tree connoting growth, we move to a dim room whose two high, tiny windows, facing earth and sea, respectively, are curtained; the lone picture has its face to the wall. Egress from the room is possible only to Clov—and not to Hamm in his armchair on castors, not to Nagg and Nell in their respective ash bins. Much of the comic stage business revolves around this circumscribed physical situation: Clov covers and uncovers the ash bin dwellers, and they themselves pop into sight and disappear. Clov climbs on a ladder to see out of the two windows; he wheels Hamm around the room and returns him to place; Hamm insists upon being first "right in" and then "more or less in" the center.

The plot of *Endgame,* like that of *Godot,* can be more easily summarized than can Beckett's later fiction. But relationships are ambiguous, and interpretation complex. Nagg and Nell are Hamm's parents, but Clov is variously called his son, menial, creature, and dog. An offstage Mother Pegg is never revealed as the mother of anybody, and like the rest of the off-stage world, she is presumably dead when the play begins. After Clov sights a small boy on the beach, he prepares to leave Hamm. The small boy, however, does not appear on scene, and Hamm, covering his face with the bloody handkerchief of the opening tableau, seems resigned to the death that has already overtaken—perhaps at his instigation—the remaining world.

The plot is nakedly built on cruelty, suffering, and death. Beckett himself describes *Endgame:* "Rather difficult and elliptic, mostly depending on the power of the text to claw, more inhuman than Godot." [3] One analysis of *Endgame* reads it as a tragedy, but a tragedy that vacillates between terror and farce.[4] In *Godot,* Vladimir complains that it hurts to laugh, but in *Endgame* Hamm and Clov reiterate that they no longer feel like laughing. Nevertheless, Clov's five brief laughs are the first sounds in *Endgame,* and the play may be interpreted as a bitterly ironic version of creation and resurrection, making incidental use of comic devices, above all repetition.

"It is finished"—the last words of Christ on the Cross, according to the Gospel of St. John—are echoed in the first words of the English version of *Endgame*—Clov's "Finished, it's finished, nearly finished, it must be nearly finished." In

Hamm's first speech, he twice declares. "It's time it ended." Shortly afterwards, when Clov wishes to withdraw from Hamm to look at his kitchen wall, Hamm sneers, "The wall! And what do you see on your wall? Mene, mene." The prophet Daniel translated *Mene* as "God hath numbered thy kingdom, and finished it" (5:26).

After Hamm's father, Nagg, tells a joke in which a pair of tailor-made trousers is exalted above God's created world, Hamm cries out, "Have you not finished? Will you never finish? Will this never finish?" Midway through the play, in one of the many duets between Hamm and Clov, Hamm pleads, "Why don't you finish us? (*Pause.*) I'll tell you the combination of the cupboard if you promise to finish me." Clov replies, "I couldn't finish you." Hamm shrugs, "Then you won't finish me." Several times, Clov repeats that the toy dog he is creating for Hamm "isn't finished." Just before Hamm embarks on his own artistic creation, he almost echoes Clov's opening phrases, "It's finished, we're finished. (*Pause.*) Nearly finished."

As the comic and intolerable emphasis on waiting summarizes the major action of *Godot,* so the many "finished's" point to the death of a world in *Endgame.* "Outside of here it's death," warns Hamm, and in the play we watch death's relentless invasion of "here." The verbal music of *Endgame* has a dying fall; the constant repetition yields macabre mirth.

There are, successively, incongruously, repetitively, "no more" bicycle wheels, pap, nature, sugarplums, tides, rugs, pain-killer, and, finally, coffins. Clov kills a flea on stage and seeks to kill a rat off stage. Nell dies on stage, Nagg no longer answers from his ash bin, Hamm and Clov both remain "*motionless*" at the final curtain. The dramatic action presents the death of the stock props of Western civilization—family cohesion, filial devotion, parental and connubial love, faith in God, empirical knowledge, and artistic creation.

With characteristic irony, Beckett accents the cruel inhumanity of *Endgame* by frequent evocation of the Bible in the light of its delineation of man's role, particularly with respect to the superhuman. Thus, Hamm, son of Nagg, instantly recalls Ham, son of Noah. Nagg, like Noah, has fathered the remnant of humanity, but rather than make a covenant with God, he tells a joke at God's expense. Biblical Noah faithfully follows God's command to perpetuate all species by thriftily introducing couples into the ark; but Beckett's Nagg is indifferent to, or unaware of, the universal death outside the shelter.

Although Noah's animals are absent from *Endgame,* the play abounds in animal associations: Hamm is an edible part of pig, and Clov either its spice accompaniment, or perhaps a reference to the cloven-hoofed animals which, pigs excepted, were the only permissible meat for biblical Jews. A nag is a small horse, and Nell a common name for a horse; Nagg-nag and Nell-knell are puns as well. Hamm refers to Clov as his dog, and Clov makes a toy dog for Hamm. Clov feeds Nagg Spratt's medium animal biscuits. An off-stage rat and an on-stage flea are objects of Clov's murderous intent, for rather than propagate all species, Nagg's progeny, Hamm and (perhaps) Clov, seek to extinguish them. The flea in Clov's trousers is fiercely and farcically destroyed lest a new evolutionary line lead to humanity again. Even a punning sex joke is made to serve the theme of universal destruction. After applying insecticide freely, with exaggerated, slapstick gestures, Clov adjusts his trousers. He has killed the flea "unless he's laying doggo."

HAMM. Laying! Lying, you mean. Unless he's *lying* doggo.
CLOV. Ah? One says lying? One doesn't say laying?
HAMM. Use your head, can't you. If he was laying we'd be bitched. (34)

In Genesis, "Ham, the father of Canaan, saw the nakedness of his father, and told his two brethren without" (9:22). Beckett's Hamm, by ironic contrast, has no brethren and cannot see; his Canaan is circumscribed to the "bare interior" of the room on the stage, and his father is relegated to an ash bin in that room. Biblical Noah curses his son for seeing him naked, and Beckett's Hamm curses his father for conceiving him. The biblical curse of Noah to Ham is: "a servant of servants shall he be unto his brethren" (9:25). Nagg also curses his son, but not with a prophecy of servitude, for Hamm is master of his domain, which is reduced to the stage room.

Hamm refers to his kingdom—an ironic name for the room before our eyes. In production, his armchair looks like a mock-throne, his toque like a mock-crown. He utters high-handed orders to Clov, a servant who is intermittently good and faithful. Both Hamm and Clov suggest that the world off stage perished by Hamm's will. Even more cruel than Hamm's own lust for destruction is that of the "I" of Hamm's story, which, like the play proper, is full of biblical reminders.

Hamm sets his chronicle on Christmas Eve, that time of birth rather than death, of peace on earth, and good will towards men. But Hamm, ironically, fills the narrator-protagonist of his tale with ill will in a desolate world, which Hamm describes in terms of numbers on thermometer, heliometer, anemometer, and hygrometer. Just as Hamm is lord of a lifeless earth, and sole custodian of its dwindling supplies, so Hamm's narrator-hero rules a similar domain. The father of a starving child crawls before him, begging for food. With charity towards none, but cruelly recalling a divine charity towards a people in exile, Hamm's "I" screams at the groveling father, "But what in God's name do you imagine? . . . That there's manna in heaven still for imbeciles like you?"

Similarly, the blindness, darkness, suffering, and above all death that fill *Endgame* comment ironically on a biblical context. The most frequently repeated line of the play is Hamm's

"Is it not time for my pain-killer?" Although Hamm is literally asking Clov for a pill, it becomes increasingly evident that the only true pain-killer is death. When Clov asks Hamm whether he believes in the life to come, the sardonic answer is, "Mine was always that." The ring of the alarm clock is "Fit to wake the dead!"

On two separate occasions, Hamm cries out in anguish, "Father, Father!" and, as Jean-Jacques Mayoux has suggested, "How can we not think of the 'Eli Eli' of that other supreme moment?"[5] Towards the end of the play, Hamm utters several phrases which derisively twist Scripture: "Get out of here and love one another! Lick your neighbor as yourself! . . . The end is in the beginning. . . . Good. . . . Good. . . . Peace to our–arses." In the French text Hamm compares the small boy outside the shelter to a dying Moses gazing at the Promised Land.

Since *Endgame* is unmistakably a play about an end of a world, there are many recollections of the Book of Revelations. In the vision of St. John the Divine, Christ says he has "the keys of hell and of death," in ironic contrast to Hamm, who knows the combination of a cupboard that presumably contains the wherewithal to keep them *alive* in their hell in the shelter.

Revelations is full of phrases about light and darkness, sea and earth, beginning and end, life and death. After the destruction of Babylon, a great voice from heaven utters the words, "It is done." In the New Jerusalem, "The length and the breadth and the height of it are equal," even as the length, breadth, and height of Clov's kitchen, whose thousand cubic feet might be a caricature reminder of the millennium of Revelations.

Within the tight text of *Endgame*, the frequency and mockery of the biblical echoes cannot be ignored in any interpretation of the play, and the fourth Gospel is crucial for such interpretation. Not only does the English *Endgame* contain the fugal variations upon Christ's last words, "It is finished," but in this gospel particularly, Christ affirms that He is the light; He speaks of "my Father" and "my Father's house." Beckett's Hamm has dispensed and extinguished light; he calls upon his father and insists that his house is the only asylum.

St. John tells the story of Lazarus, resurrected by Christ, and we learn both from that account and the Passion that in biblical times corpses were wrapped in linen clothes, a napkin around the head, and anointed with oil and spices. In *Endgame,* Clov may be a spice anointing corpses; it is he who lifts the sheets from near-corpses, but it is Hamm who focuses attention on the napkin that covers his head when the play opens and closes—even as a napkin covered the head of Lazarus and of Christ.

In the productions of *Endgame,* Clov opens the play by drawing the curtains at the two windows, and removing the sheets from the ash bins and Hamm's armchair. These gestures are performed like a ritual, or a mock-ritual. Hamm's first gestures, too, are formal—his slow lifting of the bloodstained handkerchief from his face; his meticulous wiping of eyes, face, and the dark glasses that hide his sightless eyes; his methodical folding of the handkerchief before placing it elegantly in the breast pocket of his dressing gown. Just before the final curtain, Hamm removes the handkerchief from the breast pocket over his heart, and it is seen to be stained with blood so as to suggest human features. He finally covers his head, where he previously heard his heart dripping.

Only in St. John's Gospel does doubting Thomas say, after the crucifixion: "Except I shall see in his hands the print of the nails, and put my finger into the print of the nails, and thrust my hand into his side, I will not believe." Jesus then appears to Thomas, who then believes, and Jesus admonishes: "Thomas, because thou hast seen me, thou hast believed: blessed are they that have not seen, and yet have believed."

In *Endgame,* there are apparently no believers—neither those who see (however dimly) nor blind Hamm. The onstage prayer, which Beckett refused to change upon request of the London censor, goes unanswered. The nails leave no print, or their print is perhaps no longer evidence for belief. Several critics have pointed out that Clov is *clou* is "*nail*," that Nell and Nagg derive from Germanic *naegel,* meaning "nail."[6] To these might be added the offstage Mother Pegg, for a "peg" is also a nail. Latin *hamus* is hook, a kind of crooked nail, so that Hamm may be viewed as another nail. In this sense, every proper name in *Endgame* is a nail, and "nailhood" seems sardonically to symbolize humanity, whose role is to nail Christ to the Cross. All the characters are thus instruments working towards the play's paradoxical opening word, "Finished."

But Hamm is also contained in "hammer," which strikes at nails, and is thus an even more active agent in the crucifying. If Hamm is a Christ figure, he is also a crucifier.

Hamm as biblical *Ham,* as Latin *hamus,* as contained in "hammer," indicates a revival of Beckett's early taste for puns.[7] The twisted quotation of *Murphy,* "In the beginning was the pun," parodies the opening sentence of the Gospel of St. John: "In the beginning was the Word, and the Word was with God, and the Word was God."

In *Endgame,* words serve to form not only puns but jokes, prayers, proverbs, prophecies, maledictions, chronicles, poems, and, of course, the dialogue of the play. (Joyce called words "quashed quotatoes, messes of mottage.") Clov accuses Hamm, the wielder of words, "I use the words you taught me. If they don't mean anything any more, teach me others." Near the end, Clov complains, "They [the words that remain] have nothing to say."

For all their combination into various minor genres, there

is an astonishing stinginess in the number of words Beckett allows himself in *Endgame*. Again and again, we find the same words repeated, the same words issuing from different mouths. In spite of his extraordinary vocabulary and impressive command of several languages, Beckett deliberately limits the words of *Endgame,* charging each word with an enormous burden.

"Why this farce day after day?" ask both Nell and Clov. Both exclaim nostalgically, "Once!" Nell is still able to sigh lyrically (twice), "Ah yesterday," but Clov defines yesterday as "that bloody awful day, long ago, before this bloody awful day." Time and weather are both "the same as usual." Hamm, obsessed with himself, still continues to question Clov, "How are your eyes? How are your legs?" and Nagg, "How are your stumps?" "The bastard!" exclaims Clov about his flea, and Hamm about God. Several times, Clov repeats to Hamm, and Nell to Nagg, "I'll leave you." Several times, Clov repeats to Hamm, "Something is taking its course," and Hamm retorts at last, "I'm taking my course." Even scenic directions are constantly repeated; in French *"même jeu"* virtually summarizes the action of the play. Many statements are repeated, prefaced by a "then" of resignation. Whole dialogues are built comically around a few words, as in the following example:

CLOV. So you all want me to leave you.
HAMM. Naturally.
CLOV. Then I'll leave you.
HAMM. You can't leave us.
CLOV. Then I won't leave you. (*Pause.*)
HAMM. Why don't you finish us? (*Pause.*) I'll tell you the combination of the cupboard if you promise to finish me.
CLOV. I couldn't finish you.
HAMM. Then you won't finish me.
CLOV. I'll leave you, I have things to do. (37)

In no other drama is the quantity of words so drastically reduced, mocking St. John's Words that are both with God, and God. Nevertheless, St. John's opening sentence states Beckett's fundamental and recurrent theme, and nowhere so ironically and yet so desperately as in *Endgame*. The seemingly disparate elements of the play—the end of a world, biblical fathers and sons, masters and servants, ritual and crucifixion, word and Word—do finally cohere. But the line of coherence will be more apparent if it is traced through several earlier Beckett works.

On the occasion of Joyce's fiftieth birthday, in 1934, Beckett published an acrostic poem of homage to the older Irish writer. The title "Home Olga," is a pun on *Homo Logos*, Word-Man.

J might be made sit up for a jade of hope (and exile, don't you know)
A nd Jesus and Jesuits juggernauted in the haemorrhoidal isle,
M odo et forma anal maiden giggling to death in stomacho.
E for the erythrite of love and silence and the sweet noo style,
S woops and loops of love and silence in the eye of the sun and view of the mew,

J uvante Jah and a Jain or two and the tip of a friendly yiddophile.
O for an opal of faith and cunning winking adieu, adieu, adieu;
Y esterday shall be tomorrow, riddle me that my rapparee;
C he sarà sarà che fu, that's more than Homer knows how to spew,
E xempli gratia: ecce himself and the pickthank agnus—e.o.o.e.[8]

In the last lines, Christ and Joyce are coupled, if not confused, as examples of word-men, by whom "yesterday shall be tomorrow." The implication is of a Viconian, cyclical resurrection, presumably through the Logos that tells tales (pickthank). Joyce himself viewed reality as a paradigm, and he conceived the function of the artist-maker as an obligation to recognize coincidences in time, space, and significance—a coincidence frequently compressed in the pun.

In his unpublished play, *Eleutheria,* Beckett puns on Olga and Logos. The vaguely authorial hero, Victor Krap, is engaged to the beautiful Olga Skunk. At the end of the play, hero and heroine do not marry, and, as might be expected in a Beckett work, they probably live *un*happily ever after. Beckett can see no Victor-y in the Logos, and the two characters go their respective crappy and stinking ways.

In French, Logos is usually translated by *Verbe,* not by *parole* or *mot.* In the tight prose of *L'Innommable,* the last volume of his trilogy, Beckett slips a *verbe* of biblical resonance among his torrents of *mots* into his indictment of *la parole:* "je suis tous ces mots, tous ces étrangers, cette poussière de verbe." In the second *Texte pour rien,* Beckett puns, "Les mots aussi, lents, lents, le sujet meurt avant d'atteindre le verbe, les mots s'arrêtent aussi." Literally, the subject dies before reaching the verb, but more significantly, all subjects die before being embodied in the Word.

No puns on *Verbe* or Logos appear in *Endgame,* but in the opening chapter of the Gospel of St. John, it is also written that "the Word was made flesh," and the grossest, most palpable flesh is the mammalian ham. Hamm of *Endgame* is the word made flesh, while still retaining his control over the word. Like Christ, like Joyce, Hamm is a Word-Man.

By name and dialogue, Hamm is further linked to another word-man, Shakespeare, who is described by Coleridge in almost Beckettian terms—"the great ever living dead man." Hamm, as most critics have noted, is a ham-actor, and contains at least that aspect of Hamlet. Hamm has also been compared to Prospero, and in the English text of *Endgame,* Beckett makes the parallel explicit. When Hamm has told his father his story, and betrayed his promise of a sugarplum, when Nagg, no longer able to rouse Nell, retires into his own ash bin, Hamm summarizes his situation in French, "Finie la rigolade." But the slang is not translated into English; Beckett renders the line as, "Our revels now are ended."

The words, of course, are Prospero's from Act IV of *The Tempest,* and they are surely introduced to underline the striking parallels and ironic contrasts between the two plays. Prospero's entire speech is apposite:

Our revels now are ended. These our actors,
As I foretold you, were all spirits and
Are melted into air, into thin air;
And, like the baseless fabric of this vision,
The cloud-capp'd towers, the gorgeous palaces,
The solemn temples, the great globe itself,
Yea, all which it inherit, shall dissolve,
And, like this insubstantial pageant faded,
Leave not a rack behind. We are such stuff
As dreams are made on, and our little life
Is rounded with a sleep.

Shakespeare's towers, palaces, and temples are absent from the "bare interior" of Beckett's stage, which may literally represent that container of dreams (or nightmares)—the human skull.[9] If so, each window is an eye, Shakespeare's "great globe" appearing grayly through the one, and his "multitudinous seas" as grayly through the other. All who inherit or inhabit the globe are reduced to four in *Endgame,* two in their nightcaps in ash bins, one immobilized in his dressing gown, and the fourth shrunken and unable to sit. The sleep that rounds their little life is deepened to the death that pervades the atmosphere of *Endgame* from its opening lines.

By Act V of *The Tempest,* Shakespeare returns to comedy, where, by Renaissance decorum, death has no dominion. Prospero breaks his staff, drowns his book, rewards the innocent, and pardons the guilty. While waiting for him, Ferdinand and Miranda are shown playing *chess.*

In both French and English, *Fin de Partie* and *Endgame* refer to the third and final phase of a chess game.[10] Chess is, of course, a game, a form of play, as is a work of art. Hamm's opening line, "Me to play," is emphasized by the wrenching of normal English word order (in French by the desperation of "à moi"). Like Hamlet, Hamm is responsible for a play within the play—his chronicle. But even in the direct action of *Endgame,* there are constant comic references to the play as a play.

Near the beginning, Hamm comments, "The thing is impossible." Somewhat later, "This is slow work." Several times, he encourages himself, "We're getting on." After a while, "This is not much fun." Hamm's "This is deadly," spoken while Clov is offstage, is the cue for Clov's ironic comment on the action, "Things are livening up. (*He gets up on ladder, raises the telescope, lets it fall.*) I did it on purpose. (*He gets down, picks up the telescope, turns it on auditorium.*) I see . . . a multitude . . . in transports . . . of joy. (*Pause.*) That's what I call a magnifier" (29).

As the end approaches, the references to the play as a play are more numerous and pointed. When Hamm declares that Clov can't leave him, Clov asks, "What is there to keep me here?" Hamm retorts, "The dialogue." A little later, Hamm reiterates, "Me to play," holds his handkerchief before him, repeats, "We're getting on," and folds the handkerchief back in his pocket.

Close to the end, Clov implores Hamm to stop playing, but he replies, "Never!" Hamm informs Clov angrily that he is uttering an "aside," then that he is "warming up for [his] last soliloquy." When the small boy is sighted through the window, Hamm hopes that it is "not an underplot." Abandoned by Clov—"This is what we call making an exit"—Hamm utters his final "Me to play," and reveals that from the beginning he was destined to lose, "Old endgame lost of old, play and lose and have done with losing." His exclamations of "Discard . . . Deuce" recall a card game, and further extend the generalization of play.[11] So, too, the whistle with which Hamm can no longer summon Clov has an important role in various games. The futile gesture of blind Hamm wiping his glasses, in the end as at the beginning of *Endgame,* suggests the gratuitous quality of all play, including art.

In his last lines, Hamm haltingly quotes Baudelaire,[12] then briefly continues his own chronicle. Crying out to his father for the last time, throwing away his toy dog and the whistle, crying out to Clov for the last time and hearing no answer, Hamm prepares for his end: "Since that's the way we're playing it, let's play it that way, and speak no more about it, speak no more." Although his final words are addressed to the blood-stained handkerchief, this penultimate sentence reflects ironically upon a game of words, which leads only to silence.

The last move of Hamm's game is to cover his face with the blood-stained handkerchief of the opening tableau. The recollection is of St. Veronica's handkerchief stamped with Christ's features (already used in earlier Beckett works). The suggestion is that Hamm's life is a Passion, also consummated at Golgotha, the place of a skull. But if Hamm's death closes the play, is there a resurrection?

Perhaps *Endgame,* with characteristic Beckett ambivalence, implies two resurrections—one occurring just after the curtain rises, and one just after it finally falls. As has been mentioned, the opening action, silent except for five brief laughs (possibly recalling Christ's five wounds?), is performed like a mock-ritual. Sheets are removed from inert objects, and three people come to life—slowly and feebly—on the stage. The opening word is Clov's paradoxical "Finished," but his phrases trail off in some doubt. Hamm, the word-man made flesh, is "getting on" in years. He is blind and can therefore not rely on knowledge through perception. He has relegated his parents—both their teachings and tenderness—to ash bins and nightcaps.

Far, far in the past are those days when his parents rode

through France and Italy on a tandem, when Hamm himself manipulated a bicycle, when Clov pleaded for a bicycle and rode a horse, when body was in efficient union with mind, and man and his carrier could complement each other.[13] By the time of *Endgame,* the delights of the body are grotesque anachronisms. Nagg and Nell laugh uproariously at the accident in which they lost their legs. Keats's line, "Bold lover, never, never, canst thou kiss," is hideously if hilariously caricatured when Nagg and Nell strain towards each other from their respective ash bins, their "very white" faces like death masks. Beauty is dead, truth is dead, happiness a subject for farce. "Nothing is funnier than unhappiness," Nell sets the tone of *Endgame.* Once born, or resurrected, or merely set in motion, Hamm reluctantly yet compulsively forces the show to go on.

Paralyzed himself, he directs the action, even as a director does a play, even as God perhaps directs the world. The infinitesimal movements of his armchair, human life and death—all are subject to Hamm's commands, as long as he is in command. And yet, his activities are ridiculously restricted to composing a chronicle, to praying halfheartedly when he runs out of characters, and above all to giving orders to Clov, variously designated as his dog, menial, creature, and son.

Early in the play, Hamm makes a prophecy about Clov, and we recall other blind prophets—Tiresias, Oedipus, Samson.[14] Hamm's prophecy ends, "Infinite emptiness will be all around you, all the resurrected dead of all the ages wouldn't fill it, and there you'll be like a little bit of grit in the middle of the steppe. (*Pause.*) Yes, one day you'll know what it is, *you'll be like me,* except that you won't have anyone with you, because you won't have had pity on anyone and because there won't be anyone to have pity on" (my italics).

Ironic as the word "pity" sounds in Hamm's mouth, there *is* someone for Clov to pity, once the small boy is sighted. This little child—real or imagined—is the cue for Hamm to dismiss

Clov: "I don't need you any more." Perhaps the small boy will take Clov's place as Hamm's servant, while Clov goes out to die in the desert. If, after the final curtain, Hamm is resurrected, the small boy would remove the sheets in the opening ritual, and Hamm, uncovering his face, would replay his part as hero-victim-director-actor-author. The pattern of such a resurrection would be circular.

Although Clov is the past tense of "cleave," he remains present to the final curtain. Beckett is rumored to have remarked that in *Godot,* the audience wonders whether Godot will ever come, and in *Endgame* they wonder whether Clov will ever leave. It is evident that Beckett intends the wonder in both cases, up to and beyond the end of the plays.

While the audience wonders, blind Hamm understands that he has been abandoned, and he proceeds to make himself absolute for death. In the closing scene, "*He covers his face with handkerchief, lowers his arms to armrests, remains motionless.*" If this immobility is death, and if, after the final curtain, Clov does leave the shelter, perhaps he goes only far enough to fetch the boy, so as to make of him a dog, a menial, a creature, and a son. Perhaps Clov will discover a combination to another cupboard, or perhaps he and the boy, according to some principle of parsimony, will live on leftovers in Clov's millennial kitchen. Then Clov would fulfill Hamm's prophecy with a vengeance; he would not only be like Hamm, he would *be* Hamm, word made flesh, instead of its trivial spice accompaniment. The play, perhaps on a reduced stage, perhaps in a reduced skull, would be replayed with Clov as Hamm. The pattern of such a resurrection would be cyclical.

Already, Clov at the beginning of *Endgame* has shrunk to where he needs a ladder to see out of the window (eye?) of the stage (skull?). It is Clov whose opening line echoes Christ's last words. Like Christ, he speaks of a father and his father's house. In some productions, he stands behind Hamm's chair with arms outstretched as though crucified. Once, Clov implies that "it" can end only if he sings. In his last long speech, Clov shifts from "*They* said to me" to "*I* say to myself" (my italics). Dressed though he is at the last for sun or rain, he does not actually leave the "bare interior," which is a shelter from all weathers. In the French text, Hamm's comment on Clov's discovery of the small boy is "La pierre levée" —the sign of Christ's resurrection. Clov may have invented the small boy who will serve as Clov, even as Clov may have been the small boy in Hamm's literary invention.

In all Beckett's later works, there is no way of distinguishing fact from fiction. Their inseparability and irreconcilability is a recurrent theme of his trilogy of novels. In each successive novel, the hero-narrator undergoes further physical degeneration. Ironically, composition takes place during decomposition. Just as dying had a sexual connotation for the Elizabethans, so it seems to have a creative one for Beckett—artistically creative.

The verbal spareness of *Endgame* is a startling contrast to the unparagraphed verbal rush of the trilogy, but in both works the heroes are word-men, and in both works one word-man is replaceable and (perhaps) replaced by another. In *Endgame,* Clov, Hamm, and Nagg—three generations—are also three stages of physical decomposition. Like Malone in the trilogy, it is Hamm, the middle member, who is at the height (such as it is) of his creative powers. But as the focus of *Endgame* narrows to the Hamm-Clov relationship, the tension is tautened between creator and creature until, finally, after the end of the play as played, one is (perhaps) replaced by the other, and the whole absurd, heartbreaking cycle begins again. Resurrection into another and reduced life, into another and slower death, may take place—if at all—only through the play of creation.

11
dramatic contractions

The artistic tendency
is not expansive,
but a contraction.
Proust

Except for the pantomimes, the *Acts Without Words,* Beckett composed his short dramas between 1956 and 1961, directly in English. Perhaps because he returned to his more allusive native language, perhaps because he felt that the brevity of the form imposed sufficient discipline, Beckett, in these plays, presents a somewhat less sombre picture of the human plight. Although Beckett calls the English pieces "plays," as he does the English translation of *Endgame,* perhaps the designation has come to seem less bitter to him. None of the sets seeks the suffocating atmosphere of *Endgame;* music and sound effects enliven dialogue and gesture. Nevertheless, for all his "play"fulness, Beckett harps on his old themes: solitude, absurdity, sheer dogged endurance.

Commissioned by the British Broadcasting Corporation, *All That Fall* is explicitly written for radio presentation.[1] The title is taken from David's praise of the Lord in Psalm 145, "The Lord upholdeth all that fall and raiseth up all those that be bowed down." In the play, Maddy Rooney is "bowed and bent," Dan Rooney is "bowed down over a ditch." However, neither of them actually falls during the course of the play, in spite of Maddy's fervent wish, "Oh let me just flop down flat on the road like a big fat jelly out of a bowl and never move again!"

The play opens with "*rural sounds*"; music is heard before a word is spoken—Schubert's "Death and the Maiden." Painfully, noisily, fat old Mrs. Rooney makes her way to the Boghill station to meet her blind husband on his birthday. His train is delayed fifteen minutes on a half-hour run. On their halting walk home through wind and rain, husband and wife talk of various subjects, and finally Mrs. Rooney learns from the boy who usually guides her blind husband that the train was late because a little child fell under the wheels. Both the biblical title and Schubert's music may have reference to this event, the fall and death of a child, possibly a maiden.

In spite of the grim ending, comic threads wind through the play. The name of Maddy Dunne Rooney, like various Irish predecessors in Beckett's works, suggests several puns. In connection with Maddy and Dan Rooney, we may recall linguist Molloy: "And I called her Mag because for me, without my knowing why, the letter g abolished the syllable Ma, and as it were spat on it, better than any other letter would have done. And at the same time I satisfied a deep and doubtless unacknowledged need, the need to have a Ma, that is a mother, and to proclaim it audibly. For before you say mag you say ma, inevitably. And da, in my part of the world, means father" (*Molloy*, 21–22). Perhaps the now childless *Ma*ddy and *Da*n are prototypical parents. Moreover, since the Rooneys, like the protagonists of the trilogy, are old and decrepit, we may read their family name as ruin-y; or perhaps age has nothing to do with the matter, for Maddy's maiden name is Dunne (done).

Other than the aged couple, the village inhabitants are

satirized in much the spirit of the social frame of *Watt*. Mr. Tyler does not forget the life he saved, Mr. Slocum (slow come?) is clerk at a racecourse, Christy (a menial in *Molloy*) tries to peddle dung, devout Miss Fitt (misfit) bewails the possibility of the death of her mother, who is carrying fresh sole.

Mrs. Rooney is the most moving figure in the play, and Donald Davie makes the pertinent observation that "she speaks by formula, but she does not live and feel by formula—or she strives not to, though her language continually traps her into it."[2] She attempts to resist the pat phrase by employing an exotic vocabulary (ramdam, merde), by confining herself to literal meanings ("we the unfortunate ticket-holders' nearest if not dearest," "you're just a bag of bones").

Like Beckett characters in other works, Mrs. Rooney tends to mean more than she seems to be saying: "It is suicide to be abroad. But what is it to be at home? A lingering dissolution." "Let us halt a moment and this vile dust fall back upon the viler worms." "I estrange them all." "Christ, what a planet."

Dan Rooney's role grows only gradually. Before he arrives, Mrs. Rooney twice addresses Mr. Tyler as Mr. Rooney, and this apparent absent-mindedness may well be a way of generalizing all humanity. Dan, after accusing Maddy of "struggling with a dead language," admits that he too knows the feeling. Given to counting and calculating, he adopts a "*narrative tone*" when speaking of himself outside of the immediate present. After his evasive "composition" about the train's delay, he pleads with his wife, "Say something, Maddy. Say you believe me." Maddy answers irrelevantly about a girl who died because she "had never been really born"; still another maiden has died.

Like other Beckett heroes, Dan Rooney dwells upon his physical afflictions. "The day you met me I should have been in bed. The day you proposed to me the doctors gave me up.

. . . The night you married me they came for me with an ambulance. . . . No, I cannot be said to be well." Like other Beckett heroes, Dan Rooney is filled with unmotivated cruelty: "Did you ever wish to kill a child? (*Pause.*) Nip some young doom in the bud?" Dan makes sardonic comments on his wife's biblical reminders. He and his wife "*join in wild laughter*" when Maddy quotes the biblical verse that gives the play its title. Immediately afterwards, a boy runs up to return to Mr. Rooney a ball-like object he has dropped. In answer to Mrs. Rooney's question, and in spite of Mr. Rooney's efforts to prevent the boy from speaking, it is revealed that the train was delayed when a child fell under its wheels.

JERRY. It was a little child, Ma'am.

Mr. Rooney groans.

MRS. ROONEY. What do you mean, it was a little child?

JERRY. It was a little child fell out of the carriage, on to the line, Ma'am. (*Pause.*) Under the wheels, Ma'am.

This grim finale to a relatively comic play is not unprepared for. Near beginning and end, Schubert's "Death and the Maiden" is heard. On her way to the station, Maddy reminisces about the death of Minnie, her daughter, another maiden: "In her forties now she'd be, I don't know, fifty, girding up her lovely little loins, getting ready for the change." On her way home from the station, Maddy tells Dan about attending a lecture on a little girl patient of a famous mind doctor: "The only thing wrong with her as far as he could see was that she was dying. And she did in fact die, shortly after he washed his hands of her." Death and Maiden No. 2.

The reiteration of "a little child" at the end of the play evokes the many biblical passages in which it is written that "a little child shall lead them." Perhaps it is through death that the child will lead them; perhaps it is in death that the Lord will uphold all that fall and raise those who are bowed down—even if death is inflicted by one who is himself bowed down.

Beckett's pantomimes contrast sharply with his radio plays, since in the latter, no gesture is seen, and in the former no word is heard. His first ventures in these divergent domains were both written in 1956 and produced in 1957.[3] The village of men, women, and children is reduced to "the man." The noises of farm animals, dragging feet, bicycle bell and brakes, motor and horn, "rush of train," "hissing of steam," "clashing of couplings," thudding of a blind man's stick, "tempest of wind and rain"—dissolve into a "whistle." Gesture, robbed of language, now bears the burden of the human situation.

In *Act Without Words I,* a man, flung onto the stage, mysteriously and gradually is supplied with sustenance (tree and carafe) and tools (scissors, cubes, rope). He is frustrated in his desire to return whence he came, in his several efforts to enjoy his gifts, and even in a suicide attempt. After engaging in ingenious but vain activities to conquer or circumvent invisible opposing forces, he refuses to rise any more to the bait, and indifferently allows it to dangle while he examines his own two hands.

This is slapstick comedy at the cosmological level, and the meaning is almost too explicit. It is also possible, in the light of Beckett's other works, to interpret it at the epistemological level. Perhaps sustenance and tools are man's own invention, and his frustration the result of the impossibility of ever being able to reach what may be a mirage. The mime's frequent glances at his own hands (rather than, for example, shaking his fist at the sky) would seem to lend weight to the latter view, but Beckett may well have intended to combine the two aspects in his now habitual cosmo-epistemological comedy.

Although Beckett's second pantomime, *Act Without Words II,* is only half as long as his first, it puts two characters on stage.[4] Opposed as were Mercier and Camier, Didi and Gogo, Lucky and Pozzo, Hamm and Clov, "A is slow, awkward . . . , absent. B brisk, rapid, precise." A, propped by prayer, pills, and carrot (faith, fiction, and food?), is goaded into activity, whose only result is to change the position of his sack with respect to that of B. B, propped by watch, exercises, toothbrush, comb, brush, mirror, carrot, map, compass, is goaded (by a goad on a wheel) into more feverish activity, of "approximately the same duration." The result of B's activities is to change the position of his sack with respect to that of A. When A is again goaded into activity (the goad is now on two wheels), beginning again with prayer, we have come full circle, and the curtain falls.

Beckett's dichotomized man (roughly physical versus roughly spiritual) may be goaded by increasingly complicated mechanisms, but the ironic futility of his actions is unchanged.

After experimenting with his first radio drama and his first pantomime, Beckett returned to the full resources of the theater in a "monodrama," *Krapp's Last Tape.*[5] Most of the words belong, not to Krapp as he appears on the stage, but to tape recordings of Krapp's younger voice. Dressed in "*rusty black,*" senses failing, Krapp drinks, eats bananas (to be compared with similarly phallic turnips and carrots of *Godot,* and carrots of both characters of the second pantomime), and listens to himself (the old solipsistic occupation). He engages in such slapstick pantomime as tossing banana skins offstage, knocking tapes off the table, and slipping on a banana skin. Hard of hearing, nearly blind, walking painfully, Krapp listens to a tape made in his thirty-ninth year. There are disjointed references to the death of his mother, the gift of a ball to a dog, storm and darkness, and the dissolution of a love affair. After drinking some wine, Krapp prepares his last tape, but the recording soon meanders into recollections of a literary career and a parody of a love affair. Suddenly, he interrupts his recording to replay the earlier tape, which finally *"runs on in silence"* as the curtain falls.

The pun upon Krapp is obvious, but it is heard only once in the monodrama, as opposed to the frequent repetition of the same name in the unpublished, unproduced *Eleutheria.* A slang pun upon *tape* meaning "alcoholic beverage," may also be intended. So lovingly does Krapp mouth the words "spool" and "viduity" that they take on comic incongruity, as does any word that is examined for too long.

The device of playing tapes thirty years old would in itself be a comic anachronism were the monodrama not set *"in the future,"* but that future is of course not evident on the stage. If Beckett carries out his plan for a Krapp trilogy, "Krapp with wife and child, Krapp with wife, Krapp,"[6] the movement would seem to lead, ironically, from future to past.

In the play as we have it, juxtaposition of Krapp's two voices implies an ironic comment on the insignificance of the passing of time. Separated by thirty years, the voices utter the same phrases, are prey to the same hope and despair. After familiar cosmological reflections—"Be again, be again. All that old misery. Once wasn't enough for you"—Krapp interrupts his last tape for a replaying of the end of his love affair. As always in Beckett, repetition gives emphasis, and as might be expected, the emphasis is not sentimental but epistemological. In the love scene Krapp seeks his own image in the eyes of his beloved. His insistent, "Let me in," is not only sexual in its plea, but metaphysical. If his beloved can let Krapp into her reality, they can achieve that moment of stillness even though "all moved." In the light of that moment, the rest of Krapp's life is a solipsistic "viduity," in which he communes only with himself on a "spool."

Krapp's last words—recorded thirty years earlier—are

sharply ironic in view of the miserable relic on stage: "Not with the fire in me now. No, I wouldn't want them [my best years] back." At the last, both Krapp and his tape are silent; man can no longer carry on discourse, even with himself.

Several months after *Krapp* was produced, Beckett wrote a second radio drama, *Embers*, for the BBC.[7] Like *All That Fall*, his first radio play, *Embers* has a certain surface realism, but like *Krapp's Last Tape*, it seeks reality in the past life of its hero. Henry is a name derived from German *Heimrih*, meaning head of the family. Like other Beckett heroes, however, Henry is as absorbed in his fictions as in his family.

The pun on the names of Henry's two fictions, Bolton and Holloway (Bolt-on and Hollo-way), suggests that Henry has arrived at an endgame, in which the stage is lighted by dying embers. Not only does Henry bear the brunt of the dialogue but also he calls attention to sound effects: "That sound you hear is the sea." Squeezing literalism and incongruity for pale comic echoes, he explains, "I mention it because the sound is so strange, so unlike the sound of the sea, that if you didn't see what it was you wouldn't know what it was." And of course, a radio audience cannot see. A few lines later, Henry remarks with similar comic incongruity, "Listen to the light."

In the evocation of his first fiction, Bolton, Henry constantly and flatly contradicts his composition: "shutters . . . no, hangings," "the light, no light," "sitting there in the . . . no, standing," "conversation then on the step, no, in the room," and, finally, "not a sound, only the embers, sound of dying, dying glow, Holloway, Bolton, Bolton, Holloway, old men, great trouble, white world, not a sound." Cruel cosmic irony rests heavily on the hammered negatives.

There is a noise of dripping in Henry's mind, as in Hamm's mind, and Henry calls upon his dead father (drowned at sea), upon stories, and upon his wife, Ada. Ironically, he reminisces, "Ada, too, conversation with her, that was something, that's what hell will be like, small chat to the babbling of Lethe about the good old days when we wished we were dead."

In the disconnected dialogue between Henry and Ada, she remarks that Henry's laugh and smile are what first attracted her, but he fails in his effort to laugh now. They listen to the sea, and then their daughter Addie is heard in parodies of music lessons, of riding lessons. Again the hated sound of the sea is heard, and Holloway is evoked as a doctor who may help Henry. Ada has a recollection of Henry's father seated motionless on a rock; then she leaves Henry. Calling in vain on Ada, on Christ, on his father, Henry returns to Bolton and Holloway. Contradictions again punctuate the evocation. The two fictions confront each other, Bolton looking Holloway in the eye, "the old blue eye, very glassy, lids worn thin, lashes gone, whole thing swimming. . . . Tears? (*Pause. Long laugh.*)"

Again Henry pleads, "Ada! . . . Father! . . . Christ!" In Henry's final soliloquy there is an incongruous mention of a plumber to come at nine, an oblique reference, perhaps, to the hour of Christ's death, after He asks, "My God, my God, why hast thou forsaken me?"

Forsaken by all, no longer questioning, Henry utters his last words, "Not a sound," but Beckett's closing stage direction reads cryptically, "*Sea.*" The radio drama ends with the sound of the sea, with which it began—easily drowning out the noise of Henry's boots and voice, for they make a hollow noise on a hollow way.

From the sea, Beckett moves to a scorched earth in *Happy Days.*[8] Before the "*very pompier trompe-l'oeil backcloth*" parades a host of reflections from earlier Beckett plays. Divided into two acts like *Godot,* centered on an immobile creator-protagonist like *Endgame,* spoken in virtual monologue like *Krapp,* Beckett's latest play also contains exaggerated sound effects of radio drama (nose blowing, bell ringing, music) and exaggerated gestures of pantomime (Willie's newspaper and hat business, Winnie's constant movement of hands and face). Props, too, are familiar to voyagers in Beckett country: hats as in many earlier works, the handkerchief of *Endgame,* the sack and umbrella (now a parasol) of *Mercier et Camier*, the sack of *Comment c'est* or the second pantomime; and the latter also shares with *Happy Days* some of the contents of the sack, such as toothbrush and toothpaste, comb and brush, mirror. Even more important and familiar are the invisible props—the inventory of possessions, the repetitive refrains, the constant doubts and denials, the literary echoes and creations —with which Winnie of *Happy Days,* like her predecessors in Beckett's work, attempts to fill the void of existence.

For the title, *Happy Days,* is of course ironic.

Not only is "happy" foreign to Beckett's vocabulary, but his protagonist's determined reiteration of how happy her day will be, is, and will have been, is undercut by that very determination. Once, however, she reveals that the happy day will be "when flesh melts at so many degrees and the night of the moon has so many hundred hours."

Imbedded in the earth up to her breasts, like a symbolic *tellus mater,* longing to sleep away her life—"Yes, life I suppose there is no other word"—Winnie awakens slowly, reluctantly, when a piercing bell sounds twice, first for "*say ten seconds,*" then for "*say five.*" Winnie's opening words are, "*Another* heavenly day" (my italics); with these words she links herself, buried in the earth, to the habitual heavens above, much as plain and sky are joined in the *trompe-l'oeil* backcloth.

Having opened the play, Winnie prays inaudibly for the exact intervals that the bell has sounded: "*say ten seconds,*" and "*addendum, say five.*" Winnie closes her prayer with the words of the Lesser Doxology, "World without end Amen." However, rather than a Gloria Patri, it will become apparent through the course of the play that Winnie's world without end is the familiar Beckett world of infinite human anguish.

After prayers, Winnie brushes her teeth, and as she turns to spit, she notices Willie, her invisible, inaudible husband. She envies Willie his "marvelous gift" for sleeping, oblivious to bells. Winnie, like Pavlov's dogs, needs bells to summon her to the habits of her life; her stretch of time is punctuated by bells, and sun-punctuated periods have little meaning for her. When she uses the word "day," she apologizes—"the old style."

Frequently repeated through Winnie's monologue, the very phrase "old style" is rich in its ironic reflections on the context of the play. Winnie's "old style" is implicitly contrasted with Dante's *dolce stil nuovo;* she even utters the phrase "sweet old style."[9] Dante's *dolce stil nuovo* ushered in the vigorous literature of the Renaissance, but by the time of *Happy Days* that Renaissance has become a weary decadence. Winnie herself employs comically outworn poetic words: tis, beseech, enow, bid, bon, emmet, God grant, damask cheek, dire need. Throughout the play, she repeats certain stale refrains: old things, can't be cured, genuine pure, nothing like it, there is so little one can do, that is what I always say, great mercies, that is what I find so wonderful, and another happy day. Like her toothpaste and Willie's vaseline, the words are "running out." Although Winnie still uses a gerund rather than the final "No more" of *Endgame,* we see her take the last swig of her vitalizing tonic, and hear the bottle break when she throws it away. There is no more vitality in her run-down world.

Not only does Winnie use old style words and old stale refrains, but she quotes—however inexactly—from such good old poets of the English language as Shakespeare, Milton, Herrick, Gray, Keats, Browning. Browning is the only poet mentioned by name, and then it is ambiguous whether she means the poet or her revolver. However, as she admits, to speak of dying is also to speak in "the old style," and a revolver has inevitable associations with death. Perhaps it is this association that causes her to "kiss it rapidly" when she first sees the revolver; perhaps it is this association that evokes her affectionate nickname "Brownie" (a benevolent spirit) for the gun, and that reminds her of the old times when Willie used to beg her to take the revolver from him lest he put himself out of his misery. Since Brownie is now in Winnie's possession, perhaps she did take it, so as to keep Willie in the misery that evokes her derision: "*Your* misery."

In Winnie's own happy day of Act I, three of her literary quotations paradoxically contain "woe."

woe woe is me . . . to see what I see
(from *Hamlet* III, 1:
O, woe is me,
To have seen what I have seen, see what I see!)

Oh fleeting joys—(*lips*)—oh something lasting woe.
(from *Paradise Lost* x, ll. 741–742:
O fleeting joys
Of Paradise, dear bought with lasting woes!)

something something laughing wild amid severest woe
(from Gray's "Ode on a Distant Prospect
of Eton College":
And moody Madness laughing wild
Amid severest woe.)

Two other Shakespearean quotations come from tragic moments of their respective plays. In making up her lips in the mirror, Winnie ejaculates, "Ensign crimson" and "Pale flag." When Romeo thinks Juliet lies dead before him, he addresses her:

beauty's ensign yet
Is crimson in thy lips and in thy cheeks,
And death's pale flag is not advanced there.

Under the blazing sun of *Happy Days* Winnie tests Willie's hearing with a line from *Cymbeline:* "Fear no more the heat o' the sun," quoting exactly for once. In Shakespeare's play Imogen's brothers sing this as the opening line of a dirge when they believe Imogen is dead. Thus, the literary references of *Happy Days* emphasize the *un*happiness of the human condition.

Winnie no longer waits, like Vladimir and Estragon, for Godot. She waits only for the bell that will send her to sleep, and it, like Godot, does not come. Neither in Act I nor, more painfully, in Act II.

When the curtain rises for the second time to reveal the same scorched earth and *trompe l'oeil* backcloth, Winnie is obviously in a more desperate plight. *"Imbedded up to neck"* in the earth, she can move only the muscles of her face. The bag and parasol (even though the latter has burned up in Act I) are *"as before,"* but the contents of the bag are diminished by one object, Brownie, *"conspicuous to her right on mound."*

In view of her reduced circumstances, Winnie's opening words are even more ironic than "Another heavenly day" of Act I. Now she rises to the Miltonic height of "Hail, holy light," and like Milton, she implicitly links physical and spiritual light, with the traditional neo-Platonic associations between God, the sun, and the mind. However, in Act I Winnie has already amended "holy light" to "blaze of hellish light." By Act II, though she still uses such words as "holy" and "God," Winnie no longer prays. She barely understands the particularity of words: "That day. . . . What day?" "My arms. . . . My breasts. . . . What arms? . . . What breasts?" "the reeds. . . . What reeds?" "The look. . . . What look?" Her memories of quotations are even more fragmentary than in Act I; yet she prides herself on remembering parts of the classics, and specifically summons "those unforgettable . . . exquisite . . . immortal" lines, as opposed to the merely "wonderful lines" of Act I. She actually quotes from such sentimental versifiers as Charles Wolfe, rather than from the great poets of the English language.

More than in Act I, she is turned back upon herself. She can no longer reach parasol, sack, or revolver; she can no longer crane her neck to see Willie. More than in Act I, she is driven to her "story."

In Act I, Winnie, positive that someone's eyes are upon her, has invented a spectator couple, perhaps named Shower in this "expanse of scorched grass," perhaps named Cooker in this "blaze of hellish light"—"ends in er anyway—stake my life on that." In her story, Mr. Shower or Cooker (replete with the Mr. of such earlier deity figures as Knott, Weir, and Godot) observes Winnie half-buried in the ground, and asks his female companion "his fiancée . . . or just some—loved one" coarse, pointed questions about Winnie.

By Act II Winnie invents another story about a little girl named Mildred, who has an elaborately dressed doll and memories of her mother's womb. Soon Mildred is Milly (that rhymes with Willie), and her Dolly (an off-rhyme with Willie) has a "white straw hat" like Willie's, and "China blue eyes" like his. She also wears a "pearly necklet," as Winnie did in Act I. Before the sun is up, Milly, like Willie, crawls "backwards on all fours." Abruptly, Winnie leaves Milly to wonder whether Willie has crawled headfirst into his hole, so that he is stuck there. She calls to him, but, receiving no answer, turns to "Mr. Shower—or Cooker. . . . No longer young, not yet old."[10] Suddenly, Mr. Shower or Cooker and his lady companion begin to quarrel violently—"Drop dead!"—but Winnie calms them, and watches them recede into the distance of her mind's eye: "Last human kind—to stray this way. (*Pause.*) Up to date."

When Willie still fails to reply to her calls, Winnie returns to her fictional Milly, whom she frightens with a mouse, so that Winnie screams with Milly's fright. Relieved perhaps by her shrieks, Winnie prepares to sing, to end another happy day.

Suddenly, *"dressed to kill–top hat, morning coat, striped trousers, etc., white gloves in hand,"* Willie crawls into sight and makes his way to Winnie, buried to the neck in her mound of earth. In spite of her encouragement, in spite of her mocking memories, he fails to reach her, but he does manage to utter a single syllable, "Win." *"Happy expression"* on her face, Winnie sings her song from the Waltz Duet of the *Merry Widow*. The curtain falls as Winnie and Willie look at each other, forming an absurd tableau in what may be the happiest ending that Beckett has yet devised.

For the ironic meaning of *Happy Days* is both apposite and opposite.[11]

In *Happy Days* Beckett has discovered a new stage metaphor for the old human condition–burial in a dying earth, exposure under a ruthless sun. Although Winnie's resolute cheerfulness is suspect, her happy smiles and words nevertheless lighten the atmosphere. Not only does she insist upon the happiness of her day–"old style" though it may be–but she is constantly, busily counting her blessings. Her most frequently repeated refrain, "That is what I find so wonderful," and the ability to smile remain with her almost to the final curtain of Act II. In two of her quotations about woe, there is also mention of "joys" and "laughing." In the scene from which the *Romeo and Juliet* phrases are taken, Juliet is not actually dead, and in *Cymbeline* Imogen does not die at all.

But for all Winnie's resources of good cheer, whose "end . . . is most unlikely," it is mainly to Willie that she owes her happy days. In spite of his limitations as a conversationalist, his presence protects her from becoming Hamm, whose final words are spoken into the silence, or Krapp, who speaks only to his tape recorder. Intermittently but dependably, Willie protects Winnie from the solipsistic self she calls her "wilderness."

Willie's words and deeds are prompted by Winnie's needs. His first action, while he is still invisible, is to return the parasol she has dropped. In Act I he provides her with the spectacle of himself, and it may be this fact that suggests to her that she, too, is a spectacle for other eyes. Willie allows her to see the obscene post card that he owns and enjoys. When Winnie asks Willie to show her a finger, he lifts all five, although in Act II she will claim that it was *she* who gave *him* a hand, that it was he who was "always in dire need of a hand."

When Willie first reads to Winnie from his newspaper, he evokes her sentimental reminiscences; when he reads again at the end of Act I, he enables her to pray and end her long, happy day. With the exception of the items he reads (about an opening for youth, or about events that remind Winnie of her youth), all Willie's spare dialogue is directly addressed to Winnie. He sings wordlessly for her (the melody of "I love you so" from the *Merry Widow*). He affirms that he hears her, even roaring back at her the reassuring beginning of the *Cymbeline* line: "Fear no more." He settles a point of grammar for her—that hair is singular and not plural. He identifies the burden and the motion of the emmet, "eggs" and "formication," respectively.[12] The comic, somewhat obscene overtones of these words cause them both to laugh, in part together and in part separately. In Willie's most extended speech, he defines hog for Winnie, obliquely referring to his own situation: "Castrated male swine. Reared for slaughter."

Winnie quotes from *Romeo and Juliet*, one of the great love stories of all time. Her lines contain reminiscences of Shakespeare's love sonnets (particularly 130–136, ironic poems some of which pun on "Will") and of the Song of Songs (particularly 1:2 and 5:6).

In Act II when Willie is silent, Winnie doubts his reality: "Willie. (*Pause.*) What Willie? (*Sudden vehement affirmation.*) My Willie!" But the affirmation is short-lived, and

Winnie tries to kill time with her dwindling meditations. When Winnie prepares to sing in solitude, Willie appears in splendor, suitably attired for either a wedding or a funeral.

It is ambiguous as to whether Willie means to kiss or kill when he tries to climb the mound to reach Winnie. Winnie, whose only stage kiss is for Brownie the revolver, wonders whether Willie wants a kiss, but Beckett describes Willie as being dressed *"to kill."* In the final tableau it is ambiguous as to whether Willie reaches for Winnie or Brownie as the curtain falls. But kiss or kill, either action should satisfy Winnie that Willie exists ("Ergo you are there"), that she is not alone in the wilderness, and that ergo it is indeed a happy day.

The replaying of the *Merry Widow* tune suggests that her doubts will return, that Willie will die for her again, that her solipsistic viduity will haunt Winnie even as it does Krapp. Although in Act I Willie hums the tune, and in Act II Winnie sings the first verse of the "I love you so" duet, they never sing in duet.[13]

And yet, they *do* sing the same tune. They *"laugh quietly together,"* perhaps at the same joke. Willie, summoning the will power that puns on his name, appears directly in Winnie's final line of sight. He whispers her name that puns on triumph. In Act I Winnie realizes "it does not follow . . . that because one sees the other the other sees the one." But at the end of Act II, mutually and explicitly, *"They look at each other,"* each establishing the other's reality. What more can love do, on the happiest day?

12

Samuel Beckett, self-translator

The artist has acquired his text: the artisan translates it. "The duty and the task of a writer (not an artist, a writer) are those of a translator."
Proust

As early as 1931, in his essay on Proust, Beckett distinguishes between the artist and the writer; the artist seeks his text within himself, and the artisan translates it, transmits it to the world. To translate—in its more usual meaning, Dr. Johnson's "to change into another language retaining the sense"—has been Beckett's method of improving his own craftsmanship. In the very essay from which the quotation on translation is excerpted, Beckett rendered into English passages from Proust's texts, while waiting to "acquire" his own.[1]

Beckett's first profession, like Joyce's, was that of language teacher. Grounded in Greek and Latin, a student of modern languages at Trinity College, he taught English at the Ecole Normale Supérieure in Paris, and French at Trinity College. He contributed to *transition* during that little magazine's campaign for the Revolution of the Word, and signed its "Poetry Is Vertical" manifesto, which demanded that language be mantic.

Fascinated by Joyce's verbal dexterity, Beckett explicated

Work in Progress while it *was* in progress, insisting that Joyce was making linguistic history even as Dante in the *Divine Comedy.*[2] With his French friend, Alfred Péron, Beckett prepared the first French draft of Joyce's "Anna Livia Plurabelle" from *Work in Progress.* Joyce, whose knowledge of Greek was fragmentary, consulted Beckett for some of the Greek-rooted puns of *Finnegans Wake,* and Beckett read to Joyce from Mauthner's *Beiträge zu einer Kritik der Sprache,* which presents a nominalistic view of language.[3] Years after Joyce told Beckett, "I have discovered I can do anything with language I want,"[4] the younger Irish writer echoed that opinion, claiming that Joyce "was making words do the absolute maximum of work."[5] Although he contrasts himself with Joyce—"The kind of work I do is one in which I'm not master of my material"[6]—admiration for that "superb manipulator of material" may have played its part in Beckett's moving permanently to Paris a few years before world War II. When the war was over, re-established in a Paris that had lost Joyce and many of his entourage, Beckett shifted from his native English to French for fiction and drama. At the same time, he began the series of self-translations that are unprecedented in the history of literature. By comparing original with translation, we may gain further insight into Beckett's literary intention and comic method.

Since Beckett was composing in French while he translated *Murphy,* his first English novel, into French, one might expect that some of the local idiom of the French fiction would rub off on the gallicized *Murphy.* Although that novel does not rise (or fall) to the colloquialism, vulgarity, and obscenity of its French successors, there is a definite trend in that direction, which may be conveyed by a categorical listing of sample translations.

point of bursting	point de peter
back to Teneriffe and the apes	la petite idylle de bidet portatif
God bless my soul	Que Dieu damne mon âme

Hell roast	Quelle putain
Damn	Merde
pain in the neck	mal aux couilles
tradesmen and gentry	la petite bourgeoisie et la canaille
I was not asleep	Je ne roupillais pas
man of the world	débrouillard
with his body up	de la bougeotte corporelle
the little b--- [sic]	le petit salaud
his woman	sa poule
Our medians . . . or whatever the hell they are	Nos cochonnes de médianes, si c'est bien lc terme juste
and all was in order	et vogue la galère
What are you taking, friend?	Annonce la couleur, camarade

This is not a random sampling, but one culled to exhibit the variety and color of Beckett's turn of phrase. A more extended quotation illustrates how a colloquial and vulgar French undermines the elegance of the English *Murphy*, while adding a few hilarious harmonics; Murphy complains to a waitress about his tea,

I know I am a great nuisance, but they have been too generous with the cowjuice.

Beckett as omniscient author comments,

Generous and cowjuice were the key words here. No waitress could hold out against their mingled overtones of gratitude and mammary organs. And Vera was essentially a waitress. (83)

The French introduces comic vulgarities,

—Je vous emmerde, je le sais bien, mais que voulez-vous, ils m'ont foutu tout plein de jus de vache.

"Emmerde" et "vache" furent ici les mots actifs, nulle serveuse ne pouvait résister à leurs harmoniques mélangées d'amour et de maternité. (65)

Similarly, Murphy's "My God, how I hate the charVenus and her sausage and mash sex," is vulgarized in French to "Putain de putain, ce que ça m'emmerde, la vénus de chambre et son Eros comme chez grand' mère." Moreover, Beckett adds omnisciently and ironically to the French translation, "Il [Murphy] tenait à être distinct."

Most of the changes that Beckett incorporates into the French translation of *Murphy*—insertions, deletions, or emendations—serve to heighten the comic tone. Even though the English *Murphy* is already a funny novel, there are more additions than deletions in translation; the latter are limited to extraneous, non-comic detail and to word play for which Beckett was evidently unable to find a satisfactory equivalent. Thus, the rhyme "scarlet harlot" disappears; the "striking nominative, You are not I," vanishes in French; puns are not translated—whoroscope, clinch, Murphy's irrational (surdlike) heart, Cooper's acathisia that is "deep-seated and of long standing," and Murphy's favorite pun: "Why did the barmaid champagne? Because the stout porter bitter." The book-long emphasis on Murphy's rocking chair—in the eyes of the world Murphy is most *off his rocker* when he is blissfully *on* his rocker—is lost in French.

As if to compensate for these gems, Beckett sounds several new comic notes. A "sage comme une image" is introduced ironically. In both English original and French translation, Neary curses the night he was born, then "in a bold flashback" the one in which he was conceived, but only in French does the author add "car il avait toujours été un fils respectueux" ("for he had always been a respectful son"). Frightened in both versions by a noise issuing from Murphy's room, his mistress Celia has her blood run cold, which, only in French, "elle avait cependant extrêmement chaud" ("was very hot"). Although Murphy's bed, gas stove, and tallboy are big in both languages, only the bed is masculine, and only in French.

Of interest is the substitution for English Bim of French Bom in Chapter 12 of *Murphy*. Both sadistic Clinch brothers are attendants at the Magdalen Mental Mercyseat; although they are identical twins, Bim is higher in the hospital hierarchy, and has "a fancy for Ticklepenny not far short of love." In Chapter 12 of the French translation, it is Bom (ironic pun on "bon") who is coupled with Ticklepenny in disposing of Murphy's remains.

Sometimes erudition enriches the irony in which the English *Murphy* is suffused. Thus, Murphy's garret at the MMM is compared, in French, to one where Leibniz lived and died. "Roture oblige," Murphy twists the compulsion upon *noblesse*, and his experience as a "roseau pensant" à la Pascal makes him skeptical about the sanity of the so-called sane. In neither language, however, does Beckett claim that the sane are in the Magdalen Mental Mercyseat, and that it is our world which is insane. Beckett's irony is somewhat tempered, though, when he deals with the inmates of the three M's (four M's in French, Maison Madeleine de Miséricorde Mentale). The jocular obscenitics that are introduced into the French text attack the attendants far more savagely than they do the patients.

Although new vulgarity and colloquialism are Beckett's most blatant and consistant modifications in translating *Murphy*, there are other book-long disparities between the English and French versions. From his earliest works on, Beckett ridicules sex, Ireland, and Christianity. Much of the sex comedy of *Murphy* is, in the French translation, combined with obscenity. But there are several occasions when sex, in the French version, manages to remain on a higher plane, as when Beckett mangles an English proverb into a comparably but differently mangled French one:

Women are really extraordinary the way they want to give their cake to the cat and have it. (202)

Les femmes sont vraiment extraordinaires, avec leur manie de faire coucher autrui comme elles font leur lit. (146)

Beckett's ironic treatment of Christianity is more subtle in the French, involving several "Sainte Vierge's, "Dieu's," an "impasse de l'Enfant-Jésus," and biblical echoes which do not occur in the original English. And lest anyone take these pieties at face value, Beckett comments on the insane of the Magdalen Mental Mercyseat: "Laissés en paix, ils auraient été heureux comme Dieu en France," instead of the milder English "happy as Larry, short for Lazarus, whose raising seemed to Murphy perhaps the one occasion on which the Messiah had overstepped the mark." Similarly, although the Murphy of both versions has memories of strolling around cathedrals that it is too late to enter, in French only does Beckett add, "en attendant l'ouverture de bordels" ("while waiting for the bordels to open").

Along with colloquial and ironic additions, incongruous insertions sharpen the comic tone of the translated *Murphy*. Thus, in both languages, the proto-bum Cooper is jailed for begging without singing, but "ni ambulation" in French. Again in both languages, Wylie asks the ragged Cooper to wait outside his hotel room, but adds in French, "Attention à le peinture" ("Careful, wet paint"). In French, too, the female branch of the despotic Clinch clan is incongruously enlarged by "trois tantes et quatre bâtardes, dont deux aveugles" ("three aunts and four bastards, of whom two are blind"). The patients of the mental institution play games in both languages, but in French, "à la poussette, à la marelle, à la main chaude" ("push-pin, hop-scotch, hot cockles").

The excised word play of the English *Murphy* does not seem readily replaceable in Beckett's first extended self-translation, but he makes a few attempts. The bilingual pun, "Celia s'il y a" is transferred intact. A "fake jossy" becomes a "faux fakir." One of the key motifs of the novel, that of the closed system of the horse-leech's daughter (of Proverbs) whose "quantum of wantum is fixed," has, in French, an equally "fixe . . . quantum de manquum." The derivations of "gas" from "chaos" and "cretin" from "Christian," if less supported by Littré than the *New English Dictionary*, nevertheless translate easily.

A few alterations in *Murphy* serve, not to heighten the comic, but to clarify its surface meaning for the French reader. Thus, there are money changes from "shillings" to "francs," time changes from "one o'clock" to "13 heures," a translation of the terminology of the extraordinary Murphy–Mr. Endon chess game from English to French, and changes of linear measurements to the metric equivalents, particularly in the list of Celia's measurements, calculated to deprave the male reader.

Although London remains the locale of the action, the few brand names and book titles undergo translation. In various contexts, the Pulitzer Prize becomes Le Prix Femina, and the "student of the year" becomes "un agrégé de philosophie"—not without recalling Jean-Paul Sartre, the particular *agrégé de philosophie* who was taking Paris by storm while Beckett was translating *Murphy*.

None of the early reviewers of *Murphy* recognized the philosophic import of Beckett's fiction, but his subsequent works have frequently been explicated by reference to Chapter 6 of *Murphy*, which describes its hero's mind. For the most part, the translated chapter is faithful to tone and content of the original, but there is one important deletion from the third and most mysterious zone of Murphy's mind: "Here there was nothing but commotion and the pure forms of commotion." And there are a few significant modifications in the second zone.

Here the pleasure was contemplation. This system had no other mode in which to be out of joint and therefore did not need to be put right in this. Here was the Belacqua bliss and others scarcely less precise. (111)

Ici le plaisir était esthétique. C'était un monde qui, n'étant pas affligé d'un homologue réel, n'avait pas besoin d'artifices. Ici se déroulait la vision Belacqua et d'autres à peine moins suaves. (84)

Although the changes are slight, the substitution of "esthétique" for "contemplation" and "la vision Belacqua" for "Belacqua bliss" seem to point in the direction of the writer-hero of Beckett's French fiction and away from the dreamer, Murphy, especially when we recall that Beckett borrowed Belacqua from Dante's purgatorial "bliss" to figure in his 1934 volume of short stories, *More Pricks Than Kicks.* Murphy suffers a crueler fate than Belacqua, and Beckett sardonically intensifies the cruelty in translation. Into the French text, Beckett inserts the weight of Murphy's ashes, "poids moyen d'un foetus de sept mois" ("average weight of a seven-month foetus").

Although emphasis has been placed on the differences between the English *Murphy* and its French translation, it must be stressed that none of the changes is fundamental or extensive, and that, excerpted out of context, they give a distorted view of the whole. By and large, the translation follows the original, of which, obviously, no one could have more intimate knowledge than its author-translator. And yet, nine years and a war intervened between original and translation, as a result of which, or at least after which, Beckett changed his language, both literally and figuratively. The tightening, colloquialisms, and sharpening of the comic in the French text of *Murphy* move in the sense of Beckett's own moving art.

That Beckett was able to translate without modifying is clearly demonstrated by the publication of *Three Poems* in two languages in *Transition* in 1948. In nearly word-for-word parallels, Beckett renders moods of melancholy; even the lorn rhythms are transferred from one language to the other, in spite of the rhythmic differences between French and English.[7]

It was the unexpected theatrical success of *En Attendant Godot* that catapulted Beckett from avant-garde oblivion to world fame. Pressure for an English version of the play was so strong that Beckett complied in 1954.[8] In translating now from French to English, Beckett reversed his trend towards vulgarization and colloquialization. Despite all his willingness to translate three- and five-letter French obscenities into a four-letter English norm, the French remains the more authentically colloquial of the two versions, and thereby the more comic. In contrast to Beckett's translation of *Murphy,* he deletes more than he adds to *Godot.*

As in *Murphy,* mock-Christian notes are more plentiful in translation than in the original. Thus, if a few religious and/or biblical references vanish from the English version (only in French is Lucky to be sold at the Marché du Saint-Sauveur, and only in French is Estragon asked whether he has been to "école sans Dieu"), more are introduced—a warped quotation from Proverbs 13; the term "good angel" for Lucky; the charge that Lucky is "crucifying" Pozzo; the change of Estragon's pseudonym from "Catulle" in French to "Adam" in English; the ironic suggestion that the friends give thanks for their mercies; and, at the last, a new and heartbreaking "Christ have mercy upon us" when Vladimir learns that Mr. Godot's beard is white.

A few minor modifications—the substitution of Berkeley for Voltaire, Connemara for Normandie, Puncher for Poinçon, Feckham Peckham Fulham Clapham for Seine Seine-et-Oise Seine-et-Marne Marne-et-Oise in Lucky's tirade—appeal to the changed nationality of the audience, but in both versions the two tramps have associations with France. Vladimir dreams of jumping from the Eiffel Tower, and Estragon still wants to see the Pyrenees. Curiously, Beckett changes the friends' familiarity with the Vaucluse in the French version to the Burgundian Macon country in the English; in French, Estragon was rescued by Vladimir from the Durance, in English from the Rhone.

Other minor modifications are unclear in intention. The English names of Lucky's dance—The Scapegoat's Agony and The Hard Stool—are neither funnier nor more pointed than the French—La Mort du Lampiste and Le Cancer des Vieillards. Estragon's answer, "Eleven," instead of "Demandez-lui," when Pozzo asks Vladimir's age, is more patently absurd. The longest deletion (over two pages in the French text—68–69), which concerns Pozzo's attempt to explain Lucky's behavior, deprives the English-language audience of an opportunity both to understand and to laugh. On the other hand, an Act II deletion nearly as long (148–149) tightens the play by eliminating a minimally comic dialogue between Vladimir and Estragon. The excision of Lucky's second fall (152–153) serves to tighten the play, but robs it of vaudeville slapstick comedy.

Perhaps because of these deletions, perhaps because of the less colloquial tone, the English *Godot* seems bleaker than the French. Several modifications suggest, too, that this was Beckett's intention. A proliferation of "Wait's," Vladimir's more graphic "On our hands and knees" as compared to the French "suppliants," the introduction of "wastes and pines" and "dying" into Lucky's tour de force, are illustrations in point. Vladimir's introduction of an anguished "Christ have mercy upon us" has been cited. Of cumulative menace in the English version are the references to Lucky's one refusal to obey Pozzo, and the increased hopelessness of Estragon's wait for Godot (His despairing "Ah" is uttered at the first mention of Godot in English, but in French it awaits the departure of Pozzo and Lucky). Further indications of the heightened desperation of the English version are translations of French "solitudes" to English "nothingness," French "nous

nous ennuyons ferme" to English "we are bored to death." "Si l'on s'estimait heureux" is ironically exaggerated to "If we gave thanks for our mercies?" "Mais regarde" is twisted to an ironic "as large as life." Near the end, the comment on the rope too weak to hang the friends is embittered from "Elle ne vaut rien" to "not worth a curse."

Beckett himself characterized *Endgame* as "more inhuman than *Godot.*"[9] After retaining *Fin de Partie* in French for about a year, he embarked on the translation while still working upon that of the trilogy, and he wrote to a friend, "I have nothing but wastes and wilds of self-translation before me for many miserable months to come."[10] Despite his apparent lack of zest for the task, Beckett carried it out with fidelity to the French original.

As in *Waiting for Godot,* deletion exceeds addition in *Endgame.* Particularly significant is the omission of details of the Hamm-Clov dialogue about the small boy, the one living being outside the room on stage. Other modifications accentuate the "inhumanity" of the play: echoes of the opening line, "It is finished," are heard in the various "finished's" by which Beckett translates "achevé" and "cassé," "froid" is intensified to "bitter," "happy" is repeated ironically in English; Clov, thrusting the gaff at Hamm, says in French, "Avale-la," and in English, "Stick it up"; Nell's word "comédie" is translated as "farce." In the opening and closing tableaux, the flat "vieux linge" is translated into the connotatively richer "old stancher."

There is less gratuitous jesting in this stark drama than in any previous Beckett work, and yet he exhibits unparalleled dexterity in the rendition of word play from French to English. The Hamm-home joke succeeds better in English than in the French original, and Nagg's story of the Englishman and his tailor (which casts bitter reflections on God's created world) is translated by Beckett as a paranomasial tour de force. Too long to quote, its wit is comparable to the Hamm-Clov colloquy about the flea in Clov's trousers:

CLOV.	La vache.	The bastard!
HAMM.	Tu l'as eue?	Did you get him?
CLOV.	On dirait . . . A moins qu'elle ne se tienne coïte.	Looks like it . . . Unless he's laying doggo.
HAMM.	Coïte! Coite tu veux dire. A moins qu'elle ne se tienne coite.	Laying! Lying you mean. Unless he's *lying* doggo.
CLOV.	Ah! On dit coite? On ne dit pas coïte?	Ah? One says lying? One doesn't say laying?
HAMM.	Mais voyons! Si elle se tenait coïte nous serions baisés. (51)	Use your head, can't you. If he was laying we'd be bitched. (34)

Like his mordant jokes, Beckett's literary echoes are not gratuitous but serve to enrich the spare structure. An atmospheric line from Baudelaire's "Recueillement"—"To réclamais le soir; il descend: le voici"—is diminished in translation.[11] On the other hand, the introduction into the English of a line from Shakespeare's *Tempest* carries a host of significant suggestions. Hamm's "Finie la rigolade" is translated as "Our revels now are ended." Instantly, Hamm becomes Prospero, and the Endgame "the baseless fabric of this vision." But Prospero is master of his material, whereas Hamm is a slave to his.

In the trilogy of novels, completed before *Endgame*, the dominant theme of man, the plaything of his fictions, has emerged. That theme is riddled with confusions, irrationalities, tensions, that contribute to the complex texture of the prose of the fiction, and add incalculable difficulties to the translation. It is not clear whether Beckett early envisioned translating the entire trilogy or used certain passages as finger exercises. In *Transition* in 1950—before any of the volumes of the trilogy was published in French—short sections appeared, translated into English by Beckett. When he came to the sustained translation of *Molloy*, however, in spite of his experience with *Murphy*, Beckett chose as collaborator Patrick Bowles, the South African poet.

Mr. Bowles wrote in this connection, "the strange thing would seem to be not that Beckett translated the two succeeding volumes alone but that he did not also translate *Molloy* alone. Whatever Beckett's reasons for desiring to work with a translator, I myself was glad of the privilege of working with him during that year (1953–55). Perhaps because collaboration is or at least in this case was slower than single-handed work, perhaps for a variety of reasons it would be fastidious to go into, when work on *Molloy* was over and the problem arose of each sounding out the other's feelings in the matter, Beckett and I mutually agreed he himself would tackle Malone Dies and The Unnamable alone. A task whose obstacles he surmounted with his usual mastery."[12] Mr. Bowles describes the process of translating *Molloy:* "Our method of translating Molloy varied. At first, I was in the habit of translating a page or two daily. The following morning I would meet Beckett and we would discuss the passages done. Then came a period during which Beckett and I translated jointly, working mornings. This was followed by a further period during which I translated the remaining MS in batches which were then sent to Beckett who returned them with suggestions. Of interest is the extraordinary care and concentration which Beckett devoted to this work. When the MS was finally completed both Beckett and I, separately and together, went over it several times, adding further corrections, so that when the MS was finally sent to the printers it had undergone 8 versions." Since Beckett worked so closely with Bowles, it seems safe to assume that he approved where he did not originate deviations from the French original.

At the opening of *Molloy*, there is a slight alteration that gives an interesting insight into the growth of the trilogy. In

French, Molloy says, "Cette fois-ci, puis encore une je pense," evidently suspecting that there will be another volume to his account. But by the time of translation, Beckett knew he had written a trilogy, and he adds to the English, "Then perhaps a last time"—an addition he repeats at intervals, to indicate that there are *two* succeeding volumes.

Examination of the two texts of *Molloy* reveals several atmospheric changes, but less than in *Murphy:* units of length and money are English in both languages, but "jours de fête" becomes "bank holidays"; "un pommier" is specified as "a Beauty of Bath," and "la moquette" as "Wilton"; "un petit Trianon" is reduced to a "charming home"; Isigny is changed to Blackpool, both on the sea; Moran's town Shit in French becomes the more tepid Turdy in English. A and B of the French text are changed to A and C in English, perhaps to suggest Abel and Cain. Moran's effort to *tutoyer* Gaber is, of course, eliminated, as is a pun on "assiette" favored by both Moran and Molloy.

Like *Murphy,* and unlike the two plays, English *Molloy* contains more additions than deletions, none of which exceeds a sentence in length. Again as in *Murphy,* many of the alterations heighten the comedy, especially in its ironic aspects. Introduction of paradox serves this end: "faux comme de juste" is sharpened to "wrong, very rightly wrong"; "Et me sentant soudain envahi d'une grande fatigue malgré l'heure qui était celle de ma vitalité maxima," becomes "And suddenly overcome by a great weariness, in spite of the dying day when I always felt most alive."

Comic too is the introduction of seemingly parenthetical comments by the hero-narrator. In describing his only love, Molloy mentions that she paid him each time he came to see her. "Ce n'était pas une femme pratique," he remarks in French, but the English alteration is at once funnier and more cynical, "She was an idealist." With comparable irony, mock-pious notes are introduced into the English text—"God's" and "Christ's," often followed by an obscenity.

More than in the translation of *Murphy,* heightening of the sardonic comedy reflects cosmic absurdity. Thus, Beckett turns Keats to his ironic purpose; Gaber quotes Youdi in French, "La vie est une bien belle chose . . . une chose inouïe," but in English, "Life is a thing of beauty . . . and a joy forever." Often the comic is sharpened by tightening of verbiage or concretization of metaphor. When "Les pleurs et les ris, je ne m'y connais guère," is rendered as "Tears and laughter, they were so much Gaelic to me," new laughter is provoked both by the cliché variant and the stab at Ireland.

In tone, the French *Molloy* remains more colloquial in spite of Beckett's conscientious translation of obscenities and vulgarities (already noted in *Godot* and *Endgame*). English "howl" scarcely conveys "un coup de gueule"; Molloy's final attitude, "Je ne me bilais pas," pales to "I did not fret," and the series of earlier Beckett fictions from "quelle galerie de crevés" to the more elegant "gallerie of moribunds." Even the dim man speaks more colloquially in French than in English: "Je ne m'attendais pas à trouver quelqu'un dans ce bled, dit-il, c'est une veine," becomes "What are you doing in this God-forsaken place, he said, you unexpected pleasure." Similarly, the savage and obscene despair of "Connaître le saint, tout est là, n'importe quel con peut s'y vouer," is modified to "Yes, the whole thing is to know what saint to implore, any fool can implore him." And "que la connerie prenne son vrai visage, un non-sens cul et sans issue," is rarefied to "and the whole ghastly business looks like what it is, senseless, speechless, issueless misery."

Occasionally, the increased colloquialism of the French is played against its philosophic import, creating a comic tension that the English does not quite capture. In "Et ce que j'ai ce que je suis, ça me suffit, ça m'a toujours suffi, et pour mon petit amour d'avenir aussi je suis tranquille, je ne suis pas près de m'ennuyer," the irony of the tranquillity and of the denial of boredom is more subtle than the English lack of qualms, and "good time": "And what I have, what I am, is enough, was always enough for me, and as far as my dear little sweet little future is concerned, I have no qualms, I have a good time coming."

Philosophic modifications in *Molloy* are slight. Changing "*plus* j'y songe plus j'en ai la conviction" to "the *less* I think of it the more certain I am" recalls Beckett's pronouncement in his 1931 essay on Proust: "We can only remember what has been registered in the mind by our extreme *in*attention" (my italics). A similar idea is suggested by his expanding, from French to English, on the effect of the will upon images:

> Mais ces sortes d'images, la volonté ne les retrouve qu'en y faisant violence. Elle en enlève et y ajoute. (177)

> But images of this kind the will cannot revive without doing them violence. Much of what they had it takes away, much they never had it foists upon them. (156)

These images are at the heart of Beckett's work. On the pages from which the quotations are excerpted, the image is Molloy, who, in the English text only, calls himself "neither man nor beast." But an earlier Beckett image, Watt, is suggested by the insertion, in connection with railroads, "for they had never heard of Watt."

More overtly an image-maker than Molloy, Malone, in the second volume of Beckett's trilogy, is even more incisive and savage in his expression, posing a more challenging task for his author-translator. When *Malone meurt* becomes *Malone Dies,* additions are less numerous than in the first volume, and they are more explicit in intention, for almost all of them can be ascribed to increased bitterness—"I am in chains," "an even worse place than before"—or increased irony—"There is a choice of images," "I might feel I had failed in my duty"—including mock-piety—"Ne poussez pas, nom de Dieu!" is amplified to "What in God's name are you all pushing for for Christ sake?"

Deletions, on the other hand, are often an unaccountable loss to the English-language reader, for example, the mood-setting "je me regarderai trembler" ("I will watch myself tremble"); the mordant "je n'ai jamais rencontré de semblable" ("I never met anyone like me"); a play on words concerning human habits—"combien peu on peut y compter"; a parenthesis which links a dead ass to human death—"le trou, qui n'avait pas loin de six pieds de profondeur" ("the hole about six feet deep"); the irony whereby Moll brushes her single tooth five times a day, "une fois pour chaque blessure [of Christ]" ("once for each wound"); a first description of Macmann—"c'est presque un vieillard à présent" ("he is almost an old man now"); a mention of his hat, of a beard that would relate him to Christ.

The change in language is, as usual, accompanied by several atmospheric nuances—"kilos" is rendered as "stone," "guignol" as "Punch and Judy," "Grisette" as "Whitey," "arrière-saison" as "Michaelmas," "Tweet-tweet" as "petitpetitpetit"; the rhythms of Macmann's poems are anglicized; and the Louis family of Malone's French fiction changes to Lambert in English, connecting that family more overtly—and absurdly—with Balzac's young idealist.

Some word play is untranslated—"il était reputé bon saigneur," "à cheval sur les cheveux"; but other examples are introduced into the English—"proud as punch of his fine hunch," "ulterior locomotive motive," "sweet and seventy," "Johnson, Wilson, Nicholson, and Watson, all whoresons."

As in the case of *Molloy*, the most consistent and noticeable discrepancies between original and translation are those of tone, and yet the English Malone attains a level of vulgarity that Molly-Moran did not reach. Thus, "foutu comme un magot" pales to "people would run a mile from me." The intimate relation between colloquial expression and philosophical base of the novel is sometimes not quite captured in English; for example,

Savoir pouvoir faire mieux, à s'y méconnaître, la prochaine fois, et qu'il n'y a pas de prochaine fois, et que c'est une chance qu'il n'y en ait pas, il y a là de quoi se régaler pendant un moment. (152)

To know you can do better next time, unrecognizably better, and that there is no next time, and that it is a blessing there is not, there is a thought to be going on with. (83)

Other discrepancies, like several of the additions, serve to accent the bitterness and cruelty in the English version of *Malone meurt.* In one crucial passage of the novel, where Malone reflects upon his fictions, the English is less colloquial and more desperate than the French:

Tout est prétexte, Sapo et les oiseaux, Moll, les paysans, ceux qui dans les villes se cherchent et se fuient, mes doutes qui ne m'intéressent pas, ma situation, mes possessions, prétexte pour ne pas en venir au fait, à l'abandon, en levant le pouce, en disant pouce et en s'en allant, sans autre forme de procès, quitte à se faire mal voir de ses petits camarades. (195)

All is pretext, Sapo and the birds, Moll, the peasants, those who in the towns seek one another out and fly from one another, my doubts which do not interest me, my situation, my possessions, pretext for not coming to the point, the abandoning, the raising of the arms and going down, without further splash, even though it may annoy the bathers. (107)

It is again important to stress that the translation for each work is in the main faithful, and even brilliant, particularly in the poignant passages of self-exploration of the hero-narrator. In *The Unnamable,* looking back on all fictions "from Murphy on," the unnamable hero attempts to reject "their" fictions, "their" language, in his search for independent knowledge of himself. The urgency of his seeking, gradually stripping his account of the remnants of plot and character, is conveyed in colloquial French, in rhythms that throb with the agony of struggling to be born into a distinctive self. Beckett has rendered both agony and rhythms in his own English idiom, and the discrepancies are so minor as to be of interest only to the language student.

Least interesting are the atmospheric nuances in *The Unnamable:* "rue de la Gaîeté" is translated as "fun of the fair"; "beaume tranquille" is specified as "Elliman's Embrocation"; "une fête" is again a "bank holiday"; and "guignol" is "Punch and Judy"; "Tartempion" is rendered as "Jones"; "en sixième" is "in the lower third." More curiously, "Pigalle" becomes "Montmartre," but the "Prix Goncourt" (as against the "Prix Femina" of *Murphy*) is the "Pulitzer Prize." Since time, space, and money virtually disappear from *The Unnamable,* their respective units vanish as well.

In *The Unnamable,* as in the two earlier volumes of the trilogy, additions outnumber deletions, but both are restricted to brief phrases (with a single exception—the excision of a passage on flies). Even less than in the first two volumes is the intention of the deletion always clear. On the first page, for example, the omission of "Je ne me poserai plus de questions" ("I will ask myself no more questions") robs the English-language reader of an ironic comment on the impotence of the speaker, as well as of an immediate link with the predecessors of the Unnamable, who made comic and compulsive lists of questions. Some deletions tighten the prose, but others weaken it. Ruthlessly silenced in the English are Worm's various onomatopoeic noises—"mots, rots, rires, succions, et glouglous divers." Towards the end of the book, in an abusive attempt to contrast "you" with "it," Beckett omits from the English, "Voilà pour le vous, nous voilà fixés sur le vous" ("So much for the you, we have no doubt about the you"), and the English-language reader is less sure, in the packed context, of what or who is being contrasted with "it."

Many of the additions are inserted to sharpen the philosophic tension—the principal bulk and subject of this extraordinary novel. Thus, there is meticulous addition of "on these matters" to the translation of "Je n'ai pas d'opinion," and addition of "I mean up above me" to "là-haut." To the French anguish about "ma peine" is added "my crime is my punishment." But the French "si je bougeais, si je comprenais" ("if I moved, if I understood") does not stress the Cartesian mind-body split as strongly as the English "if my body stirred, if my head understood." New "I don't know's" appear here and there, and a significant insertion is "you say that for something to say, you say anything for something to say" in a passage which, like much of the Unnamable's novel, castigates "their" words.

The play upon sound and meaning of words is germane to the content of *The Unnamable* in either language, and, as in the other novels, it sometimes remains untranslated, as in "le cuculte," "du savoir-crever," "le peux un peu," "un vieux de la vieille," "mielleuse et fielleuse," "fourré dans un fourré"; "l'oeil se fait tirer l'oreille" pales to "the eye is hard of hearing." However, as in the other translations, English word play is introduced—"the teller and the told," "defame my defamer," "upon my word," "off it goes on," "wordy-gurdy," "the last at last," "this eye is an oversight," "shit . . . the right word, one has only to seek, seek in vain, to be sure of finding in the end, it's a question of elimination."

To the English *Unnamable* are added more mock-pieties than to any of the previous translations; numerous "please God's" and "God knows's," but also a "good God" and a "God forbid." Other ironic additions are "let us be just . . . let us be impartial," "just for the fun of it . . . fun, what fun we've had, what fun of it." Most pathetic is the insertion into the last paroxysmic five-page sentence, "the words fail." All-important is the addition of the penultimate fragmentary phrase, "I can't go on," before the final and heroic, "I'll go on."

As each staccato phrase contributes to the cumulative anguish of the entire book, of the entire trilogy, the hero's quest becomes at once more single-minded and more chaotic. In the human search for identity through fiction and language—its impossibility and its inevitability—each word is relevant, each tight phrase is at once a construction and a destruction. Even more than in the translations of the first two volumes of the trilogy, one cannot but be impressed by the astounding conviction and precision of a translation that transcends minor discrepancies. Towards the end of the book, where words, stories, and an unnamable self are confounded and confused, Beckett provides a masterly rendition of the fragmented, cumulative anxiety of our time:

je suis en mots, je suis fait de mots, des mots des autres, quels autres, l'endroit aussi, l'air aussi, les murs, le sol, le plafond, des mots, tout l'univers est ici, avec moi, je suis l'air, les murs, l'emmuré, tout cède, s'ouvre, dérive, reflue, des floccons, je suis tous ces flocons, se croisant, s'unissant, se séparant, où que j'aille je me retrouve, m'abandonne, vais vers moi, viens de moi, jamais que moi, qu'une parcelle de moi, reprise, perdue, manquée, des mots, je suis tous ces mots, tout ces étrangers, cette poussière de verbe (204)[13]

I'm in words, made of words, others' words, what others, the place too, the air, the walls, the floor, the ceiling, all words, the whole world is here with me, I'm the air, the walls, the walled-in one, everything yields, opens, ebbs, flows, like flakes, I'm all these flakes, meeting, mingling, falling asunder, wherever I go I find me, leave me, go towards me, come from me, nothing ever but me, a particle of me, retrieved, lost, gone astray, I'm all these words, all these strangers, this dust of words (159)

In addition Beckett has transferred his first *Texte pour rien* from French to English, and he has collaborated with Robert Pinget on the translation into French of his radio play *Embers.* In 1958, an anthology of Mexican poetry was published, translated from Spanish into English by Beckett. Through the years, Beckett the artist acquires his texts more painfully, but he persists in perfecting his craft, which Proust characterized as "the duty and the task of a writer."

Beckett in 1961 was engaged in his most challenging and arduous self-translation—that of *Comment c'est.* The opening pages testify to the staggering difficulties of working without punctuation and within poetic rhythms.[14] Although the single excerpt that has been published is too short to permit of generalization, it is evident that the English is, as always, less comically colloquial than the French. The most frequent refrain of the book, "quelque chose là qui ne vas pas," is rendered as "something wrong there," and one is tempted to echo, "something wrong *there*" for so inadequate a translation. The puns on Pim, Bom, and quaqua are, of course, untranslatable, as are the many French connotations of sack and cord. Several "I quote's" are introduced into the English, as are an "I see me," a "hear that there," and an "I recapitulate."

For all the similar recapitulation of phrases, the English version is more condensed than the French. Compare, for example,

autre image déjà une femme lève la tête et me regarde les images viennent au début première partie elles vont cesser je le dis comme je l'entends le murmure dans la boue les images première partie comment c'était avant Pim je les vois dans la boue ça s'allume elles vont cesser une femme je la vois dans la boue (13)

image a woman raises her head from her needlework and looks at me the images are all at the beginning part one I say it as I hear it I see them in the mud soon they will cease (61)

Two verses are combined, as well as condensed, from French to English:

je me tourne vers ma main la libre je la porte vers mon visage c'est une ressource quand tout fait défaut images rêves sommeil matière à réflexion quelque chose là qui ne va pas

et défaut les grands besoins le besoin d'aller plus loin le besoin de manger et vomir et les autres grands besoins toutes mes grandes catégories d'existence (17)

I turn towards my hand my free hand draw it to my face that's a help when all fails food for thought images dreams sleep and the great needs when the great needs fail the need to go to eat to vomit and the baser needs all my great categories of being (64)

Characteristically, Beckett does not appear to be climaxing his career as translator in a blaze of glory. His last "novel," poorer than ever before in plot, characters, and sheer number of words, is even further impoverished in translation, for the compression of the puns and the connotations of the colloquialisms no longer work for him.

13

a comic complex and a complex comic

Somthing old, something new,
Something borrowed, something blue.

The old wedding jingle may be used to symbolize and summarize Beckett's work, much as he himself used the round song about the dog in *Godot,* or Schubert's "Death and the Maiden" in *All That Fall,* or the duet from *The Merry Widow* in *Happy Days.* At first glance, a marriage rhyme might seem singularly inappropriate for an author haunted by man's loneliness and alienation, and yet Beckett conveys man's essential solitude through various couples, from Belacqua and his sundry *amours* to Winnie-Willie of *Happy Days,* passing through several sets of master and servant, friend and friend, Molloy and his mother, Moran and his son, Krapp and his tape recorder.

Even the first line of the wedding rhyme, "Something old, something new," may be illustrated by a double view of a single characteristic. Thus, the illiberal jest so central to Beckett's work is at least as old as the *Iliad,* but Beckett plays it for a new metaphysical resonance. Similarly, man's fate is one of the oldest themes of literature, but Beckett composes in a minor key that is constantly enriched by fresh comic overtones. Beckett's heroes are old fools in the old fool tradition of the one who gets slapped, but Beckett inveigles us to laugh at the slap and the slapper, as well as at the one who gets slapped.

The Beckett hero incorporates other features of the fool tradition—his appearance of physical freak, his inspired idiocy that borders on wisdom, his alienation from a society that is criticized through his comic gift. And again Beckett, with comic astringency, gives new depth to these old traditions. Often a dwarf or cripple, the traditional fool is as splendid as a Greek statue by comparison with Beckett's protagonists in their various stages of disintegration. The wisdom of Beckett's heroes, bolstered by his own considerable learning, is maintained by tenacious ignorance in the face of modern stockpiling of information. Beckett's fools are alienated not only from society but from all the modern world. Beckett's buffoon rejects a social role, and yet by his fierce obsession with himself in a hostile world, he stands for every individual in that world. A sacrificial victim, Beckett's fool no longer achieves anyone's catharsis, least of all his own.

One of the best-educated men of our time, Beckett has undoubtedly read the major philosophers from Aristotle, "qui savait tout," to Sartre, possibly the "agregé de philosophie" of the French *Murphy*. He adheres to no school, denying Existentialist affiliations. Yet he has mingled and published with French Existentialists; his theater has been called a "theater of existence."[1] Like the Existentialists, Beckett is haunted by death, and his ghosts react raucously to this climactic event of human life.

Beckett's first hero, the poet Belacqua Shuah, dies quietly enough on the operating table. His second hero, Murphy, is in a rocking trance when he is burned to death in his garret retreat. Watt seems too busy to have time for death. But Beckett's French heroes long explosively for death while they endure the sentence of their lives. From Molloy, the first of the writing heroes, each of them has to earn his way to death through his works. The process of writing becomes an approach to death; composition takes place during decomposition. In living, we slowly kill ourselves; however agonizing, however farcical, life kills time. It is a cruelly comic Beckett paradox: While we live, we die; we must compose while we decompose. And faced with death, what attitude can we adopt?

Just before his fatal operation, Beckett's Belacqua ponders this question:

> At this crucial point the good God came to his assistance with a phrase from a paradox of Donne: *Now among our wise men, I doubt not but many would be found, who would laugh at Heraclitus weeping, none which would weep at Democritus laughing.* This was a godsend, and no error. . . . Belacqua snatched eagerly at the issue. Was it to be laughter or tears? It came to the same thing in the end, but which was it to be *now*? . . . He [Belacqua] must efface himself altogether and do the little soldier. It was this paramount consideration that made him decide in favour of Bim and Bom, Grock, Democritus, whatever you are pleased to call it. ("Yellow," 235–237)

Even though tragic and comic "came to the same thing in the end," both Beckett and Belacqua consciously choose laughter some few hours before the latter's death. They ride in the wake of Bim and Bom, who joke about the things that other people would be shot for saying; of Democritus, the laughing philosopher of antiquity; and of Grock, the clown who mimicked human failure—"Nicht möglich."

Later Beckett heroes are less able than Belacqua to make this clear-cut choice between tears and laughter. In *Watt,* the hero's predecessor, Arsene, and his successor, Arthur, are both practiced laughers, but Watt himself alternates between smiles and tears. Moran "at the thought of the punishments

Youdi might inflict . . . was seized . . . with mighty silent laughter and [his] features composed in their wonted stillness and calm." Malone, fighting the gravity into which he was born, "plays the clown." The Unnamable wonders whether his constant flow of tears can be tears of mirth at this joke of a life; later, however, he admits to weeping to keep from laughing, and he invokes Democritus as the last proper name in a comedy of namelessness. In *Godot,* it hurts Vladimir to laugh; in *Endgame,* Hamm muses, "You weep, and weep, for nothing, so as not to laugh." In *Embers,* Henry can only laugh a "long horrible laugh." The crawling creature of *Comment c'est* at first wants to laugh all the time, then only sometimes, three times out of ten, four out of fifteen, but he finally settles for "trois quatre rires réussis de ceux qui secouent un instant ressuscitent un instant puis laissent pour plus mort qu'avant" ("three four successful laughs of those that shake one an instant revive one an instant then leave one more dead than before"). Winnie asks Willie after a laugh, "How can one better magnify the Almighty than by sniggering with him at his little jokes, particularly the poorer ones?" At no time is there a hint of catharsis to be achieved through laughter, either for Beckett's characters or for us.

Of all Beckett's characters, the specialist in laughing matters is Arsene, Watt's predecessor and mentor at Mr. Knott's house. Arsene's hierarchy of laughs, "the bitter, the hollow, and the mirthless," suggests the ironic complexity of Beckett's own comic:

> The bitter laugh laughs at that which is not good, it is the ethical laugh. The hollow laugh laughs at that which is not true, it is the intellectual laugh. . . . But the mirthless laugh is the dianoetic laugh, down the snout—Haw!—so. It is the laugh of laughs, the *risus purus,* the laugh laughing at the laugh, the beholding, saluting of the highest joke, in a word the laugh that laughs—silence please, at that which is unhappy. (48)

Practitioners of the *risus purus,* Beckett's heroes laugh at suffering. Like the Surrealists, they laugh helplessly at cosmically illiberal jests upon themselves or others, and like the Surrealists, too, they enter into the cruel cosmic spirit by perpetrating sadistic jokes of their own. Responding to cosmic cruelty with "black laughter," the Surrealist hero defied and transcended his fate, triumphantly expelling a laugh with his last lungful of breath. But Beckett's laughter—the laughter he expresses and the laughter he evokes—is a mask for, not a release from, despair. It may start with a bang, but it trails off in a whimper; it is "yellow laughter," often rasped out in spite of the laugher. It defies no one and transcends nothing. Such laughter is as automatic and anguished as a response to tickling.

From Beckett's earliest writing, callousness and cruelty evoke bitter ethical laughter. An execution amuses Belacqua Shuah; the sadistic routines of the Magdalen Mental Mercyseat are itemized for our amusement; and all the heroes of Beckett's French fiction invite our laughter at their savage drives—Moran's towards his son, Molloy's towards his mother, Malone's towards his creations, the Unnamable's towards his creators. Vladimir and Estragon turn their stichomythic humor to suicide and murder. Hamm and Clov engage in verbal torture, to their and our ironic appreciation. In *Comment c'est* all men are paradoxically and statistically revealed as both victim and executioner, and the more one suffers, the more wildly one laughs: "j'ai toute la souffrance de tous les temps je m'en soucie comme d'une guigne et c'est le fou rire dans chaque cellule" ("all suffering of all time is mine but it doesn't phase me and it's the wild laugh in every cell"). Winnie quotes: "laughing wild amid severest woe."

By Arsene's definition, the dianoetic laugh is the obverse of the ethical laugh. The latter is inspired by the executioner, the former by the victim. Beckett's heroes swing from one to the other, from sadism to suffering and back again. Midway between the ethical and dianoetic laughs, Arsene situates the hollow or intellectual laugh, and, in a somewhat broader definition than Arsene allows, the middle range of laughter undergoes the most significant modification through Beckett's successive works.

Intellectual laughter, aroused by deviation from truth, may be compared to Bergsonian laughter, aroused by mechanical rigidity imposed upon the authentic free flow of life, which is a kind of truth. Beckett's early works exhibit the twists of plot, distortion of character, and tricks of language, much as Bergson analyzed them. Thus, in *More Pricks Than Kicks,* Beckett twists plots for comic effect when Belacqua abandons a damsel in distress, urges his fiancée to take a lover, is himself the object of a lady's lust, and is finally supplanted in the arms of his third wife by his best friend. In *Murphy* the hero consents to take employment so that his prostitute-mistress need not continue hers. After Murphy's death, his ashes, instead of being flushed down the toilet of Dublin's Abbey Theater, are dispersed in a busy London bar—in crooked comic comment on Murphy's teetotaling, solipsistic life.

From *Watt* on, however, Beckett's plots are so unpredictable that they cannot be twisted, since there is no norm from which to twist. One seemingly senseless incident follows another without sequence or motivation. Place, time, and season are described at inappropriate intervals; day and night, land and sea, town and forest, light and dark, cathedral and slaughterhouse figure incongruously in the plots. From volume to volume, these excursions into "reality" are reduced until in *Comment c'est* the narrator's encounters with Pim and Bom are maddeningly and ridiculously rehearsed. Amorphous and non-concatenated, the volumes of the French trilogy mock the well-made novel. Pointed and repetitive, *Comment c'est* mocks the traditional novel by diminishing plot to human situation.

In Beckett's fiction there is an almost straight-line movement to a single human center. The debonair and detached elegance of *More Pricks Than Kicks* is soon perforated by the embryonic philosophical explorations of *Murphy*. In *Watt*, the hero painstakingly attempts to make sense of his world; both his efforts and his failure are conveyed in a comic mode, and yet traditional comic distance is shortened as Beckett moves us closer and closer to his hero's suffering, for his predicament is that of everyman, is our own.

In the French fiction, with increased control and concentration in each successive work, Beckett channels man's absurd fate into anguish at that fate. As fiction follows fiction, Beckett reduces his plots, diminishes his characters, and compresses his language. It is perhaps partly this voluntary impoverishment that caused Beckett to turn from English to French, where the vocabulary is more limited, and where there is a greater divergence than in English between the literary language to which Beckett was habituated and the colloquial discourse his narrators employ.

As early as 1929, Beckett observed in his essay on Joyce, "No language is so sophisticated as English. It is abstracted to death." He compared English to Medieval Latin in order to establish an analogy between Dante's use of the vulgar tongue and Joyce's creation of one. Perhaps the all-powerful language of Joyce inhibited Beckett's development in English. Beckett himself contrasted the two: "The more Joyce knew the more he could. He's tending toward omniscience and omnipotence as an artist. I'm working with impotence, ignorance."[2]

The emphasis should be placed on "working." It is a simple fact that Beckett's erudition compares with that of Joyce. Although they work differently, they both strive for maximum inclusiveness in their fiction. Joyce's reach is encyclopedic; he finds a syllable or symbol to suggest everything, from the most trivially accidental to the most mythically universal. Omniscient and omnipotent, detached and smiling, he creates a universe of unparalleled linguistic wealth. Beckett, in contrast (and perhaps in direct reaction), seeks ignorance, impotence, nakedness. He comes as close to them as literature can, but he cannot achieve them. He may change his language so that he speaks an alien tongue literally as well as metaphorically, but he cannot do away with language and still manage to think. And that is his curse, as it is ours—that man is, as Descartes defined him, "a thing that thinks."

Thus sentenced, thus cursed, Beckett's protagonists insist upon the ridiculous details of their physical situations—Murphy in his rocker, Molloy on his compulsive voyage, Malone in bed, the Unnamable in limbo, an uprooted Gogo and Didi by their rooted tree, a defenseless Hamm and Clov in their shelter, the partner of Pim and/or Bom in the mud, Winnie and Willie on a scorched earth beneath a hellish blazing sun. Mobile or immobile, in frantic activity or absurd tableau, they evoke laughter at their physical situations and pity for their metaphysical situation. Seeking sense and sensibility in an indifferent cosmos, reflecting the Absurdity of the Macrocosm in the absurd details of his microcosm, the Beckett hero cries out in the frustration of his humanity, which is our own.

A poet and not a philosopher, Beckett had to work through his own creations to attain his bleak, comic vision of the human condition. Thus, the early English fiction is inhabited by caricatures, and only for the heroes does Beckett modify his attitude between *More Pricks* and *Murphy.* In the short stories, Belacqua is seen through detached and mocking eyes, but Beckett tacitly admits his sympathy for Murphy: "All the puppets in this book whinge sooner or later, except Murphy, who is not a puppet." In the Magdalen Mental Mercyseat, Murphy's mind is even vouchsafed a vision of what the French heroes will seek in vain to glimpse: "that rare postnatal treat . . . the Nothing, than which in the guffaw of the Abderite naught is more real." Appropriately enough,

Murphy's response—like Belacqua's in the hospital, like that of Democritus the laughing Abderite—is laughter.

Watt, who cannot laugh, is a grotesque throwback to Cooper, a servant in *Murphy*, and a grotesque foreshadowing of the French heroes, who finally cast off servitude. The grotesque has been identified by its assimilation of animal and human worlds, of real and dream worlds.[3] In *Watt*, termites, frogs, rats, dogs, men, are confused. Although Watt's concerns are not with reality, it is nevertheless a kind of reality that he seeks at Mr. Knott's establishment, where events are as illogical and inexplicable as in dreams.

Ungainly and plodding, Watt consecrates his life to trying to understand Mr. Knott's establishment. Sam the narrator pokes fun at Watt's senses and reason, which fail their owner in his time of need, but Sam Beckett's sympathy for Watt (an ironic, ambivalent sympathy, to be sure) peeps through the account of Sam, surname unknown. Not so completely detached from Watt as he would have us believe, Sam-narrator dwells on the same physically disgusting and mentally agonizing details that preoccupy Sam Beckett in his French works, and, through Sam Beckett, his French heroes. Far from Bergson's analysis of the comic as mechanical aberration imposed on the *élan vital*, Beckett's comic heroes are limp rags of life lost in a stone-cold universe.

Beckett neither discovered nor invented the coldness of the cosmos, nor is he alone in finding indifference in the so-called moral as well as the natural order. The hypocrisy of faith, the stupidity of hope, and the brutality of charity are familiar attitudes in the contemporary scene, and contemporary art is riddled with the breakdown of belief, motivation, and communication. As the painter Burri expresses the poignancy of the human situation with his ludicrous sacks and scarlet gashes, Beckett's comic, violent bums become a metaphor for modern man, fallen too low for the contingencies of history or religion.

Unlike the biblical patriarchs who are ironically reflected in Watt, faithful servant of Mr. Knott, Beckett's French heroes have no job. Vagrants, paralytics, beggars, they move compulsively or do not move at all. Molloy is semiparalyzed, Malone is completely paralyzed, and the Unnamable is virtually bodiless except for a possible head and rump. Hilariously incongruous collections of impulse and habit, they are sentenced to recount their experience in all its unreconstructed absurdity. In those accounts, events blend into one another, along with places and times; characters change names, pop up and vanish, are invented and expunged; paragraphs disappear, sentences expand and contract, and phrases reflect forwards and backwards, suddenly denied or repeated. But the haphazard, irrational surface is actually a mosaic of extraordinary conceptual and linguistic control.

Trapped between birth and death, Beckett's French heroes fill the interim with stories, "And all funny; not one not funny." In the long interval between birth and death, while yearning for an exit through womb or tomb, these compulsive narrators spawn words as incoherent as the cries of the newborn, as incoherent as the death rattle, but the incoherence is calculated by Beckett.

To arrive at these approximations of the noises of the nascent and moribund, Beckett underwent intensive linguistic discipline. His early characters share with him a penchant for comic verbal elegance that depends upon breadth of vocabulary and reference. The titles of the early works, like the works themselves, contain puns: *Whoroscope, More Pricks Than Kicks,* "Enueg," *Murphy* (where Beckett declares, "In the beginning was the pun"). In these works, an intellectual laugh springs from linguistic techniques that are indifferent or irrelevant to truth: polished paradox, sneering irony, twisted quotation, erudite jargon. Even the heavier humor of misplaced literalism is lightly and elegantly applied. Beckett's wit glitters mainly in parody, where the tone is sometimes riotously, sometimes grotesquely, out of key with its subject. *Watt,* the bulk of whose prose is a heavy-handed parody of the workings of the rational understanding, opens and closes in light social satire, and it is enlivened midway by a caricature of an academic committee. But *Watt* also abounds in verbal repetition, flat contradiction, and ambivalent irony, all later transferred intact into Beckett's French work.

From the first burst into French prose, an incisive and vulgarly colloquial tongue replaces the elegant language of *Murphy* and the laborious logic of *Watt.* The cultivated English smile explodes into a Rabelaisian guffaw when pedantic jawbreakers give way to Basic-French-and-dirty-words, when a Latinate syntax gives way to pygmy phrases and giant sentences. The twisted quotations turn no longer about literature but about biblical or commonplace sayings, and, unlike the polished gems of the English fiction, they are deeply imbedded in the philosophic context. Only incidental in the English work, ingenuous literalism, flat self-contradiction, and hammered repetition become tools for comic creation and epistemological exploration. They are blunt, clumsy instruments, extensions of the hands that hold them, of the heads that conceive them. They do not, finally, discover or construct a universe; we laugh, finally, at the outlandish idea that they ever could, and yet the tension of their effort supports all of Beckett's work, inspiring bitter, hollow, mirthless laughter at their failure, which reflects ours.

In Beckett's latest work, Arsene's three laughs are merged; the ethical laugh is aroused by cruelty, the intellectual laugh by ignorance, but cruelty and ignorance dissolve in suffering. Bitter and hollow laughter are drowned in mirthless, dianoetic laughter—the only possible reaction to the impossible human situation, in which we live.

Cursed with a mind, man cannot be content with his animal body. Cursed with a body, he cannot retire into the life of the spirit. Forever alone, he is immersed in words, married to phenomena, and he spawns reasons before he knows what is happening to him; he spends the rest of his life foisting names on things, and things on names. If he is lucid beyond logic, he attempts to understand raw experience, but the pattern of ready-made things, names, and values intrudes upon his efforts at an intimate and idiosyncratic interpretation. He comes to doubt everything, and even to doubt the interpreting subject; his "I" is a working hypothesis that no longer works, and yet there is no one else he can be. Unable to penetrate into his microcosm, unable to break out into a macrocosm, he agonizes, poised awkwardly between them, and he is aware of his precarious position: "on the one hand the mind, on the other the world, I don't belong to either."

Beckett's extraordinary achievement has been to give dimension to this tightrope-walker, so that we care profoundly about his equilibrium. Beckett's is an intellectual accomplishment, for all the vaunted ignorance of his heroes. Using comic cliché phrases, he farcically deprives us of ready-made concepts. Using ludicrously simple events, he ironically invests them with metaphysical meaning. But he does not deal in philosophical problems; he plunges us into an emotional situation so that we alternate between panic and hilarity, as we anxiously watch the tottering of subject and object, of world and self, or *our* world and *our* self.

In Beckett's work, coherence is jarred at every level—the cosmos, the plot, the person, the sentence. In the "wordygurdy" of his protagonists' monologues, we are persuaded by our dizziness of his heroes' authenticity. They know no respect for time or place; they disdain sequence and proportion. But they must not be too readily confused with their creator. Unlike Sartre and Camus, who paint an absurd world in logical language and syntax, Beckett strives for a more mimetic art. Cosmic absurdity is reflected by non-concatenation of incidents, as in the fiction of Kafka; personal disintegration is reflected by syntactical fragmentation, as in the drama of

Ionesco. Beckett uses the words and moods of our time, but he weaves them into a fabric of impressive design; the surface gibberish is packed with significance, the surface chaos with symbolism. Beckett's precise workmanship is readily apparent if we examine his revisions. Successive versions of his stories contain no modification in the abrupt *non sequiturs,* but there are many phrasal changes in order to achieve ludicrous incongruity, syntactical ambiguity, symbolic ambivalence, and more intense rhythms.

By use of a first-person, alogical narration, Beckett links his presentation of cosmic irony with his heroes' consciousness of that irony. Introspectionists who descend from Descartes, his protagonists show how miserably the line has deteriorated. Grotesque, ancient, crippled, hysterically caressing what they scarcely dare call possessions, thinking tenderly of their hats, clinging frantically to pencil, stick, or sack, Beckett's French "I's" mock themselves as they suffer. Gradually stripped of possessions and clothes, they grow larger in meaning as their silhouettes shrink. In *Comment c'est* the narrator is naked even of hat, bereft even of pencil, and literally dumb, reduced to voiceless, sentenceless, significant phrases. In *Happy Days* Winnie is reduced to a hatted head, thinking staccato thoughts in fewer and older phrases. As the very number of words is reduced, the tension is tautened between knowledge and ignorance, between sense and non-sense. With consummate verbal skill, Beckett involves us more deeply in his heroes, as they become more obsessively involved with themselves. And at the same time, we are more involved with *our*selves. Beckett's fellow playwright Ionesco speaks for Beckett's heroes too when he writes: "By expressing my deepest obsessions, I express my deepest humanity." [4]

Instead of laughing in a civilized and detached way at comic figures whom we do not resemble, instead of reforming after laughing at our own weakness as seen in another, we come, in Beckett's work, to doubt ourselves through our laughter. But through the obsessions of Beckett's heroes, we understand our own deepest humanity. Since names are interchangeable, perhaps we too are nameless and unnamable. We laugh at the leg ailments, verbal difficulties, ignorance, and passion of Beckett's heroes, but our laughter is nervous and anxious. Are *our* feet solidly grounded, *our* words expressive of *our* meaning, *our* tears of grief or mirth? What shall we take as fact? We laugh in fear as we realize that there is no fact, only fiction. "Know thyself." What, that fiction? "Connaître, c'est mésurer." What, a fiction?

Beckett has achieved an ambiguously ironic confusion and communion of identity: Beckett, his creation the "I" who creates, his creation, the "I" who sees. At this late stage of human history, when man cannot decipher his identity from the comic complexity of fictions and words, he nevertheless is compelled to seek that identity. Life and letters alike become a dianoetic joke of creations feeding upon their creators, with whom they are assimilable and irreconcilable. The artistic condition is no longer a pinnacle of privilege from which one may nod in neighborly fashion at God the Creator. Instead, creator and creature wallow together in dust or mud, whence they came. Or perhaps they never left it.

The modern man of letters who turns against letters was not fathered by Beckett, but no other modern writer--not Proust or Gide or Joyce or Mann—has integrated the act of creation so consistently and ironically into his own creation. Joyce held that the greatest love of a man was for his own lies, and yet the artist-liar is only one of his mythic prototypes. For Beckett, all literature and all life reduce to his portrait of the artist-liar as old bum: "You either lie or hold your peace," says Molloy, and Beckett's heroes do not hold their peace. Do we?

Beckett's art-lies, his fictions, know each other, if they know anything at all. Murphy's mind contains Belacqua, and the voiceless narrator of *Comment c'est,* recounting his life as the penitential task that all Beckett's heroes perform, likens himself to Belacqua, comically turned on his side in the slime. In Beckett's unpublished novel, Mercier speaks to Watt of Murphy, for the one reminds him of the other. Moran refers to Murphy, Watt, Yerk, Mercier. Malone groups himself with other Beckett fictions: "Then it will be all over with the Murphys, Merciers, Molloys, Morans and Malones, unless it goes on beyond the grave." Perhaps it does, since the Unnamable carries on a discourse with Molloy and Malone, Mahood and Worm, and others "from Murphy on"; he insists in vain that he is not they "who told me I was they, who I must have tried to be, under duress, or through fear, or to avoid acknowledging me." The crawling, voiceless creature of *Comment c'est* intermittently encounters and is Pim and Bom, voiced and voiceless aspects of Beckett's earlier fictions. So, all knowledge is a dialogue between man and his fictions; reason and calculation, emotion and imagination—all are taught to man through his fiction, even if the fiction is himself, and the dialogue reduced to a monologue of ready-made phrases, stubbornly, clumsily, ironically, searching for an individual and independent self. But the search itself is paradigmatic of all human endeavor.

Like his fiction, Beckett's drama focuses on man as artist-liar, often in the guise of artist-actor. It is this accent that distinguishes his drama from the comparably comic anti-plays of Ionesco. Although Beckett and Ionesco both have learned from Artaud and Jarry to express serious theatrical concerns in spectacular farcical terms, it is Beckett for whom theater is the more immediate metaphor of the world. The worn-out acts of vaudeville and the threadbare devices of drama emphasize our presence at a spectacle, and symbolize our lives. In *Godot* each of the characters performs for an audience, and conflicting testimonies thread through the play. In *Endgame,* the artist is the hero whose chronicle seems to relate to his life in the penitential fashion that Belacqua's dream relates to his. In *Embers,* Henry's fictions, Bolton and Holloway, are possible doctors to cure him. In *Krapp's Last Tape,* Krapp attempts to fix the flux of himself through a tape recorder, for love has not accomplished this task. In *Happy Days,* Winnie needs the spectacle of Willie, as she needs to feel herself a spectacle in other eyes.

Beckett's heroes are aware of playing a role, as though they had read Epictetus the Stoic: "Remember that you are an actor in a drama, of such a kind as the author pleases to make it. . . . For this is your business, to act well the character assigned to you; to choose it is another's."[5] We are all actors, playing stock parts in the repertoire of the *commedia dell'arte.* Although ad lib dialogue is encouraged, it must be couched in familiar phrases and re-enforced by violent slapstick. If there ever was a script, we cannot know it; much less can we know an author or audience.

Dramatic or fictional, Beckett's work paints an ironic portrait of man, Everyman, as artist-liar. He paints in words—in the words that his heroes revile and unravel, in the words he weaves into one of the masterly prose styles of our time. Superbly controlling his medium, Beckett probes both source and product of language. The succinct redundancy of his dramatic dialogue is in ironic contrast to the logorrhea of his fictional narrators.

Within each literary genre, Beckett undermines that very genre—fictional formulae in the fiction and dramatic conventions in the drama. By mocking the literary form within that form, Beckett questions the boundary between art and life, between fiction and fact. Such interrogation is part of the traditional stock in trade of the fool, and Beckett plays it for all its farcical, metaphysical worth. He pommels existence with the questions of his characters, or with their frenzied affirmations immediately followed by more frenzied negations. These questions slap at life as well as art; for any interpretation of life is a construction, a game, a work of art, bordering on a reality that is necessarily unknown, unknowable, and frustratingly seductive.

"I'm working with impotence, ignorance," Beckett has explicitly admitted. "My little exploration is that whole zone of being that has always been set aside by artists as something unusable—as something by definition incompatible with art. I think anyone nowadays, who pays the slightest attention to his own experience finds it the experience of a non-knower, a non-can-er." [6]

"A non-knower, a non-can-er" is, however, still another role, that of the old comic Eiron or self-deprecator, the fool of his fictions. Aristotle, "qui savait tout," wrote that comedy paints men as worse than they are, and the Eiron paints himself as worse than he is. Beckett's comic ironist is ugly, small, poor, cruel, ignorant, miserable, and infinitely vulnerable. It is above all in that vulnerability that we recognize ourselves. As long as man remains ugly, small, poor, cruel, ignorant, miserable, and vulnerable, Beckett's ironic works will have lively and deadly relevance for us.

Through the years Beckett has hacked at his plots and characters; he has decimated his sentences and the number of his words, until he is left with a single protagonist in the generalized human situation, an "I" in quest of his "I" through fiction, who is in quest of his "I" through fiction, who, etc. Perhaps the old wedding jingle should be applied with a shotgun, for each "I" conceives another who conceives another who conceives another until we arrive full circle laughing—hysterical perhaps at our plight.

appendix

Whoroscope

Text

Ooftish

Translation of Watt's Anti-Language

Whoroscope

What's that?
An egg?
By the brothers Boot it stinks fresh.
Give it to Gillot.

Galileo how are you,
and his consecutive thirds!
The vile old Copernican lead-swinging son of a sutler!
We're moving he said we're off—Porca Madonna!
the way a boatswain would be, or a sack-of-potatoey charging
  Pretender.
That's not moving, that's *moving*.

What's that?
A little green fry or a mushroomy one?
Two lashed ovaries with prostisciutto?
How long did she womb it the feathery one?
Three days and four nights?
Give it to Gillot.

Faulhaber, Beeckman, and Peter the Red,
come now in the cloudy avalanche or Gassendi's sun-red crystally cloud
and I'll pebble you all your hen-and-a-half ones
or I'll pebble a lense under the quilt in the midst of day.

To think he was my own brother, Peter the Bruiser,
and not a syllogism out of him
no more than if Pa were still in it.
Hey! pass over those coppers,
sweet millèd sweat of my burning liver!
Then were the days I sat in the hot-cupboard throwing Jesuits out of the skylight.

Who's that? Hals?
Let him wait.

My squinty doaty!
I hid and you sook.
And Francine my precious fruit of a house-and-parlor foetus!
What an exfoliation!
Her little grey flayed epidermis and scarlet tonsils!
My one child
scourged by a fever to stagnant murky blood—
blood!
Oh Harvey belovèd
how shall the red and white, the many in the few,
(dear bloodswirling Harvey)
eddy through that cracked beater?
and the fourth Henry came to the crypt of the arrow.

What's that?
How long?
Sit on it.

A wind of evil flung my despair of ease
against the sharp spire of the one
lady:
not once or twice but . . .
(Kip of Christ hatch it!)
in one sun's drowning
(Jesuitasters please copy)
So on with the silk hose over the knitted, and the morbid leather—
what am I saying! the gentle canvas—
and away to Ancona on the bright Adriatic,
and farewell for a space to the yellow key of the Rosicrucians.
They don't know what the master of them that do did,
that the nose is touched by the kiss of all foul and sweet air,
and the drums, and the throne of the faecal inlet,
and the eyes by its zig-zags.
So we drink Him and eat Him
and the watery Beaune and the stale cubes of Hovis
because He can jig
as near or as far from His jigging Self
and as sad or lively as the chalice or the tray asks.
How's that, Antonio?

In the name of Bacon will you chicken me up that egg.
Shall I swallow cave-phantoms?

Anna Maria!
She reads Moses and says her love is crucified.
Leider! Leider! she bloomed and withered,
a pale abusive parakeet in a mainstreet window.
No I believe every word of it I assure you.
Fallor, ergo sum!
The coy old frôleur!
He tolle'd and legge'd
and he buttoned on his redemptorist waistcoat.

No matter, let it pass.
I'm a bold boy I know
so I'm not my son
(even if I were a concierge)
nor Joachim my father's
but the chip of a perfect block that's neither old nor new,
the lonely petal of a great high bright rose.

Are you ripe at last,
my slim pale double-breasted turd?
How rich she smells,
this abortion of a fledgling!
I will eat it with a fish fork.
White and yolk and feathers.
Then I will rise and move moving
Toward Rahab of the snows,
the murdering matinal pope-confessed amazon,
Christina the ripper.
Oh Weulles spare the blood of a Frank
who has climbed the bitter steps,
(René du Perron . . . !)
and grant me my second
starless inscrutable hour.

Beckett's Notes on Whoroscope

René Descartes, Seigneur du Perron, liked his omelette made of eggs hatched from eight to ten days; shorter or longer under the hen and the result, he says, is disgusting.
He kept his birthday to himself so that no astrologer could cast his nativity.
The shuttle of a ripening egg combs the warp of his days.

l. 3 In 1640 the brothers Boot refuted Aristotle in Dublin.

4 Descartes passed on the easier problems in analytical geometry to his valet Gillot.

5–10 Refer to his contempt for Galileo Jr. (whom he confused with the more musical Galileo Sr.), and to his expedient sophistry concerning the movement of the earth.

17 He solved problems submitted by these mathematicians.

21–26 The attempt at swindling on the part of his elder brother Pierre de la Bretaillière–The money he received as a soldier.

27 Franz Hals.

29–30 As a child he played with a cross-eyed girl.

31–35 His daughter died of scarlet fever at the age of six.

37–40 Honoured Harvey for his discovery of the circulation of the blood, but would not admit that he had explained the motion of the heart.

41 The heart of Henri IV was received at the Jesuit college of La Flèche while Descartes was still a student there.

45–53 His visions and pilgrimage to Loretto.

56–65 His Eucharistic sophistry, in reply to the Jansenist Antoine Arnauld, who challenged him to reconcile his doctrine of matter with the doctrine of transubstantiation.

68 Schurmann, the Dutch blue-stocking, a pious pupil of Voët, the adversary of Descartes.

73–76 Saint Augustine has a revelation in a shrubbery and reads Saint Paul.

77–83 He proves God by exhaustion.

91–93 Christina, queen of Sweden. At Stockholm, in November, she required Descartes, who had remained in bed till midday all his life, to be with her at five o'clock in the morning.

94 Weulles, a Peripatetic Dutch physician at the Swedish court, and an enemy of Descartes.

Reprinted from Hours Press edition, Paris 1930.

Text

Come come and cull me bonny bony doublebed cony swiftly my springal and my thin Kerry twingle-twangler comfort my days of roses days of beauty week of redness with mad shame to my lips of shame to my shamehill for the newest news the shemost of shenews is I'm lust-be-lepered and unwell oh I'd rather be a sparrow for my puckfisted coxcomb bird to bird and branch or a coalcave with goldy veins for my wicked doty's potystick trimly to besom gone the hartshorn and the cowslip wine gone and the lettuce nibbled up nibbled up and gone nor the last beauty day of the red time opened its rose and struck with its thorn oh I'm all of a galimaufry or a salady salmafundi singly and single to bed she said I'll have no toadspit about this house and whose squab was I I'd like to know that from my cheerfully cornuted Dublin landloper and whose foal hackney mare toing the line like a Viennese Tabchen take my tip and clap a padlock on your Greek galligaskins before I'm quick and living in hope and glad to go snacks with my twingle-twangler and grow grow into the earth mother of whom clapdish and foreshop.

Reprinted from *New Review* (April, 1932), 57.

Ooftish

offer it up plank it down
Golgotha was only the potegg
cancer angina it is all one to us
cough up your T. B. don't be stingy
no trifle is too trifling not even a thrombus
anything venereal is especially welcome
that old toga in the mothballs
don't be sentimental you won't be wanting it again
send it along we'll put it in the pot with the rest
with your love requited and unrequited
the things taken too late the things taken too soon
the spirit aching bullock's scrotum
you won't cure it you—you won't endure it
it is you it equals you any fool has to pity you
so parcel up the whole issue and send it along
the whole misery diagnosed undiagnosed misdiagnosed
get your friends to do the same we'll make use of it
we'll make sense of it we'll put it in the pot with the rest
it all boils down to the blood of the lamb

Reprinted from *transition* 27 (April-May, 1938), 33.

Translation of Watt's Anti-Language

Most of day, part of night, now with Knott. Up till now, oh so little seen, oh so little heard. From morning till night. What then, this I saw, this I heard. Dim, quiet thing. Ears, eyes, also failing now. So I moved in mist, in hush. (164)

Two orb, pale blur, dark bulk. Two drum, puff low, puff low. To skin, mass grows, mass grows. To smell, stale smell stale smell. To tongue, tart sweat, tart sweat. (165)

Abandoned my little to find him. My little to learn him forgot. My little rejected to have him. My little reviled to love him. This body homeless. This mind ignoring. These emptied hands. This emptied heart. To him I brought. To the temple. To the teacher. To the source. Of nought. (166)

What did need? Knott. What had got? Knott. Was cup full? Pah! But did need? Perhaps not. But had got? Know not. (166)

He'd say, Shave. When had got things ready to shave, the bowl, the brush, the powder, the razor, the soap, the sponge, the towel, the water, he'd say, No. He'd say, Wash. When had got things ready to wash, the basin, the brush, the glove, the salts, the soap, the sponge, the towel, the water, he'd say, No. He'd say, Dress. When had got things ready to dress, the coat, the drawers, the shirt, the shoes, the socks, the trousers, the vest, the waistcoat, he'd say, No. (167)

For time, lived so. Not sad, not gay. Not asleep, not awake. Not dead, not alive. Not spirit, not body. Not Knott, not Watt. Go to, came day light. (167)

Side by side, two men. All day part of night. Dumb, numb, blind. Knott look at Watt? No. Watt look at Knott? No. Watt talk to Knott? No. Knott talk to Watt? No. What then did us do? Nix, nix, nix. Part of night, all day. Two men, side by side. (168)

notes and bibliography

notes

chapter 1

1. "Dante . . . Bruno. Vico . . . Joyce," *transition* 16–17 (June, 1929), 248.
2. *Proust* (New York: Grove Press Evergreen edition, 1957), pp. 64, 67.
3. "Denis Devlin," *transition* 27 (April–May, 1938), 289.
4. "Three Dialogues," *Transition* (1949), 103.
5. "Hommage à Jack B. Yeats," *Lettres Nouvelles* (April, 1954), 619. The quotation is a backhanded slap at Ireland and W. B. Yeats.
6. Meyer Howard Abrams, *The Mirror and the Lamp* (New York, 1953), pp. 26–28.
7. Interesting parallels between the Symbolist poet and the ironic fiction writer are discussed by Northrop Frye, *Anatomy of Criticism* (Princeton, 1957), p. 60.
8. "Three Dialogues," p. 102.
9. "Dante . . . Bruno. Vico . . . Joyce," p. 242.
10. Aristotle's *Ethics* is germinal for the one approach, and his *Poetics* for the other.
11. This distinction is traced by Mary Grant, *Ancient Rhetorical Theories of the Laughable* (Madison, 1924).
12. Some propounders of the corrective theory of comedy are Cicero, Sidney, Jonson, Molière, Voltaire, Meredith. Often the conception is traced to a Horatian source in Verse 334 of the *Art of Poetry;* "prodesse aut delectare" is usually read as "prodesse et delectare."
13. Social normalization through comedy is stressed by Albert Cook, *The Dark Voyage and the Golden Mean* (Cambridge, 1949); Frye, *Anatomy of Criticism;* Katherine Lever, *The Art of Greek Comedy* (London, 1956).

    Lane Cooper, *An Aristotelian Theory of Comedy* (New York, 1922), p. 86, quotes a nameless Elizabethan writer: "Tragedy dissolves life, and comedy consolidates it."
14. Euripides is the great classic example, Shakespeare the great modern.

Sidney, in the *Defense of Poesie,* mentions "mungrell tragy-comedie."

15. *Anatomy of Criticism,* pp. 60–61.
16. Alan Reynolds Thompson, *Dry Mock: A Study of Irony in Drama* (Berkeley, 1948), p. 24.
17. *Anatomy of Criticism,* p. 39.
18. *Ibid.,* p. 81.
19. Thompson, *Dry Mock,* locates dramatic irony, even as Bergson in *Le Rire* locates comedy, in event, character, or language. George Soule, however, in an unpublished doctoral dissertation, "Irony in Early Critical Comedy" (Stanford, 1959), convinces me that irony of character depends upon event or language, and does not exist per se.
20. An empirical classification of techniques of the comic was my first approach to this study. Bergson's analysis of the comic as mechanical aberration groups him with the correctionists; by laughing at a semimechanical comic figure, we reimmerse ourselves in the *élan vital.* Bergson says explicitly in *Le Rire*: "Le rire est, avant tout, une correction. Fait pour humilier, il doit donner à la personne qui en est l'objet une impression pénible."

chapter 2

1. Biographical information on Beckett is not readily available; details have been gathered from flyleaves of his books, from newspaper clippings, from Rayner Heppenstall, *The Fourfold Tradition* (London, 1961), pp. 254–58, and from Martin Esslin, *The Theatre of the Absurd* (New York, 1961), pp. 1–8.
2. Reprinted in *Poems in English* (London, 1961). All Hours Press publications were printed in 300 copies, and Beckett still possesses several copies of *Whoroscope,* which are now collectors' items (conversation with Vivian Mercier). See the Appendix.
3. Descartes believed that bleeding would be the death of him, and it is not certain that he was wrong.
4. Although this quotation from Beckett's *Proust* does not refer to Descartes, Beckett links Descartes and Proust in that monograph: "The mystical experience and meditation of the narrator in the Cartesian hot-cupboard of the Guermantes library." (New York: Grove Press Evergreen edition, 1957, p. 51.)
5. Warren Ramsay, *Jules Laforgue and the Ironic Inheritance* (New Haven, 1953), pp. 35–37, distinguishes between irony of ordinary discourse, where the meaning is opposite, and the irony of connotative language "where meaning is both opposite and apposite."
6. Page references are to *transition* 16–17 (June, 1929).
7. Page references are to the Grove Press Evergreen edition, 1957.
8. Katherine Lever, *The Art of Greek Comedy* (London, 1956), p. 111, characterizes the matter (as opposed to the complex rhythmic structure) of parabasis: "The parabasis proper belongs particularly to the poet. There Aristophanes tells the audience about his life and art. He states his political beliefs, casts aspersions upon his rivals, rebukes the spectators for their lack of appreciation, and in general says freely whatever he has in mind."

9. *New Review* (April, 1932), 57. See the Appendix.
10. Published in London in 1934. "Dante and the Lobster" was republished by Grove Press in *Evergreen Review*, Vol. 1, No. 1 (1957), to which page numbers refer. Page references to the other stories are to the original edition of *More Pricks*.
11. Northrop Frye, *Anatomy of Criticism* (Princeton, 1957), p. 81.
12. Even irony has been defined as "an incongruity that rouses both pain and amusement." Alan Reynolds Thompson, *Dry Mock: A Study of Irony in Drama* (Berkeley, 1948), p. 247.
13. Cantos XXI and XXIII of the *Inferno*. The poem repeats several phrases from p. 270 of "Draff," and both owe Scarmiglione to Dante. As late as *The Unnamable*, Beckett recalls Malacoda: "I shall transmit the words as received . . . roared through a trumpet into the arsehole" (86).

chapter 3

1. Israel Shenker, "Moody Man of Letters," New York *Times*, May 6, 1956, sec. 2, p. 1, gives 1936; Grove Press flyleaves give 1937 as the year Beckett took up permanent residence in Paris.

   Page references to *Murphy* are to the Grove Press American edition of 1957.
2. March 12, 1938, 172:1, and March 26, 1938, 220:2. The latter hashes and reprints the former, under the new title, "Political and Social Novels."
3. *transition* 27 (April–May, 1938), 293. The phrase "sublunary excrement" occurs in *Murphy*, p. 138. Both perhaps derive from Marston's *Malcontent*: "the very muck-hill on which the sublunary orbs cast their excrements." (Act IV, scene 5)
4. *Proust* (New York: Grove Press Evergreen edition, 1957), p. 62.
5. Cf. the passage from "Yellow" quoted on p. 35.
6. Samuel Mintz, "Beckett's *Murphy*: A 'Cartesian' Novel," *Perspective* (Autumn, 1959), 156–65.
7. French version only; Editions de Minuit edition, p. 119.
8. In spite of the assonance with Heaven, Helen seems curious in this context. Perhaps this Helen is Descartes's mistress, as Celia is Murphy's. In the French translation of this passage, Beckett deletes both Celia and Helen, replacing them by further parody of biblical creation.
9. Proverbs 30:15.
10. In the third dark zone of Murphy's mind, all is a "flux of forms."
11. In this connection, it may be mentioned that a year after *Murphy* was published, appeared Flann O'Brien's *At Swim-Two-Birds*, constructed entirely of literary-parody characters and themes. Joyce, in a letter to Adrienne Monnier, couples the two works, "qui au juste se ressemblent comme diable et l'eau bénite." Letter dated March 28, 1940, is printed in *Mercure de France* (January, 1956), 123.
12. Examples are Maurice Nadeau, *La Littérature présente* (Paris, 1952), p. 277; Claude Mauriac, *L'Alittérature contemporaine* (Paris, 1958), pp. 84, 88. Mintz, "Beckett's *Murphy*," 164–65, recognizes the irony,

but interprets it as Beckett's defensive gesture against a dominant Logical Positivist philosophy.

13. The first comparison recalls Laforgue's "Autre Complainte de Lord Pierrot":

 Celle qui doit me mettre au courant de la femme–
 Nous lui dirons d'abord, de mon air le moins froid:
 "La somme des angles d'un triangle, chère âme,
 Est égale à deux droits."

 The circle suggests Murphy-solipsist. The reference to the two thieves is the first of several in Beckett's works.

14. There is also a pun on *adieux* and *à* Madameoiselle *Dew*. Actually, we catch another brief glimpse of her, after Murphy's death.

15. Murphy has already established the derivation of "gas" from "chaos." Richard Ellmann, *James Joyce* (New York, 1959), p. 714, mentions that Joyce "pleased Beckett by quoting from memory the description of the disposal of Murphy's body."

16. *transition* 27 (April-May, 1938), 33. See the Appendix.

chapter 4

1. Israel Shenker, "Moody Man of Letters," New York *Times*, May 6, 1956, sec. 2, p. 1.

2. The Olympia Press Paris edition is, by error, dated 1958. Page references are to the Grove Press American edition, 1959.

3. Christine Brooke-Rose, "Samuel Beckett and the Anti-Novel," *London Magazine* (December, 1958), 38–46:

 Claude Mauriac, *L'Alittérature contemporaine* (Paris, 1958); the English translation, *The New Literature*, does not preserve this flavor.

 In France today, the much-discussed "Nouveau Roman" is frequently dubbed an "anti-roman." Sartre, in his introduction to Nathalie Sarraute's *Portrait of a Man Unknown*, calls that work an anti-novel, but *Watt* would, I feel sure, be classified by him as "fantasy." Many of Sartre's penetrating remarks about the works of Kafka and Blanchot are applicable to *Watt*, e.g., "It is a contradictory world in which mind becomes matter, since values look like facts, a world in which matter is eaten away by mind, since everything is both ends and means, a world in which, without ceasing to be within, I see myself from without. Better still, we cannot ponder it at all." Quoted from *Literary Essays* (New York, 1957), p. 68.

4. *Ibid.*, p. 67.

5. Quoted in Friedrich George Jünger, *Über das Komische* (Zurich, 1948, p. 18. (My translation.)

6. Examples of paragraphic *non sequitur* occur on pp. 8, 12, 15, 26, 30, 38, 45, 69, 87, 117, 120, 127, 136, 138, 145, 157, 199, 208, 222, 238, of *Watt*. Some of the comic resonance of Arsene's monologue, Sam's notes, the social dialogues, and particularly Arthur's Louit-Nackybal tale, depends upon sentence *non sequitur*, bolstered by removal of quotation marks for direct discourse.

7. On p. 96 of *Watt*, Beckett is careful to distinguish between *a* dog and *the* dog.
8. For the interpretation of a Logical Positivist Watt, I am indebted to discussions with Jacqueline Hoefer, as well as to her article, "*Watt*," *Perspective* (Autumn, 1959), 166–82.
9. See the Appendix. Perhaps the anagrammatic method was suggested to Watt by Mr. Spiro, who cites the winning entry in his contest to rearrange the fifteen letters of Jesus, Mary, Joseph, to form a question and answer: "Has J. Jurms a po? Yes" (27).
10. Cf. Apollinaire in his Preface to *Les Mamelles de Tirésias:* "There is no symbol in my play, which is very clear, but you are free to see in it all the symbols you like, and to unravel a thousand meanings, as in Sibylline oracles." (My translation.)
11. The irony of the pun on Watt, and the double pun on Mr. Knott, has been pointed out by Jacqueline Hoefer, "*Watt*," 172. Probably the combination "what not" is meant to suggest the triviality of the nondescript or bric-a-brac, for all combinations of the human and divine. Nor is it impossible that the knotty aspect of Mr. Knott's name owes assonance and mystery to Kafka's hermetic Klamm of *The Castle.*
12. Cf. Lord Gall of Wormwood, Miss Rosie Dew's only client in *Murphy.* There, however, the pun appears to be gratuitous joking.
13. Who is the pianist? No pianist appears in the text of *Watt*, but in the Addenda we discover a description of a second painting in Erskine's room—of a naked pianist with pale red moustache. Watt is red-haired, and he has no difficulty in identifying the chord being played by the man in the picture. The strong probability is that he is the pianist, and he is certainly doomed.
14. *Con,* a French obscenity (as I learned through its homonym Cohn), is thus ironically twinned with *Art*—frail lads both. In the Addenda an Art Conn O'Connery is mentioned; he may be Mr. O'Connery, painter of the picture of the nude pianist in Erskine's room.
15. One sentence, "Do not come down the ladder, they have taken it away," is lifted almost textually from *Murphy* (p. 188, to be compared with p. 44 of *Watt*). See Hoefer, "*Watt*," p. 180, for a possible explanation of this line as a reference to the ladder mentioned by Wittgenstein near the end of his *Tractatus.* That explanation is strengthened by Beckett's insertion of *Louis* into the French translation of this sentence in *Murphy,* possibly for *Ludwig* von Wittgenstein.
16. Even the farcical cube root is not haphazardly chosen. When the academic committee suggests the possibility of square roots, Mr. Louit retorts, "Did he rise on the second day?"
17. After Watt leaves Mr. Knott's establishment, he tries in vain to designate a mysterious moving figure (the only nameless character in the novel) as man, woman, priest, or nun. Not only does he fail to identify the figure but he becomes terribly agitated that, for all its steady movement, it makes "no more headway than if it had been a millstone."
18. Towards the end of his stay at Mr. Knott's house, Watt comes to realize that Erskine sped feverishly up and down stairs when he did not know Mr. Knott's whereabouts. Watt, in the same situation, merely waits.

19. Mr. Nixon's confidence in Watt's honesty may be ill-founded, for though he lent Watt five shillings, or six and ninepence to buy a single boot, we learn from Watt he bought the boot "for eightpence, from a one-legged man." He found the other. Watt offers to pay Mr. Nixon four and fourpence, but does not say how he obtained that sum.

    On the problem of Watt's single boot, it is interesting that his pre-Knott *amoureuse* was the one-legged Mrs. Watson. Her name—Watt's son—and single leg suggest that Watt sought, or created, his love in his own image.
20. See Hoefer, "*Watt*," pp. 179–81, for a link between Watt and Mr. Hackett, who fell off a ladder when he was young.
21. In both this and the next passage, it is essential to know that in vulgar French *bander* means "to have an erection."
22. Vivian Mercier, "The Mathematical Limit," *Nation* (February 14, 1959), 144–45; Niall Montgomery, "No Symbols Where None Intended," *New World Writing* No. 5 (New York, 1954), pp. 324–37; Christine Brooke-Rose, "Samuel Beckett and the Anti-Novel," *London Magazine* (December, 1958), 38–46.
23. Nathalie Sarraute, *L'Ere de soupçon* (Paris, 1956). This collection of four critical essays on the modern novel discusses the problem of the credibility of authorial presence in fiction. Although the essays were published separately between 1947 and 1956, their appearance in book form caused a good deal of discussion.
24. Michel Carrouges, *André Breton et les données fondamentales du surréalisme* (Paris, 1952), p. 112. (My translation.)

chapter 5

1. *Transition* (1948), p. 146.
2. Niklaus Gessner, *Die Unzulänglichkeit der Sprache* (Zurich, 1957), p. 32 n.
3. "Poèmes 38–39" were not published until November, 1946, in *Temps Modernes*. Poem number XI is omitted, and I have been unable to find out, by writing the review, what happened to it.
4. Three stories are included in the volume *Nouvelles et Textes pour rien* (Paris: Editions de Minuit, 1955); a preliminary note explains: "Les *Nouvelles* sont de 1945, les *Textes pour rien* de 1950." In a letter from Beckett to his American publisher, dated December 27, 1958, he wrote: "*Mercier et Camier* novel (?) 1945 (?); *Premier Amour* short story, 1946 (?) written at same time as and intended to go with the 3 nouvelles of *Nouvelles et Textes Pour Rien*; Eleutheria play in 3 acts (1947?)."

    "La Fin" was translated by Richard Seaver in collaboration with the author, and quotations are from the translation, reprinted in *Evergreen Review*, Vol. 4, No. 15 (November-December, 1960), 22–41. Translations from the other works are mine.

    Through his publishers, Grove Press, Beckett granted me permission to read the unpublished works. Professor Hugh Kenner was kind enough to interrupt his own work on these typescripts so that I might see them.

5. Lawrence Harvey, "Art and the Existential in *En Attendant Godot,*" *PMLA* (March, 1960), 139, n. 6.
6. "The Cartesian Centaur," *Perspective* (Autumn, 1959), 135.
7. In a letter of February 16, 1952, Beckett wrote me: "Yes, I had read Céline before the war." Since the sharp colloquialisms of Céline's French are rarely caught in the English translation, it has been necessary to quote the original French. Translations are by John H. P. Marks, from the New Directions edition.
8. The incoherence of the plot may be gauged from the fact that approximately half of "La Fin" appeared as "Suite" in *Temps Modernes* (July, 1946), but it was not continued in any subsequent issue, and presumably no one noticed that it was incomplete.
9. For the importance of Geulincx to Beckett, see Samuel Mintz, "Beckett's *Murphy,*" *Perspective* (Autumn, 1959), 156–65, and my note in *Comparative Literature* (Winter, 1960), 93–94.
10. Cf. the solipsism of Belacqua, Murphy, and Arsene, as well as the circularity of *Watt,* leading from Watt's to Mr. Knott's single boot.
11. I disagree with the conception of stream of consciousness in literature that is maintained both by Robert Humphrey, *Stream of Consciousness in the Modern Novel* (Berkeley, 1954), and Melvin Friedman, *Stream of Consciousness: A Study in Literary Method* (New Haven, 1955). Professor Humphrey summarizes this view: "We may define stream-of-consciousness fiction as a type of fiction in which the basic emphasis is placed on exploration of the prespeech levels *for the purpose, primarily, of revealing psychic being of the characters*" (p. 4; my italics to indicate where I disagree). Professor Humphrey's fine textual analyses implicitly reject his own definition.

    Fiction is thus reduced to do-it-yourself psychoanalysis. A good deal of immature, unimportant writing does this, but Woolf, Joyce, and Faulkner do not. Rather, they make use of the discoveries of post-Freudian psychology to free the *forms* of fiction for greater esthetic achievement. Their purpose is not only to reveal psychic being but to use the techniques of psychological exploration to reveal symbolic depth or to delineate form. Their work is sharply to be contrasted with Surrealist writing, which is prespeech psychic exploration, and is often insignificant as literature. Beckett has quoted Joyce as saying that the Surrealists could not justify their obscurity, whereas he could justify every syllable of *Finnegans Wake.* David Hayman, *Joyce et Mallarmé* (Paris, 1956), p. 125 n. For generalizations about the Surrealist climate of the thirties, which may have influenced Beckett, see Wallace Fowlie, *Age of Surrealism,* "Epilogue" (Bloomington, 1960).

chapter 6

1. *Molloy,* translated into English by Beckett and Patrick Bowles, was published by Grove Press in 1955. *Malone Dies* and *The Unnamable,* translated by Beckett, were published by Grove Press in 1956 and 1958, respectively. Page numbers refer to these editions.
2. Plots are evidently difficult, too, at the factual level. I have noted the following errors:

Kenneth Allsop, *Angry Decade* (London, 1958), finds Malone clubbed to death in an insane asylum.

Warren Lee, "The Bitter Pill of Samuel Beckett," *Chicago Review* (Winter, 1957), has Moran setting off on a bicycle.

Dan Davin, "Mr. Beckett's Everymen," *Irish Writing* 34 (Spring, 1956), has Molloy killing the charcoal-burner.

Gouverneur Pauling, "*Malone Dies,*" New York *Herald Tribune,* September 16, 1956, sec. 5, p. 2, sees the hatchet being wielded by a "trusted inmate" of the asylum.

William York Tindall, "Beckett's Bums," *Critique* (Spring-Summer, 1958), finds Moran writing in bed.

Several critics find the Unnamable (instead of Worm) in a jar before the slaughterhouse.

3. William York Tindall, "Beckett's Bums," p. 9, points out that Baille is Gaelic for Dublin. Although I do not agree with Professor Tindall that *Molloy* is even in part a "loose parody of *Ulysses,*" it is possible that *Jacques* Moran was suggested by *James* Joyce. Jacques is French for James, and both are middle-class Irish Catholics, driven to create. In this connection, Joyce's remark is apposite: "There are only two forms of love in the world, the love of a mother for her child and the love of a man for lies." Richard Ellmann, *James Joyce* (New York, 1959), p. 303.
4. Beckett himself speaks of the three novels as a trilogy, according to Barney Rosset of Grove Press. But this does not necessarily impose chronological continuity.
5. William York Tindall, "Beckett's Bums," p. 13. Professor Tindall believes the two parts of *Molloy* must happen simultaneously, but gives no reason for this hypothesis.
6. Edith Kern, "Moran-Molloy: The Hero as Author," *Perspective* (Autumn, 1959), 183–93, traces the process whereby Moran becomes Molloy.
7. In apocalyptic imagery, there is an equation of stone to sheep to tree to man to Christ; Northrop Frye, *Anatomy of Criticism* (Princeton, 1957), p. 141. In *Malone Dies,* Malone says that "pebbles . . . stand for men and their seasons" (63), as they do in the reasoning of Eurytus the Pythagorean.
8. Israel Shenker, "Moody Man of Letters," New York *Times,* May 6, 1956, sec. 2, p. 1.
9. Kern, "Moran-Molloy."
10. Hugh Kenner, "The Cartesian Centaur," *Perspective* (Autumn, 1959), 132–41, interprets the Cartesian bicycle as mind and body in efficient union. Thus unified, they may kill God with impunity.
11. Kern, "Moran-Molloy," p. 186.
12. Although Louis Lambert is the only unmistakable borrowing from Balzac, the letter may also have suggested to Beckett other names that their works share: Arsene, Arthur, Sophie, and a Godeau who never appears. Balzac's Louis Lambert is obsessed with and destroyed by the conflict between the angelic and physical side of man, and he fails to bridge the gap between them. Malone's Lambert, in contrast, is completely and cruelly physical.
13. Just before creating Moll, Malone asks himself, "For why be discouraged, one of the thieves was saved, that is a generous percentage" (83).

This percentage is judged merely "reasonable" by Vladimir while he waits for Godot. Mercier and Camier are compared to the two thieves looking for Christ.

14. Maurice Nadeau, "Samuel Beckett ou le droit de silence," *Temps Modernes* (January, 1952), 1280, mentions that Lemuel is Samuel in the third person, but I am not sure what to make of this, unless that Sam, the asylum companion of Watt, has evolved into Samuel-Lemuel, the sadistic attendant of *Malone Dies*. Beckett's Christian name is, of course, Samuel, and his friends call him Sam.
15. This is one of the rare examples when the English joke is more scatalogical than its French original.

    The "he's" of the English text have Malone as antecedent (33), but the French original reads Mahood. I pointed out the discrepancy to Grove Press, who wrote to Beckett about three examples of this misprint. He replied, "Ruby Cohn is quite right. The three Malone's (33, 44, 68) should be Mahood's."
16. Kern, "Moran-Molloy," p. 185.
17. In *Transition* (1950), where the passage first appears, French "balance" is translated into English "scales," but English "balance" in the book version restores the biblical echo of "Thou art weighed in the balances, and art found wanting." Daniel 5:27.
18. The French, "je mourrais aujourd'hui même, si je voulais, rien qu'en poussant un peu, si je pouvais vouloir, si je pouvais pousser" was at first translated, "I could die before tonight, if I wished, simply by putting my mind to it, if I could wish, if I could make an effort." *Transition* (1950), 105. The revision emphasizes by repetition and qualification.
19. Also reminiscent of *Watt* is Malone's first nameless fiction: "If I said, Now I need a hunchback, immediately one came running, proud as punch of his fine hunch that was going to perform." Like Watt, Malone is reminded by the stars of a stay in London, and he too has a single boot.
20. Molloy was already able to conceive of the bliss of Worm's ignorance: "For to know nothing is nothing, not to want to know anything likewise, but to be beyond knowing anything, to know you are beyond knowing anything, that is when peace enters in, to the soul of the incurious seeker" (p. 86).
21. Ellmann, *James Joyce*, p. 162.
22. *Essais*, Book 3, Chapter 9. Cf. too, "I'll let down my trousers and shit stories" (*The Unnamable*, p. 130).
23. English version only (103).
24. Rayner Heppenstall, *The Fourfold Tradition* (London, 1961), p. 261, quotes a letter from Beckett on the Montparnasse slaughterhouse: "Through the railings is or was to be seen on a high pedestal the bust of M. Decroix. I think there is a café across the street. Of a real Marguerite or Madeleine I know nothing. This episode is one of Mahood's stories."
25. French critics such as Gaston Bachelard, Georges Poulet, Jean-Pierre Richard, and above all Maurice Blanchot, have been concerned with this aspect of literature, which is summarized by the poet and critic Yves Bonnefoy, "Critics English and French," *Encounter* (July, 1958), 44: "The essence of literature is not to be found in what it explicitly asserts but in its continual annihilation of the meanings which language forces it to compound with, in its flight towards its goal of silence."

Recently, Professor Northrop Frye interpreted the trilogy in this light; "The Nightmare Life in Death," *Hudson Review* (Autumn, 1960), 442–48.

26. One can trace this theme as far back as Beckett's 1931 monograph on Proust: "Art is the apotheosis of solitude. . . . Either we speak and act for ourselves–in which case speech and action are distorted and emptied of their meaning by an intelligence that is not ours, or else we speak and act for others–in which case we speak and act a lie" (47).
27. A "Mahood" on p. 87 of the French text is translated to "they" on p. 59 of the English.
28. Davin, "Mr. Beckett's Everymen," p. 39.
29. Oliver de Magny, "La Nouvelle Littérature romanesque," *Esprit* (July-August, 1958), 16.
30. Martin Gerard, "Is Your Novel Really Necessary?" *X*, Vol. I, No. 1 (November, 1959), 50.

chapter 7

1. The poem groups are *Echo's Bones* and "Poems 38–39," published in *Temps Modernes* (November, 1946), from which XI is omitted. Joyce's first collection of poems, *Pomes Penyeach,* also numbered thirteen, the baker's dozen.

   Dante may be at the root of Beckett's thirteen and M. Dante assigns the date 1300 to his vision, and in Canto X of the *Purgatorio,* he sees thirteen stone images of the fallen proud. In Canto XXIII of the *Purgatorio,* the starved, bony faces of the repentant gluttons are compared to the letter M. If Beckett did have the fallen proud and repentant gluttons in mind, the kinship with his own heroes is highly ironic, for it would be difficult to imagine characters with less pride or gluttony.
2. A poem "Text" appeared in *New Review* (Winter 1931–32), 338–39; a prose poem "Text" in the same magazine (April, 1932), 57. The *Textes pour rien* were published in the volume *Nouvelles et Textes pour rien* (Paris: Editions de Minuit, 1955), 127–220.
3. Israel Shenker, "Moody Man of Letters," New York *Times,* May 6, 1956, sec. 2, p. 1.

   Miss Judith Schmidt of Grove Press wrote me in May, 1959, that the texts were being translated "under Mr. Beckett's supervision," but not by him. *Evergreen Review,* Vol. 3, No. 9 (Summer, 1959), 21–24, carries Beckett's translation of Texte I. In a letter of February 2, 1960, Miss Schmidt wrote me, "It is possible Mr. Beckett will translate more of the *Textes pour rien*–but we don't know when. Same situation holds true for the nouvelles." Quotations are from the French edition of Editions de Minuit, 1955, and translations are mine, except for those from Texte I, which are Beckett's.
4. Shenker, "Moody Man of Letters."

   Niklaus Gessner, *Die Unzulänglichkeit der Sprache* (Zurich, 1957), p. 32 n.
5. "Three Dialogues," *Transition* (1949), 98. Of the three painters, Tal

Coat, André Masson, and Bram van Velde, Beckett finds only the last succeeds in Beckett's own aims for art.

6. *Evergreen Review,* Vol. 1, No. 3 (1957), 83–91.
7. Cf. the comments on the ironic mode, Chapter I.

chapter 8

1. *Comment c'est* was published in 1961 by Editions de Minuit. A fragment, "From an Unabandoned Work," was translated by Beckett and published in *Evergreen Review,* Vol. 4, No. 14 (September-October, 1961), 58–65. I place (B) after quotations from Beckett's translation; the others are mine.
2. The latter is already the excuse of the "I" of the fifth Texte.
3. Cf. Texte I: "d'abord j'y avais seulement été, maintenant j'y suis toujours, tout à l'heure je n'y serai pas encore" (132) "at first I had only been here, now I'm here still, soon I won't be here yet" (23).
4. Cf. the closing lines of *Fin de Partie:*
"HAMM. Vieux linge! Toi-je te garde."
5. Beckett is not daunted by the fact that the galactic Coalsack is rarely visible in London, where Murphy lives.
6. *X,* Vol. I, No. I (November, 1959), 35–37.
7. In the French Bible, God creates man from "limon" rather than "dust."
8. At one point (28) the narrator of *Comment c'est* compares himself to Belacqua turned on his side.

chapter 9

1. Beckett thinks his first play, *Eleutheria,* was written in 1947. To Jean-Jacques Mayoux he wrote: "J'ai écrit *Godot* en 47 ou 48, je ne me rappelle pas exactement. Je l'ai écrit d'une traite." *Eleutheria* has been neither produced nor published, although M. Lindon of Editions de Minuit had scheduled its publication. *Godot* was published in 1952 (before production) by Editions de Minuit. It was produced by Roger Blin January 5, 1953. Translated into English by Beckett, it was published by Grove Press in 1954.
2. With the exception of Roger Blin as Pozzo, the original French cast has played all over the world.
3. *L'Express* (June 1, 1961), 43.
4. In "Home Olga," *Contempo* (February, 1934), quoted and interpreted by Richard Ellmann, *James Joyce* (New York, 1959), pp. 714–15. Since the poem was published in 1934, and *Murphy* in 1938, Professor Ellmann errs (as he confirms in his March 3, 1960, letter to me) in stating: "Beckett reciprocated [in recognition of Joyce's appreciation of the passage on the disposal of Murphy's body] with an acrostic, 'Home Olga.'"
5. Rosette C. Lamont, "The Metaphysical Farce: Beckett and Ionesco," *French Review* (February, 1959), 319–28.

6. *Arts* (January 27, 1953), 1. Edith Kern's translation in "Drama Stripped for Inaction," *Yale French Studies* No. 14, (1954), p. 41.
7. Jean-Jacques Mayoux, "The Drama of Samuel Beckett," *Perspective* Autumn, 1959), 142.
8. Niklaus Gessner, *Die Unzulänglichkeit der Sprache* (Zurich, 1957), p. 102n, says that Beckett thought of naming the work *En Attendant.* William Barrett, *Irrational Man* (New York, 1958), p. 16, claims that the phrase comes from Heidegger. But see above all Martin Esslin, *The Theatre of the Absurd* (New York, 1961), pp. 16–17, for the relevance of Simone Weil's *Attente de Dieu* and Balzac's *Mercadet.*
9. Israel Shenker, "Moody Man of Letters," New York *Times,* May 6, 1956, sec. 2, p. 1.
10. Alfonso Sastre, "Siete notas sobre 'Esperando a Godot,'" *Primer Acto,* No. I (April, 1957), 46–52. I have not seen the original article; the translation is by Leonard Pronko of Pomona College.
11. Esslin, p. 15, points out many other characteristics that oppose them.
12. Cf. Basil in *The Unnamable,* and Clov in *Endgame.*
13. In *Murphy* Neary says, "Humanity is a well with two buckets . . . one going down to be filled, the other coming up to be emptied" (58). This is probably an echo of Marston's *Malcontent*: "Did you e'er see a well with two buckets: whilst one comes up full to be emptied, another goes down empty to be filled? Such is the state of all humanity." (Act III, scene 3) These buckets are comparable to the pots that appear in Beckett's novels subsequent to *Murphy,* but, strangely, Beckett never uses them as comic stage props, unless the ash bins of *Endgame* are to be considered as mammoth pots.
14. Charlie Chaplin is Charlot in French. Various critics–Edith Kern, Eric Bentley, Lawrence Harvey–have made this point. The "god" words are listed by J. Chadwick, "*Waiting for Godot*: A Logical Approach," *Symposium* (Winter, 1960), 252–57.
15. Northrop Frye, *Anatomy of Criticism* (Princeton, 1957), p. 172.
16. See Gessner for a detailed study of disintegration of language in *Godot.*
17. An old vaudeville joke is repeated from "What a Misfortune": When Estragon mocks Pozzo, who has just lost his pulverizer, "My left lung is very weak! . . . But my right lung is sound as a bell," he is reversing lungs on the remark of Otto Olaf to Hermione.
18. Cf. *The Unnamable,* p. 128.
19. Cf. Mr. Knott's family in *Watt.*
20. Cf. Gaber in *Molloy.*
21. English version only.
22. "The Long Wait," *Times Literary Supplement* (May 5, 1961), 277.
23. Günther Anders, "Sein Ohne Zeit zu Beckett's Stück *En Attendant Godot,*" *Die Antiquiertheit des Menschen* (Munich, 1956), p. 227.
24. Enid Welsford, *The Fool* (New York, 1961), p. 27.
25. See, e.g., G. S. Fraser, "*Waiting for Godot,*" in *English Critical Essays: Twentieth Century* (London, 1958), 324–32, first published anonymously in *Times Literary Supplement* (February 10, 1956), where it inspired much correspondence, summarized in an editorial in that newspaper on April 13, 1956. Mr. Fraser recognizes that his Christian interpretation clashes with the tone of the novels, but he feels that the

Christian imagery, and the explicit rejection of Nietzschean and Liberal philosophies, render *Godot* Christian, whatever Beckett's intention.

See also Ronald Gray, "*Waiting for Godot:* A Christian Interpretation," *Listener* (January 24, 1957), 160–61. Mr. Gray also reads Kafka's *Castle* as a novel of Christian grace.

See also Charles McCoy, "*Waiting for Godot*: A Biblical Approach," *Florida Review* (Spring, 1958), 63–72.

See also Esslin's intelligent discussion, pp. 19–24.

26. Lawrence Harvey, "Art and the Existential in *En Attendant Godot*," *PMLA* (May, 1960), 137, points out how early the rope motif is introduced, when Estragon asks Vladimir if they are "tied" to Godot (13, 14). The French lack of liaison between "pas" and "encore" (perceptively noted by Professor Harvey) is lost in translation, but the English adds new irony in a word play on being tied "down."
27. Relevant, too, is the definition of John Fletcher, the major writer of tragicomedy in English: "A tragi-comedy is not so called in respect of mirth and killing, but in respect it wants deaths, which is enough to make it no tragedy, yet brings some near it, which is enough to make it no comedy, which must be a representation of familiar people, with such kind of trouble as no life be questioned; so that a god is as lawful in this as in a tragedy, and mean people as in a comedy."

chapter 10

1. Jean-Jacques Mayoux, "Le Théâtre de Samuel Beckett," *Etudes Anglaises* (October, 1957), 350 n, quotes a letter from Beckett to him: "La rédaction définitive de *Fin de Partie* est de 56. Mais j'avais abordé ce travail bien avant, peut-être en 54. Une première puis une seconde version en deux actes ont précédé celle en un acte que vous connaissez."

   In spite of the success of *Godot,* Roger Blin was unable to find a Paris theater manager who would risk producing the grimmer *Fin de Partie,* and the first production (in French) therefore took place at the Royal Court Theatre in London on April 3, 1957. The French publication by Editions de Minuit appeared a month later, and Beckett's English translation, *Endgame,* was published by Grove Press in 1958.
2. Johan Huizinga, *A Study of the Play Element in Culture* (Boston, 1955), p. 132.
3. *Village Voice,* March 19, 1958, pp. 8, 15.
4. Richard Eastman, "The Strategy of Samuel Beckett's *Endgame,*" *Modern Drama* (May, 1959), 36–44.
5. "The Theatre of Samuel Beckett," *Perspective* (Autumn, 1959), 149.
6. E.g., Thomas Barbour, "Beckett and Ionesco," *Hudson Review* (Summer, 1958), 271–75.
7. The most pyrotechnic display of paronomasia in *Endgame* is Beckett's translation of Nagg's multipunning joke from French (36–38) to English (22–23).
8. *Contempo* (February 2, 1934), 3.
9. Roger Blin's set, in the French production supervised by Beckett, was vaguely oval. The interior of a skull, owner unknown, is a recurrent locale in Beckett's fiction.

10. For fuller discussion of chess in *Endgame,* see Eastman, "The Strategy of Beckett's *Endgame"*; Vivian Mercier, "How to Read *Endgame," Griffin* (June, 1959), 10–14.
11. Charles Shattuck of the University of Illinois suggested this point to me.
12. Leonard Pronko of Pomona College called the Baudelaire line to my attention.
13. For fuller discussion of Beckett's bicycles, see Hugh Kenner, "The Cartesian Centaur," *Perspective* (Autumn, 1959), 132–41.
14. In *Godot,* blind Pozzo of Act II denies the prophetic powers of the blind.

chapter 11

1. Beckett wrote Jean-Jacques Mayoux: "J'ai écrit *All That Fall* très rapidement, en 56. C'est la première fois, depuis 45, que j'écris directement en anglais." First broadcast January 13, 1957, it was published by Grove Press shortly afterwards. It was subsequently translated into French as *Tous ceux qui tombent* by Robert Pinget in collaboration with the author.
2. "Kinds of Comedy: *All That Fall," Spectrum* (Winter, 1958), 26.
3. *Acte sans paroles* (as it was called before Beckett wrote his second pantomime) was written originally in French, produced and published with *Fin de Partie in* 1957, and was subsequently translated by him, and published in 1958 by Grove Press.
4. Written in French, translated by the author into English, *Act Without Words II* was first published and produced in 1959. Grove Press subsequently included it in the 1960 Evergreen collection, *Krapp's Last Tape and Other Dramatic Pieces.*
5. First produced at the Royal Court Theatre in London, October 28, 1958, *Krapp's Last Tape* was published separately in 1959, and then in 1960 in the collection *Krapp's Last Tape and Other Dramatic Pieces.* In 1959 it was translated into French as *La Dernière Bande* by Pierre Leyris, with the collaboration of the author.
6. Herbert Blau, "Meanwhile Follow the Bright Angels," *Tulane Drama Review* (Autumn, 1960), 90–91.
7. *Embers* was first broadcast on June 24, 1959, and was published the same year; it was subsequently included in the 1960 Evergreen collection, *Krapp's Last Tape and Other Dramatic Pieces.* In 1960, too, it was translated into French by Robert Pinget and the author.
8. Written in English, *Happy Days* received its first production at the Cherry Lane Theatre in New York City on September 17, 1961. It was directed by Alan Schneider (who also directed New York productions of *Godot* and *Endgame*). Ruth White played the maximal role of Winnie, and John C. Becher the minimal one of Willie. The play was published in 1961 by Grove Press.
9. Cf. Beckett's phrase "sweet noo style" in his poem of homage to Joyce.
10. Cf. the aging of the fictional Joe Breem to "le pauvre père Breem" in "Le Calmant."
11. See note 5, Chapter II.
12. Cf. the description of the egg as "like a little white ball" with Dan Rooney's ball-like object in *All That Fall.*

13. I am grateful to Lisa Giraud for obtaining for me *The Merry Widow,* with Adrian Ross's English libretto, which Beckett used.

chapter 12

1. *Proust* (New York: Grove Press, 1957), p. 64. The quotation within the quotation is Beckett's translation of Proust's, "Le devoir et la tâche d'un écrivain sont ceux d'un traducteur."
2. "Dante . . . Bruno. Vico . . . Joyce," *transition* 16–17 (June, 1929), 242–53.
3. Richard Ellmann, *James Joyce* (New York, 1959), pp. 661–62.
4. *Ibid.,* p. 715.
5. Israel Shenker, "Moody Man of Letters," New York *Times,* May 6, 1956, sec. 2, p. 1.
6. *Ibid.*
7. Reprinted in *Poems in English* (London, 1961).
8. Niklaus Gessner, *Die Unzulänglichkeit der Sprache* (Zurich, 1957), p. 32, asserts that Beckett also closely superintended the German translation by Elmar Tophaven.
9. *Village Voice,* March 19, 1958, p. 8.
10. *Ibid.*
11. I am grateful to Leonard Pronko of Pomona College for identifying this line.
12. Letter of March 14, 1960, from Patrick Bowles to Norman Moss, who asked the former several questions for me.
13. Even in this highly accomplished translation, not all the nuances are conveyed. Of special relevance in an article on Beckett's translation is the foreignness implicit in "étranger" but not in "stranger." Of primary significance is the biblical resonance of "poussière de verbe," which is virtually absent in "dust of words."
14. "From an Unabandoned Work," *Evergreen Review* Vol. 4, No. 14 (September, October, 1960), 58–65. In a letter of February 16, 1962, Beckett wrote me: "I have finished first draft of *How It Is.* Very unsatisfactory."

chapter 13

1. Jacques Guicharnaud, *Modern French Theatre from Giraudoux to Beckett* (New Haven, 1961), p. 219. The analysis of Beckett's theater is remarkably fine in this book.
2. Israel Shenker, "Moody Man of Letters," New York *Times,* May 6, 1956, sec. 2, p. 1.
3. Wolfgang Kayser, *Das Groteske* (Oldenburg, 1957).
4. Georges Ionesco, "The Avant-Garde Theatre," *World Theatre VIII,* No. 3 (Autumn, 1959), quoted in Martin Esslin, "The Theatre of the Absurd," *Tulane Drama Review* (May, 1960), 7.
5. Quoted by Jean-Jacques Mayoux, "The Theatre of Samuel Beckett," *Perspective* (Autumn, 1959), 142.
6. Shenker, "Moody Man of Letters."

bibliography

published works of Samuel Beckett

1929 "Assumption." *transition* 16–17 (June, 1929), 268–71. Reprinted in *transition Workshop* (New York, 1949), pp. 41–43.

"Dante . . . Bruno. Vico . . . Joyce." *transition* 16–17 (June, 1929), 242–53. Reprinted in *Our Exagmination Round his Factification for Incamination of Work in Progress.* Paris: Shakespeare and Company, 1929; New York: New Directions, 1939.

"Malacoda." *transition* 16–17 (June, 1929), 204. Reprinted in *Echo's Bones.* Paris: Europa Press, 1935.

1930 *Whoroscope.* Paris: Hours Press. 4 pp. Reprinted in *Poems in English.* London: Calder, 1961.

"For Future Reference." *transition* 19–20 (June, 1930), 342–43.

1931 "Anna Livia Plurabelle." *Nouvelle Revue Française* (May, 1931), 637–46.

Proust. London: Chatto and Windus, 72 pp. New York: Grove Press, 1957.

"Return to the Vestry." *New Review* (August-September-October, 1931), 98–99.

"Text." *New Review* (Winter, 1931–32), 338–39.

1932 "Sedendo et Quiescendo." *transition* 21 (March, 1932), 13–20.
"Text." *New Review* (April, 1932), 57.
"Dante and the Lobster." *This Quarter* (December, 1932), 222–36.
Revised story published in *More Pricks Than Kicks*. London: 1934. And in *Evergreen Review*, Vol. 1, No. 1 (1957), 24–36.

1934 "Home Olga." *Contempo* (February, 1934), 3.
More Pricks Than Kicks. London: Chatto and Windus.

1935 *Echo's Bones*. Paris: Europa Press. 30 pp. Reprinted in *Poems in English*. London: Calder, 1961.

1938 *Murphy*. London: Routledge; New York: Grove Press, 1957. 282 pp.
"Ooftish." *transition* 27 (April-May, 1938), 33.
"Denis Devlin." *transition* 27 (April-May, 1938), 289.

1946 "Suite." *Temps Modernes* (July, 1946), 107–19. Revised and republished as first part of "La Fin" in *Nouvelles et Textes pour rien*. Paris: Editions de Minuit, 1955.
"Poèmes 38–39." *Temps Modernes* (November, 1946), 288–93.
"L'Expulsé." *Fontaine* (December, 1946–January, 1947), 685–708. Revised version published in *Nouvelles et Textes pour rien*. Paris: Editions de Minuit, 1955.

1947 *Murphy*. Translated by the author. Paris: Bordas. 201 pp. Reprinted by Editions de Minuit.

1948 "Three Poems." *Transition* (1948), 96–97. Reprinted in *Poems in English*. London: Calder, 1961.
"Peintres de l'empêchement." *Derrière le Miroir* 11–12 (June, 1948), 4–5, 7.

1949 "Three Dialogues." With Georges Duthuit. *Transition* (1949), 97–103. Reprinted in part in *Bram van Velde*. New York: Grove Press, 1960. Pp. 9–13.

1951 *Molloy*. Paris: Editions de Minuit, 272 pp.
Malone meurt. Paris: Editions de Minuit. 217 pp. Excerpts previously published in *Temps Modernes* (September, 1951), 385–416.

1952 *En Attendant Godot*. Paris: Editions de Minuit. 163 pp.

1953 *Watt.* Paris: Olympia Press. 279 pp. Erroneously dated 1958. Reprinted by Grove Press, New York, 1959. 254 pp.
L'Innommable. Paris: Editions de Minuit. 262 pp. Excerpt previously published in *Nouvelle Nouvelle Revue Française* (February, 1953), 214–34.

1954 *Waiting for Godot.* Translated by the author. New York: Grove Press. [116 pp.]
"Hommage à Jack B. Yeats." *Lettres Nouvelles* (April, 1954), 619.
"The End." Translated by Richard Seaver in collaboration with the author. *Merlin* (Summer, 1954). Reprinted in *Evergreen Review,* Vol. 4, No. 15 (November-December, 1960), 22–41.

1955 *Nouvelles et Textes pour rien.* Paris: Editions de Minuit. 220 pp. Contains "L'Expulsé," "Le Calmant," "La Fin," and thirteen texts.
Molloy. Translated by Patrick Bowles in collaboration with the author. New York: Grove Press. 241 pp. Excerpts previously published in *Transition* (1950), *Paris Review* (1954), *New World Writing* No. 5 (1954).

1956 *Malone Dies.* Translated by the author. New York: Grove Press. 120 pp. Excerpts previously published in *Transition* (1950), *Irish Writing* 34 (Spring, 1956).

1957 *All That Fall.* New York: Grove Press, 59 pp. Reprinted in *Krapp's Last Tape and Other Dramatic Pieces.* New York: Grove Press, 1960.
Tous ceux qui tombent. Paris: Editions de Minuit. Translated by Robert Pinget in collaboration with the author.
Tous ceux qui tombent. Translated by Robert Pinget in collaboration with the author. Paris: Editions de Minuit.
Fin de partie and *Acte sans paroles.* Paris: Editions de Minuit. 124 pp.
"From an Abandoned Work." *Evergreen Review,* Vol. 1, No. 3 (1957), 83–91.

1958 *The Unnamable.* Translated by the author. New York: Grove Press. 179 pp. Excerpt previously published in *Spectrum* (Winter, 1958), 3–7.

Endgame and *Act Without Words.* Translated by the author. New York: Grove Press, 91 pp.

Anthology of Mexican Poetry. Compiled by Octavio Paz. Translated by Beckett. London: Thames and Hudson. 213 pp.

"Krapp's Last Tape." *Evergreen Review,* Vol. 2, No. 5 (Summer, 1958), 13–24. Reprinted in *Krapp's Last Tape and Other Dramatic Pieces.* New York: Grove Press, 1960.

1959 "La Dernière Bande." Translated by Pierre Leyris. *Lettres Nouvelles* (March 4, 1959), 5–13.

"Text I." Translated by the author. *Evergreen Review,* Vol. 3, No. 9 (Summer, 1959), 21–24.

"Embers." *Evergreen Review,* Vol. 3, No. 10 (November-December, 1959), 28–41. Reprinted in *Krapp's Last Tape and Other Dramatic Pieces.* New York: Grove Press, 1960.

"Act Without Words II." *New Departures* (Summer, 1959), 89–91. Reprinted in *Krapp's Last Tape and Other Dramatic Pieces.* New York: Grove Press, 1960.

"L'Image." *X,* Vol. 1, No. 1 (November, 1959), 35–37.

"Cendres." Translated by Robert Pinget and the author. *Lettres Nouvelles* (December 30, 1959), 3–14.

1960 *Krapp's Last Tape and Other Dramatic Pieces.* New York: Grove Press. 141 pp. Contains "Krapp's Last Tape," "All That Fall," "Embers," "Act Without Words I," and "Act Without Words II."

1961 *Comment c'est.* Paris: Editions de Minuit. 177 pp.

"From an Unabandoned Work." Translated by the author. *Evergreen Review,* Vol. 4, No. 14 (September-October, 1961), 58–65.

Happy Days. New York: Grove Press. 64 pp.

a checklist of Beckett criticism

Abel, Lionel. "Joyce the Father, Beckett the Son," *New Leader* (December 14, 1959), 26–27.

Allsop, Kenneth. *The Angry Decade.* London, 1958. Pp. 37–42.

Anders, Gunther. "Sein Ohne Zeit zu Beckett's Stück *En Attendant*

Godot," *Die Antiquiertheit des Menschen über die Seel im Zeitalter der zweiten industriellen Revolution.* Munich, 1956.

Anon. "Life in the Mud," *Times Literary Supplement* (April 7, 1961), 213.

———. "Paradise of Indignity," *Times Literary Supplement* (March 28, 1958), 168.

———. "Puzzling about Godot," *Times Literary Supplement* (April 13, 1956), 221.

———. "The Train Stops," *Times Literary Supplement* (September 6, 1957), 604.

———. "Trilogy," *Times Literary Supplement* (June 17, 1960), 381.

Barbour, Thomas. "Beckett and Ionesco," *Hudson Review* (Summer, 1958), 271–77.

Barr, Donald. "One Man's Universe," New York *Times* (June 21, 1959), sec. 7, p. 4.

Barrett, William. "How I Understand Less and Less Every Year," *Columbia Forum* (Winter, 1959), 44–48.

———. "Real Love Abides," New York *Times* (September 16, 1956), sec. 7, p. 5.

———. "The Works of Samuel Beckett Hold Clues for an Intriguing Riddle," *Saturday Review of Literature* (June 8, 1957), 15–16.

Bataille, Georges. "Le Silence de Molloy," *Critique* (May 15, 1951), 387–96.

Bentley, Eric. "The Talent of Samuel Beckett," *New Republic* (May 14, 1956), 20–21.

Blanchot, Maurice. "Où Maintenant? Qui Maintenant?" *Nouvelle Nouvelle Revue Française* (October, 1953), 676–86; reprinted in *Le Livre à Venir.* Paris, 1959, pp. 256–64.

Blau, Herbert, "Meanwhile Follow the Bright Angels," *Tulane Drama Review* (Autumn, 1960), 90–91.

Boisdeffre, Pierre de. "Samuel Beckett ou l'au-delà," *Une Histoire vivante de la littérature d'aujourd'hui.* Paris, 1957.

Bowles, Patrick. "How Samuel Beckett Sees the Universe," *Listener* (June 19, 1958), 10.

Brick, Allan. "The Madman in His Cell: Joyce, Beckett, Nabokov and the Stereotypes," *Massachusetts Review* (October, 1959),

40–55. "A Note on Perception and Communication in Beckett's *Endgame*," *Modern Drama* (Summer, 1961), 20–22.
Briggs, Ray. "Samuel Beckett's World in Waiting," *Saturday Review of Literature* (June 8, 1957), 14.
Brooke-Rose, Christine. "Samuel Beckett and the Anti-Novel," *London Magazine* (December, 1958), 38–46.
Chadwick, C. "*Waiting for Godot:* A Logical Approach," *Symposium* (Winter, 1960), 252–57.
Champigny, Robert. "Interprétation *d'En Attendant Godot*," *PMLA*, LXXV (June, 1960), 329–31.
Chapsal, Madeleine. "Un célèbre inconnu," *L'Express* (February 8, 1957), 26–27.
Clurman, Harold. "Theater," *Nation* (May 5, 1956), 387–90.
Cmarada, Geraldine. "*Malone Dies:* A Round of Consciousness," *Symposium* (Fall, 1960), 199–212.
Cohn, Ruby. "The Comedy of Samuel Beckett," *Yale French Studies* No. 23, pp 11–17.
———. "*Endgame:* the Gospel According to Sad Sam Beckett," *Accent* (Autumn, 1960), 223–34.
———. "A Note on Beckett, Dante, and Geulincx," *Comparative Literature* (Winter, 1960), 93–94.
———. "Preliminary Observations on Samuel Beckett," *Perspective* (Autumn, 1959), 119–31.
———. "Samuel Beckett: Self-Translator," *PMLA*, LXXVI (December, 1961), 613–21.
———. "Still Novel," *Yale French Studies* No. 24, 48–53.
———. "Waiting is All," *Modern Drama* (Fall, 1960), 162–67.
———. "*Watt* in the Light of *The Castle*," *Comparative Literature* (Spring, 1961), 154–66.
Curtis, Anthony. "Mood of the Month–IV," *London Magazine* (May, 1958), 60–65.
Davie, Donald. "Kinds of Comedy," *Spectrum* (Winter, 1958), 25–31.
Davin, Dan. "Mr. Beckett's Everymen," *Irish Writing* 34 (Spring, 1956), 36–39.
Dobrée, Bonamy. "The London Theater," *Sewanee Review* (Winter, 1958), 149–52.

Dort, Bernard. "En Attendant Godot," *Temps Modernes* (May, 1953), 1842–45.

Driver, Tom F. "Beckett by The Madeleine," *Columbia University Forum* (Summer, 1961), 21–25.

Eastman, Richard. "The Strategy of Samuel Beckett's *Endgame*," *Modern Drama* (May, 1959), 36–44.

Esslin, Martin. "The Theatre of the Absurd," *Tulane Drama Review* (May, 1960), 3–15.

Esslin, Martin. "Samuel Beckett: the Search for the Self," *The Theatre of the Absurd*. New York, 1961. Pp. 1–46.

Fiedler, Leslie. "Search for Peace in a World Lost," New York *Times* (April 14, 1957), sec. 7, p. 27.

Fletcher, John. "*Comment c'est*," *Lettres Nouvelles* (April, 1961), 169–71.

Fowlie, Wallace. "Fallen Out of the World," New York *Herald Tribune* (November 23, 1958), sec. 4, p. 4.

Fraser, G. S. "*Waiting for Godot*," *Times Literary Supplement* (February 10, 1956), published Anon. Reprinted in *English Critical Essays: Twentieth Century*. London, 1958. Pp. 324–32.

Friedman, Melvin. "The Achievement of Samuel Beckett," *Books Abroad* (Summer, 1959), 278–81.

———. "The Novels of Samuel Beckett: An Amalgam of Joyce and Proust," *Comparative Literature* (Winter, 1960), 47–58.

———. "Samuel Beckett and the Nouveau Roman," *Wisconsin Studies in Contemporary Literature* (Spring-Summer, 1960), 22–36.

Frye, Northrop. "The Nightmare Life in Death," *Hudson Review* (Autumn, 1960), 442–48.

Gerard, Martin. "Molloy Becomes Unnamable," *X* (October, 1960), 314–19.

Gessner, Niklaus. *Die Unzulänglichkeit der Sprache*. Zurich, 1957.

Gibbs, Wolcott. "*Waiting for Godot*," *New Yorker* (May 5, 1956), 89.

Gray, Ronald. "*Waiting for Godot:* A Christian Interpretation," *Listener* (January 24, 1957), 160–61.

Gregory, Horace. "Beckett's Dying Gladiators," *Commonweal* (October 12, 1956), 88–92.

Gresset, Michel. "Le 'parce que' chez Faulkner et le 'donc' chez Beckett," *Lettres Nouvelles* (November, 1961), 124–38.

Grosvogel, David. "Beckett," *The Self-Conscious Stage in Modern French Drama.* New York, 1958. Pp. 324–34.

Guicharnaud, Jacques. *Modern French Theater from Giraudoux to Beckett.* New Haven, 1961. Pp. 193–220.

Hamilton, Kenneth. "Boon or Thorn? Joyce Cary and Samuel Beckett on Human Life," *Dalhousie Review* (Winter, 1959), 433–42.

Hartley, Anthony. "Samuel Beckett," *Spectator* (October 23, 1953), 458–59.

Harvey, Lawrence. "Art and the Existential in *En Attendant Godot,*" *PMLA,* LXXV (March, 1960), 137–46.

Hicks, Granville. "Beckett's World," *Saturday Review of Literature* (October 4, 1958), 14.

Hobson, Harold. "Samuel Beckett, Dramatist of the Year," *International Theatre Annual* No. 1. London, 1956.

Hoefer, Jacqueline. "*Watt,*" *Perspective* (Autumn, 1959), 166–82.

Hooker, Ward. "Irony and Absurdity in the Avant-Garde Theater," *Kenyon Review* (Summer, 1960), 436–54.

Johnston, Denis. "Waiting with Beckett," *Irish Writing* (Spring, 1956), 23–28.

Karl, Frederick R. "Waiting for Beckett," *Sewanee Review* (Autumn, 1961), 661–76.

Kennebeck, Edwin. "The Moment of Cosmic Ennui," *Commonweal* (December 31, 1954), 365–66.

Kenner, Hugh. "The Absurdity of Fiction," *Griffin* (November, 1959), 13–16.

———. "The Beckett Landscape," *Spectrum* (Winter, 1958), 8–24.

———. "The Cartesian Centaur," *Perspective* (Autumn, 1959), 132–41.

———. "Samuel Beckett vs. Fiction," *National Review* (October 11, 1958), 248–49.

———. "Samuel Beckett: The Rational Domain," *Forum* (Summer, 1960).

———. "Voices in the Night," *Spectrum* (Spring, 1961), 3–20.

Kermode, Frank. "Beckett, Snow, and Pure Poverty," *Encounter* (July, 1960), 73–76.

Kern, Edith. "Drama Stripped for Inaction," *Yale French Studies,* No. 14 (1954), pp. 41–47.

———. "Moran-Molloy: The Hero as Author," *Perspective* (Autumn, 1959), 183–92.

Lamont, Rosette C. "The Metaphysical Farce: Beckett and Ionesco," *French Review* (February, 1959), 319–28.

Lee, Warren. "The Bitter Pill of Samuel Beckett," *Chicago Review* (Winter, 1957), 77–87.

Leventhal, A. J. "Close of Play," *Dublin Magazine* (April-June, 1957), 18–22.

Loy, J. Robert. " 'Things' in Recent French Literature," *PMLA,* LXXI 1956), 27–41.

McCoy, Charles. "*Waiting for Godot:* A Biblical Approach," *Florida Review* (Spring, 1958), 63–72.

Magny, Olivier de. "Panorama d'une nouvelle littérature romanesque," *Esprit* (July-August, 1958), 3–18.

Mannes, Marya. "A Seat in the Stalls," *Reporter* (October 20, 1955), 43.

Mauriac, Claude. "Samuel Beckett," *L'Alittérature contemporaine.* Paris, 1958. Pp. 77–92. Translated as *The New Literature.* New York, 1959.

Mauroc, Daniel. "*Watt,*" *Table Ronde* (October, 1953), 155–56.

Mayoux, Jean-Jacques. "Le Théâtre de Samuel Beckett," *Etudes Anglaises* X (October-December, 1957), 350–66. Translated in *Perspective* (Autumn, 1959), 142–55.

———. "Samuel Beckett et l'univers parodique," *Vivants Piliers.* Paris, 1960. Pp. 271–91.

Mercier, Vivian, "Beckett and the Search for Self," *New Republic* September 19, 1955), 20–21.

———. "Savage Humor," *Commonweal* (May 17, 1957), 188–90.

———. "The Mathematical Limit," *Nation* (February 14, 1959), 144–45.

———. "How to Read *Endgame,*" *Griffin* (June, 1959), 10–14.

———. "Samuel Beckett and the Sheela-Na-Gig," *Kenyon Review* (Spring, 1960), 299–328.

Micha, René. "Une Nouvelle Littérature allégorique," *Nouvelle Nouvelle Revue Française* (April, 1954), 696–706.

Miller, Karl. "Beckett's Voices," *Encounter* (September, 1959), 59–61.

Mintz, Samuel I. "Beckett's *Murphy:* A 'Cartesian' Novel," *Perspective* (Autumn, 1959), 156–65.

Montgomery, Niall. "No Symbols Where None Intended," *New World Writing* No. 5 (New York, 1954), pp. 324–37.

Moore, John R. "A Farewell to Something," *Tulane Drama Review* (September, 1960), 49–60.

Nadeau, Maurice. "Samuel Beckett, l'humour et le néant," *La Littérature présente* (Paris, 1952), 274–79.

———. "Samuel Beckett," *Mercure de France* (August, 1951), 693–97.

———. "Samuel Beckett ou le droit de silence," *Temps Modernes* (January, 1952), 1273–82.

———. "*Comment c'est*," *L'Express* (January 26, 1961), 25–26.

Norès, Dominique. "La Condition humaine selon Beckett," *Théâtre d'Aujourd'hui* (September-October, 1957).

Paris, Jean. "The Clock Struck 29," *Reporter* (October 4, 1956), 39.

Paulding, Gouverneur. "*Malone Dies*," New York *Herald Tribune* (September 16, 1956), sec. 5, p. 2.

Piatier, Jacqueline. "*Comment c'est*," *Le Monde* (February 11, 1961), 9.

Pingaud, Bernard. "*Molloy*," *Esprit* 9 (1951), 423–25.

Politzer, Heinz. "The Egghead Waits for Godot," *Christian Scholar* XLII, 46–50.

Pouillon, Jean. "*Molloy*," *Temps Modernes* (July, 1951), 184–86.

Pronko, Leonard. "Beckett, Ionesco, Schéhadé: The Avant-Garde Theatre," *Modern Language Forum* XLII (1958), 118–23.

Robbe-Grillet, Alain. "Samuel Beckett, auteur dramatique," *Critique* (February, 1953), 108–14.

Rousseaux, André. "L'Homme desintégré de Samuel Beckett," *Littérature du XXe siècle.* Paris, 1955. Pp. 105–13.

Sastre, Alfonso. "Siete notas sobre 'Esperando a Godot,'" *Primer Acto* No. 1 (April, 1957), 46–52.

Schneider, Alain. "Waiting for Beckett," *Chelsea Review* (Autumn, 1958), 3–20.

Seaver, Richard. "Samuel Beckett: An Introduction," *Merlin* (Autumn, 1952), 2.

Selz, Jean. "L'Homme finissant de Samuel Beckett," *Lettres Nouvelles* (July-August, 1957), 120–23.

Shenker, Israel. "Moody Man of Letters," New York *Times* (May 6, 1956), sec. 2, p. 1.

Spender, Stephen. "Lifelong Suffocation," New York *Times* (October 12, 1958), sec. 7, p. 5.

Stottlar, James. "Samuel Beckett: An Introduction and an Interpretation." Unpublished Master's Thesis, Columbia University, 1957.

Strauss, Walter A. "Dante's Belacqua and Beckett's Tramps," *Comparative Literature* (Summer, 1959), 250–61.

Tindall, William Y. "Beckett's Bums," *Critique* (Spring-Summer, 1959), 3–15.

Unterdecker, John. "Samuel Beckett's No-Man's Land," *New Leader* (May 18, 1959), 24–25.

Walker, Roy. "Love, Chess, and Death," *Twentieth Century* (December, 1958), 532–40.

———. "Shagreen Shamrock," *Listener* (January 24, 1957), 167–68.

background materials

Aristotle. *Poetics, Ethics* (Butcher translation, Dover edition).

Auerbach, Erich. *Mimesis*. New York, 1957.

Balzac, Honoré de. *Louis Lambert* (Edition de la Pléiade).

Barrett, William. *Irrational Man*. New York, 1958.

Bergson, Henri. *Le Rire*. Paris, 1899.

Bonnefoy, Yves. "Critics English and French," *Encounter* (July, 1958).

Breton, André. *Anthologie de l'humour noir*. Paris, 1940.

Carrouges, Michel. *André Breton et les données fondamentales du surréalisme*. Paris, 1952.

Céline, Louis-Ferdinand. *Voyage au bout de la nuit*. Paris, 1932.

Cook, Albert. *The Dark Voyage and the Golden Mean*. Cambridge, 1949.

Cooper, Lane. *An Aristotelian Theory of Comedy*. New York, 1922.

Dante. *Divine Comedy* (Temple Classics bilingual edition).

Descartes, René. *Discours de la méthode, Méditations, Lettres* (Edition de la Pléiade).

Ellmann, Richard, *James Joyce*. New York, 1959.

Fowlie, Wallace. *Age of Surrealism.* Bloomington, 1960.

Freud, Sigmund. "Wit and its Relation to the Unconscious," in the *Basic Writings of Sigmund Freud* (Modern Library Edition).

Friedman, Melvin. *Stream of Consciousness: A Study in Literary Method.* New Haven, 1955.

Frye, Northrop. *Anatomy of Criticism.* Princeton, 1957.

Gerard, Martin. "Is Your Novel Really Necessary?" *X*, Vol. 1, No. 1 (November, 1959), 46–52.

Goth, Maja. *Franz Kafka et les lettres françaises 1928–1955.* Paris, 1956.

Grant, Mary. *Ancient Rhetorical Theories of the Laughable.* Madison, 1924.

Hartman, Geoffrey. *The Unmediated Vision.* New Haven, 1954.

Hayman, David. *Joyce et Mallarmé.* Paris, 1956.

Heppenstall, Rayner. *Fourfold Tradition.* London, 1961.

Horace. *Art of Poetry* (Everyman Edition).

Huizinga, Johan. *A Study of the Play Element in Culture.* Boston, 1955.

Humphrey, Robert. *Stream of Consciousness in the Modern Novel.* Berkeley, 1954.

Jünger, Friedrich George. *Über das Komische.* Zurich, 1948.

Kayser, Wolfgang, *Das Groteske.* Oldenburg, 1957.

Land, J. P. M., *Arnold Geulincx.* The Hague, 1895.

Langbaum, Robert. *The Poetry of Experience.* London, 1957.

Lever, Katherine. *The Art of Greek Comedy.* London, 1956.

Mathewson, Louise. *Bergson's Theory of the Comic in the Light of English Comedy.* Lincoln, 1920.

Meredith, George. *An Essay on Comedy.* Doubleday Edition, New York, 1956.

Montaigne, Michel de. *Essais* (Edition de la Pléiade).

O'Brien, Flann. *At Swim-Two-Birds.* New York, 1939.

Potts, L. J. *Comedy.* London, 1957.

Pouillon, Jean. *Temps et Roman.* Paris, 1946.

Ramsay, Warren. *Jules Laforge and the Ironic Inheritance*. New Haven, 1953.

Sarraute, Nathalie. *L'Ere de soupçon*. Paris, 1956.

Sharpe, Robert Boies. *Irony in the Drama*. Chapel Hill, 1959.

Sidney, Sir Philip. "Defense of Poesie," in *Tudor Poetry and Prose*, ed. Hebel, Hudson *et al.*

Soule, George. *Irony in Early Critical Comedy*. Unpublished doctoral dissertation, Stanford University, 1959.

Sypher, Wylie. "The Meanings of Comedy," *Comedy*, ed. L. J. Potts. New York, 1956.

Terraillon, Eugène. *La Morale de Geulincx dans ses rapports avec la philosophie de Descartes*. Paris, 1912.

Vivas, Eliseo. *Creation and Discovery*. New York, 1955.

Welsford, Enid. *The Fool*. New York, 1961.